Ultrasonics

journal homepage: www.elsevier.com/locate/ultras

invasive therapeutic ultrasound: Ultrasound-guided ultrasound
ı neuro-oncology

ːrg[a], Smruti Mahapatra[b], Alexander Perdomo-Pantoja[e], Francisco Chavez[c],
n[c], Kah Timothy Xiong[c], Nao J. Gamo[d], Stephen Restaino[d], Nitish Thakor[b],
di[b], Rajiv Iyer[e], Betty Tyler[e], Nicholas Theodore[b,e], Mark G. Luciano[b,e],
,[e], Mari Groves[e], Alan R. Cohen[e], Amir Manbachi[b,e,*]

ːtology, Johns Hopkins University, Baltimore, MD, USA
ːdical Engineering, Johns Hopkins University, Baltimore, MD, USA
Bothell, WA, USA
nt Center, Baltimore, MD, USA
surgery, Johns Hopkins University, Baltimore, MD, USA

F O

ːd

ːrgery

A B S T R A C T

Introduction: To improve patient outcomes (eg, reducing blood loss and infection), practitioners h toward noninvasive and minimally invasive surgeries (MIS), which demand specialized toolki trasound, for example, facilitates thermal ablation from a distance, thereby reducing injury t tissue. Focused ultrasound can often be performed noninvasively; however, it is more difficult neuro-oncological tumors, as ultrasound is dramatically attenuated while propagating through shortcoming has prompted exploration of MIS options for intracranial placement of focused ultra such as within the BrainPath™ (NICO Corporation, Indianapolis, IN). Herein, we present the de ment, and *in vitro* testing of an image-guided, focused ultrasound prototype designed for use in M This probe can ablate neuro-oncological lesions despite its small size.

Materials & Methods: Preliminary prototypes were iteratively designed, built, and tested. The f consisted of three 8-mm-diameter therapeutic elements guided by an imaging probe. Probe fun validated on a series of tissue-mimicking phantoms.

Results: Lesions were created in tissue-mimicking phantoms with average dimensions of 2.5 × and 3.4 × 3.25 × 9.36 mm after 10- and 30-second sonification, respectively. 30 s sonificatio power at 50% duty cycle generated a peak temperature of 68 °C. Each ablation was visualized in r built-in imaging probe.

Conclusion: We developed and validated an ultrasound-guided focused ultrasound probe for use dures. The dimensional constraints of the prototype were designed to reflect those of BrainPath are MIS tools used to create atraumatic access to deep-seated brain pathologies.

sound is an appealing tool for use in both noninvasive vasive surgical (MIS) procedures, as it can ablate pa- om a distance [1–3]. This is particularly helpful in ed with inoperable tumors [4,5]. In neurosurgery, scranial) focused ultrasound systems have been suc- treat movement disorders, including Parkinson and [6]. However, their use for ablation of neuro- oncological tumors faces certain drawbacks [3]; namely attenuation of the ultrasonic wave during propagation which requires high powers directed at the patient's h response to these drawbacks, MIS focused ultrasound ap been contemplated, necessitating miniature probes tracranial lesions from within the cranium [10,11].

One such example is a minimally invasive, focused u capable of being placed within the BrainPath™ (NIC Indianapolis, IN), a device that allows atraumatic

uthor at: Department of Biomedical Engineering, Johns Hopkins University, 3400 N. Charles Street, Clark Hall 208F, Baltimo
Amir.Manbachi@jhu.edu (A. Manbachi).

1016/j.ultras.2020.106210
2019; Received in revised form 28 May 2020; Accepted 12 June 2020

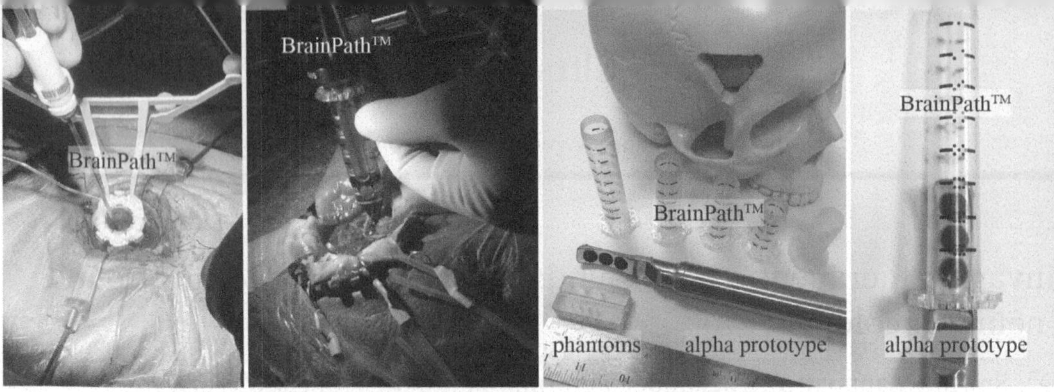

ainPath™ is a minimally invasive neurosurgical toolkit that can accommodate neuroendoscopic devices. (A&B) The BrainPath™ tro
create atraumatic surgical access to deep-seated lesions. (C&D) The ultrasound-guided focused ultrasound alpha prototype prob
in relation to the BrainPath™ dimensions. *A and B contain original images presented with permission from NICO Corporation.*

., deep-seated tumors) in MIS settings (Fig. 1). The de-
products like BrainPath™ represents a growing trend to-
tions in healthcare, where surgical interventions are in-
ing performed with minimally invasive approaches or
edures to enhance patient outcomes and reduce blood loss
12]. Of course, this trend requires development of novel,
ature surgical instruments. Although larger transducer
allow for better energy deposition, MIS encourages in-
aller probes to reduce incision sizes and dissection re-
and this tradeoff demands better understanding of
gns to balance both criteria [13–15]. In this study, we
preliminary focused ultrasound configurations for use in
particularly for use in ablation of neuro-oncological le-
ve report the development and *in vitro* testing of an initial
e designs small enough for use in MIS, yet with a large
ducer surface area to generate the focal point ablations.
ement of the probe within the BrainPath, all anatomies in
be within 4–5 cm. As a result, such a focal length enables
of brain lesions from within the BrainPath trocar.

and methods

tic elements

the dimensions of BrainPath™ and the guidelines for MIS
doscopy techniques (i.e., burr holes measuring 18 mm or
focused ultrasound transducer was designed to fit within a
perture of 9 × 32 mm (Figs. 1 and 2) [16–18]. In order to
e the anatomy of a typical adult brain, where a tumor may
way from the probe placement within the BrainPath™, a
h a 45-mm radius of curvature (RoC) was designed to
focal point lesion 4–5 cm away. Building upon our prior
es that investigated the effects of variations in trans-
RoC, and power on the thermal dose and energy de-
we developed and manufactured 2 alpha prototype
with center frequency of 1.5 MHz (full width half
h: 1.20–1.80 MHz) for *in vitro* validation (Fig. 2)
a 1-piece, 9 × 32 mm, cylindrically curved rec-
h 45 mm RoC. Design II contained three 8-mm-
ents placed on the curved geometry described
array had a width of 12 mm casing, which
ccommodate a built-in imaging array, as de-

2.2. Imaging elements

To reduce the need for intraoperative magnetic re
(MRI) guidance, a built-in ultrasound imaging probe
demonstrate proof-of-concept for the ultrasound-guid
sound (USgFUS) approach studied here. An "off-the-sh
imaging probe from Sonic Concepts (Bothell, WA) was
element, one-dimensional phased array (center freq
was placed within the device housing and was tilted 30
time visualization of the ablation lesion. Customized
veloped to drive the probe and to store, study, and mo
software was developed on MATLAB (MathWorks Inc,
installed on a Vantage 64 LE system (Verasonics Inc,

2.3. Experimental assessment

In vitro testing of the preliminary prototype wa
submerging the device in a 4-gallon test tank filled
Water was degassed to reduce the amount of dissolved
tank. Water temperature throughout experimental te
with less than 1 °C variation. An acoustic absorber was
tank to reduce acoustic reflections from the tank ed
oscilloscope as well as voltage and current probes were
the voltage, current, and subsequently the net pow
under test conditions. Using a three-dimensional (3D
created on a commercial 3D printer (Objet260, Connex
Eden Prairie, MN), blocks of solid water phantoms w
the focal point. Solid water is a tissue-mimicking phan
to Sonic Concepts, with acoustic properties (i.e., atte
pagation velocity) similar to those of water. The abso
at 1 MHz is ~0.01 dB/cm. Sound speed is 1500 m/
were used to create predictable lesions and correlate
brated hydrophone measurements. Lesion generatio
both visually and via the built-in imaging probe driven
LE system (Verasonics, Inc., Kirkland, WA). The exper
shown in Fig. 3.

A 1.620-MHz sonification waveform with a pulse
and 50% duty cycle was generated. The solid water
cated for 10 s. To test the built-in imaging probe
brightness-mode (B mode) images were recorded us
transducer described above.

The solid water sample was raised 5 mm parallel to
the device and, using the aforementioned paramete
lesion was created. This process was repeated to

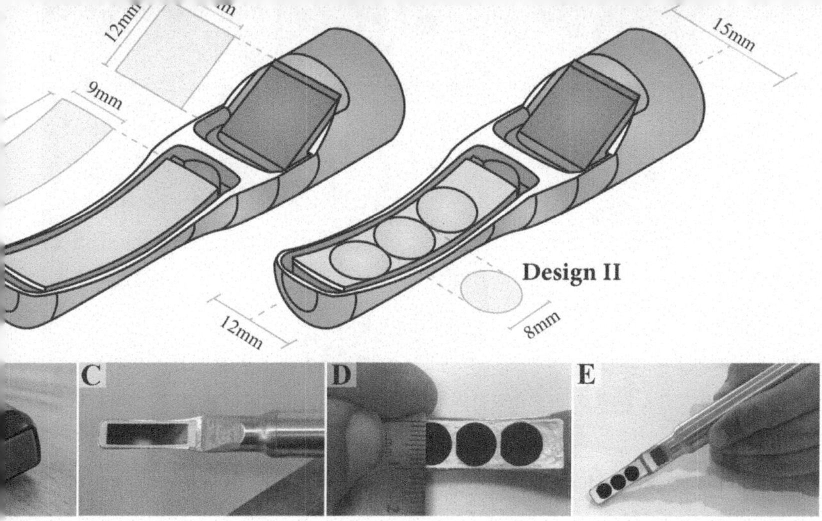

tains. (A) Two late-stage de
custom probe containing a 1
imaging transducer adjacent
apeutic component. Design I
9 × 32mm, cylindrically curve
aperture with 45 mm RoC. D
tains 3 circular therapeutic e
suring 8 mm in diameter, arr
9 × 32mm, cylindrically curve
aperture with 45 mm RoC. Th
array fits within a casing 12
meter, which widened to 15 m
modate the built-in imaging
commercial imaging probe (Sc
IP-105, center frequency: 5 MH
integrated into our custom
guided probe; (C) functional
the custom probe (Design I)
stainless steel casing; (D) 8-
circular therapeutic elements (
complete prototype of Design
both the imaging and therap
nents.

bove-described procedure was repeated; however, a was now performed for 3 trials. Axial, lateral, and ons of the lesions were measured using a slide mi- icroscope.

another block was placed in the water-filled tank at num, as experimentally detected by a hydrophone (Y- sity Hydrophones, Sonic Concepts Inc.). A thermo- oled using a Type T thermocouple connector (SMPW- neering, Karvina, Czech Republic) and a 40-gauge uple wire with formvar enamel insulation (Pelican

uple was inserted into the block at the acoustic max- ure measurements were acquired using a micro- neter (HH23, OMEGA Engineering). Per the afore- eters, a 30 s sonification was performed with ature measurements. As mentioned previously, peak d at 50% duty cycle.

evice based on Design I (Fig. 2) was built, but the design was abandoned due to lateral mode effects that multiple unwanted focal points and overheating during ini second prototype (Design II) was developed and underwe testing. At 118 W and 50% duty cycle, Design II generated l tissue-mimicking phantoms (Fig. 5 & Supplementary Vide cation of 10 s resulted in lesions with average din 2.5 × 1.2 × 6.5 mm (lateral, elevation, and axial alignr sonification resulted in lesoins with average dim 3.4 × 3.25 × 9.36 mm (Table 1).

Peak temperatures reached 42 °C at 10 s and 68 °C at nification. B-mode images acquired before, during, and af resulted in lesion generation (Fig. 6 & Supplementary Vide ablation was visualized by the built-in imaging probe durin and 30 s sonifications of the phantom blocks.

4. Discussion

Focused ultrasound devices facilitate targeted tissue abl distance, providing a means to treat pathology previously inoperable due to inaccessibility. Noninvasive, transcran ultrasound is limited by the acoustic properties of skull

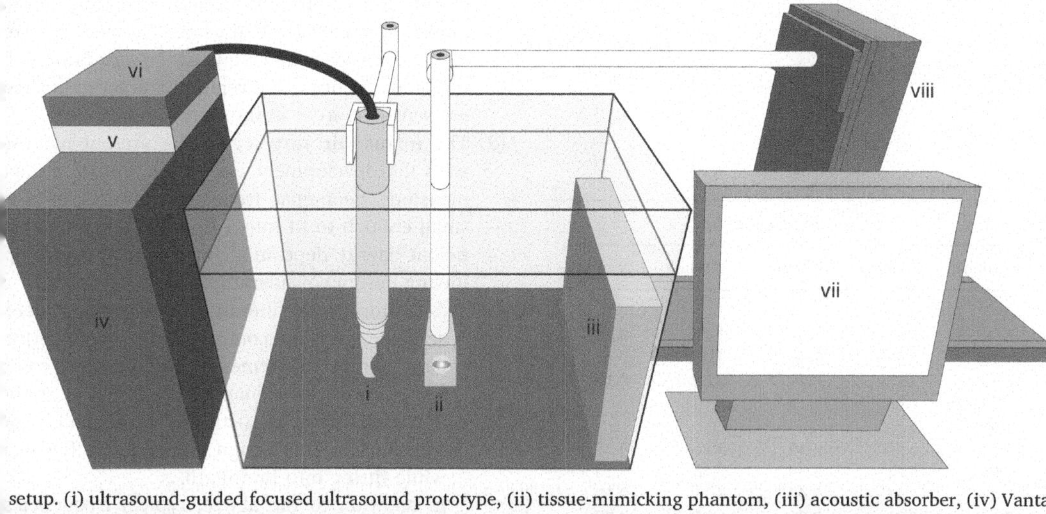

setup. (i) ultrasound-guided focused ultrasound prototype, (ii) tissue-mimicking phantom, (iii) acoustic absorber, (iv) Vantage 64 L atching network, (vii) screen for real-time monitoring of ablation, and (viii) stepper motor to raise solid water tissue-mimicking ph

ːion of the prototype. (A) Device aligned with the 3D-printed holder. (B) The prototype generated lesions in tissue-mimicking phan
l holder.

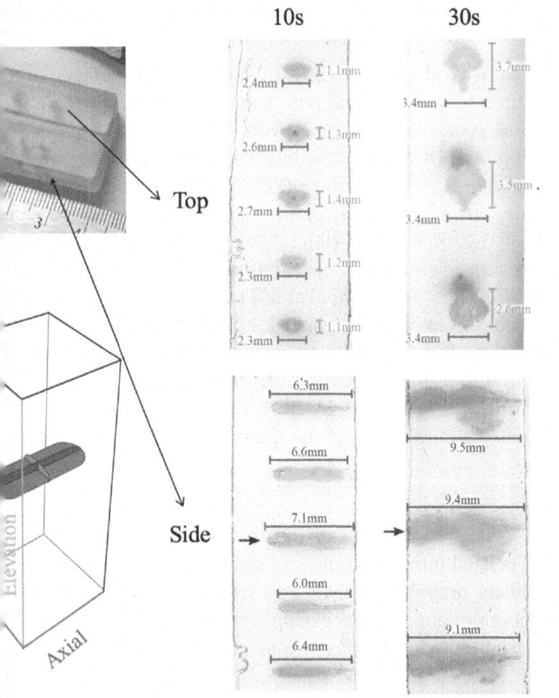

ts of 10- and 30-second ablation of solid water samples. The
ear dimension of each lesion created was measured using a slide
nder microscope.

surements. *SD, standard deviation.

10 s sonification			30 s sonification		
Z (mm)	Y (mm)	X (mm)	Z (mm)	Y (mm)	X (mm)
2.29	1.09	6.45	3.39	3.71	9.53
2.33	1.19	6.01	3.42	3.50	9.43
2.71	1.43	7.11	3.40	2.56	9.15
2.60	1.29	6.63			
2.36	1.08	6.32			
2.46	1.22	6.50	3.40	3.26	9.37
2.29	1.08	6.01	3.39	2.56	9.15
2.71	1.43	7.11	3.42	3.71	9.53
0.19	0.15	0.41	0.01	0.61	0.20

Minimally invasive, intracranial focused ultrasound
limitations, particularly in patients with excessively
However, developing focused ultrasound devices f
challenging. Although acoustic physics favors larger t
areas to achieve ablation, MIS demands tools with in
dimensions [13,14,15]. The optimal geometry for fun
focused ultrasound devices is not well studied [13]
marizes a first step in the development of a focused
small enough for use in MIS procedures such as
treatment performed with BrainPath™.

The novelty of the ultrasound transducer report
script is two-fold:

(1) The **clinical novelty** of the present manuscript is
new surgical technique that allows remote treatm
tumors, primarily those in hard-to-reach regions
cannot be removed surgically because of their lo
in most of these procedures, the BrainPath troca
the brain lesion, not outside the lesion. Howeve
investigated in this study allows for BrainPath de
a manner that enables HIFU systems to be house
treat a lesion that is farther away. This may ev
tumors considered to be inoperable due to thei
sensitivity of the surrounding tissue. As a result,
application of BrainPath required design, devel
dation of a new HIFU device. This new device
surgical approach can allow us to place BrainPath
region of the brain and remotely target tumor reg
are sensitive areas in the intervening space.

(2) The **ultrasonic novelty** of the present manusc
with the development and validation of a trans
mensions, geometry, frequency, number of elem
small enough to fit into a BrainPath, yet capable
ficient energy deposition for tumor ablation. Sp
lowing design considerations were key:

According to the literature, a major considera
array design is the compromise between perfor
large number of elements), and cost and comp
small number of elements) [22,23]. Our study
mm wide) array, consisting of three small, 8-mr
transducers. This design allows for sufficient e
while fitting into BrainPath.

In addition to the above, typical frequencies

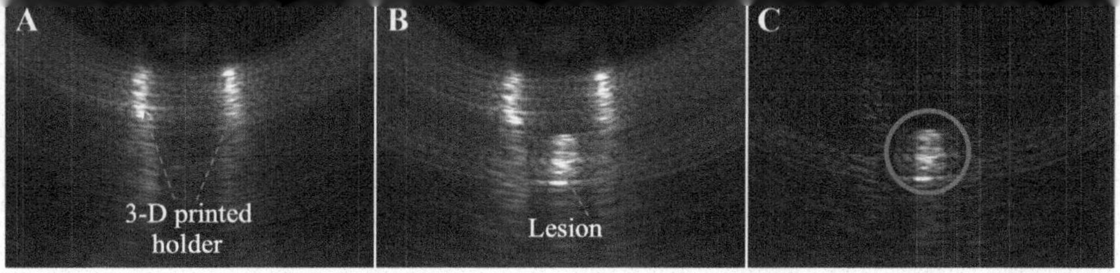

ation of solid water phantom as visualized by the built-in imaging probe: (A) pre ablation, (B) post ablation, and (C) the difference
the lesion. (For interpretation of the references to colour in this figure legend, the reader is referred to the web version of this a

edical's NeuroBlate) are in the lower range compared other organs (less than2 MHz) [24]. As the necessity equencies requires larger transducers, the design of a), low-frequency, transducer proves even more chal- r our ultrasound probe to fit within the BrainPath diameter has to be smaller than 18 mm.

t decade, other clinical applications have witnessed ns and developments. An example includes a transe- reported in 26. Their device consists of eight con- ic annular rings and one imaging transducer in the of 14 mm). In this study, we have reported a new e therapeutic piston transducers (each 8 mm in dia- these designs may look similar at a first glance, it is t they are quite dissimilar—for example, the circular herapeutic in our new design (see the circular yellow), whereas in the formerly reported transesophageal ar transducer is the imaging probe [26]. Finally, the n that paper were larger, while their probe was at t to our 1.5 MHz, in this study.

evice presented in this study demonstrated a possible which with further iterations and miniaturizations, development of new minimally invasive USgFUS de- those designed for use in neuro-oncological settings.

nd future directions

eported in this study was validated using tissue-mi- ns within a controlled test tank, left in 23 °C water. rmal dose needed to achieve ablation is known to vary d possessing 37 °C [25]. As a result, additional studies n brain tissue with histologic evaluation are needed to al focal point tissue necrosis and the effect on sur- oreover, further *in vivo* testing is required to examine ebrospinal fluid and perfusion on focal point and sur- heating. Future studies involving a larger number of an investigate electronic delays as means to replace ing of the probe to target lesions in 3D space.

ugh the built-in imaging probe of this device offered ation of the ablation, the image resolution resulting ansducer was deemed by our clinical team as "*accep- of improvement*" for identification of lesions on the phantoms. Therefore, for real patients with vascu- r complex adjacent anatomies, the resolution and age guidance will most likely need to be enhanced.

ports the development and validation of a USgFUS MIS procedures. The dimensional constraints of the

pathologies. Laboratory testing demonstrated that the prototype successfully created lesions in tissue-mimicki and surpassed threshold temperatures for therapeutic Real-time visualization was also achieved with a buil probe. Although this study demonstrates successful *in v* principle, future studies should explore cadaveric validati tional probe miniaturization for use in MIS procedures.

Funding

This study was funded by Maryland Technology Corporation's Maryland Innovation Initiative, Coulter National Science Foundation's I-Corps program and Jo University, Whiting School of Engineering's Cohen Funding opportunities.

Financial disclosures

Kyle Morrison, Francisco Chavez, and Kah Timothy X ployees of Sonic Concepts, Inc. Dr. Brem is a consulta Medical Advisory Board Chairman for InSightec. He is also of directors for Galen Robotics. Dr. Nao J Gamo is the foun of Neurosonics Medical, Inc. Dr. Stephen Restaino is th Engineering at Maryland Development Center, a startup porting local medical device innovations.

Declaration of Competing Interest

The authors declare the following financial interests, lationships which may be considered as potential compet Kyle Morrison, Francisco Chavez, and Kah Timothy Xi ployees of Sonic Concepts, Inc. They developed the reporte transducer under contract from Johns Hopkins Universit Brem is a consultant serving as Medical Advisory Board InSightec, a company active in the space of ultrasound for r applications. He is also member of the board of directo Robotics. Dr. Nao J Gamo is the founder and CEO of Medical, Inc. Dr. Stephen Restaino is the Director of Er Maryland Development Center, a startup studio supportin ical device innovations.

Acknowledgments

The authors would like to thank Sonic Concepts, I Washington) for manufacturing the custom probe, as well Development Center and Dr. Gil Blankenship for support development. NICO Corporation's Joe Mark and Michele acknowledged for providing their minimally invasive Bra duct for free.

Appendix A. Supplementary material

fre, A. Bouakaz, Therapeutic Ultrasound, first ed., Springer International , 2016.
bold, Foundations of biomedical ultrasound, in: Foundations of Ultrasound, Oxford University Press, Oxford, 2007.
nold, G.T. Clement, P. Black, F. Jolesz, K. Hynynen, Transcranial magance imaging- guided focused ultrasound surgery of brain tumors: initial 3 patients, Neurosurgery. 66 (2) (2010) 323–332, http://dx.doi.org/10. EU.0000360379.95800.2F discussion 332.
, A.J. Kim, J.A. Winkles, H.M. Eisenberg, G.F. Woodworth, V. Frenkel, applications of therapeutic ultrasound in neuro-oncology: moving beyond ation, Neurosurgery 79 (5) (2016) 643–654, http://dx.doi.org/10.1227/)00000001399.
va, H.M. Strunk, M. Rauch, et al., High-intensity focused ultrasound tumor pain relief in inoperable pancreatic cancer : Evaluation with the tion scale (SES), Schmerz 31 (1) (2017) 31–39, http://dx.doi.org/10. 82-016-0140-7.
esonance-guided focused ultrasound neurosurgery for essential tremor: a nology assessment. Ont. Health Technol. Assess Ser. 18(4) (2018) 1–141.
, D. Levine, Physics of ultrasound, in: Diagnostic Ultrasound, fifth ed., c., Philadelphia, 2018, pp. 1–33.
, M. Tanter, MR-guided transcranial focused ultrasound, in: ffre, A. Bouakaz (Eds.), Therapeutic Ultrasound, first ed., Springer, 2016, .
E. Barger, Acoustical properties of the human skull, J. Acoust. Soc. Am. 78) 1576–1590.
hi, J. Siewerdsen, N. Ellens, et al., Flexible control and guidance of invasive focused ultrasoundle (2018).
Minimally Invasive Focused Ultrasound (MIFUS) for Brain Surgery, 2018.
, H. Abou-Al-Shaar, C. Cavallo, Minimally invasive cranial neurosurgery century, J. Neurosurg. Sci. 62 (6) (2018) 615–616, http://dx.doi.org/10. 390-5616.18.04600-3.
, V.A. Salgaonkar, C.J. Diederich, Modelling of endoluminal and intersound hyperthermia and thermal ablation: applications for device deack control and treatment planning, Int. J. Hyperth. Off. J. Eur. Soc. mic Oncol. North Am. Hyperth. Gr. 29 (4) (2013) 296–307, http://dx.doi. 09/02656736.2013.800998.
R. Berriet, L. Chupin, et al., High intensity therapeutic ultrasound performance and characterisation, in: 2010 IEEE International s Symposium, San Diego, 2010, pp. 876–885. doi:10.1109/ULTSYM. 910.
[16] Minimally invasive Neuroendoscopy. Johns Hopkins Medicin hopkinsmedicine.org/neurology_neurosurgery/centers_clinics/ treatment/surgery/neuroendoscopy.html. Published 2019.
[17] E.S. Sussman, C.P. Kellner, E. Nelson, et al., Hemorrhagic co triculostomy: incidence and predictors in patients with intrace Neurosurg. 120 (4) (2014) 931–936, http://dx.doi.org/10.31 JNS131685.
[18] S.A. Chowdhry, A.R. Cohen, Intraventricular neuroendoscopy avoidance and management, World Neurosurg. 79 (2 Suppl) (org/10.1016/j.wneu.2012.02.030 S15.e1-10.
[19] M. Belzberg, F. Chavez, K.T. Xiong, et al., Minimally invasive trasound: design and instrumentation towards a miniaturized focused ultrasound probe, in: Proc SPIE 10951, Med Imaging Proced Robot Interv Model, 2019, pp. 109512Y.
[20] X. Zhang, N. Ellens, M. Belzberg, et al., Design of a low-powe high intensity focused ultrasound device for ablative applica cology: a simulation study, 59th AAPM (American Associatio Medicine) Annual Meeting & Exhibition, Denver, 2017.
[21] N.Y. Jung, I. Rachmilevitch, O. Sibiger, et al.. Factors related transmission of focused ultrasound through a skull : a study in its comparison with clinical experiences. J. Korean Neurosurg. jkns.2018.0226.
[22] G. Malietzis, L. Monzon, J. Hand, et al., High-intensity focus vances in technology and experimental trials support enhanc ultrasound surgery in oncology, Br. J. Radiol. 86 (1024) (201 dx.doi.org/10.1259/bjr.20130044.
[23] P.R. Patel, A. Luk, A. Durrani, et al., In vitro and in vivo eva effective beam width for heat deposition using a split focus h sound (HIFU) transducer, Int. J. Hyperthermia 24 (7) (2008) doi.org/10.1080/02656730802064621.
[24] Insightec ExAblate Neuro system components: https://www.i products/exablate-neuro/system-components (accessed 20 M
[25] G.C. Van Rhoon, T. Samaras, P.S. Yarmolenko, M.W. Dewhir N. Kuster, CEM43°C thermal dose thresholds: A potential gui sonance radiofrequency exposure levels? Eur. Radiol. 23 (8) http://dx.doi.org/10.1007/s00330-013-2825-y.
[26] E. Constanciel, W.A. N'Djin, F. Bessière, et al., Design and ev sophageal HIFU probe for ultrasound-guided cardiac ablation: mini-maze procedure and preliminary ex vivo trials, IEEE Tr Ferroelectr. Freq. Control 60 (9) (2013) 1868–1883, http://d TUFFC.2013.2772.

The manufacturer's authorised representative in the EU is Springer Nature Customer Service Centre GmbH, Europaplatz 3, 69115 Heidelberg, Germany. If you have any concerns regarding our products, please contact ProductSafety@springernature.com

Printed and bound by CPI Group (UK) Ltd, Croydon, CR0 4YY
05/10/2026
02227747-0001

Law and Visual Jurisprudence

Volume 5

The Series Law and Visual Jurisprudence seeks to harness the diverse and innovative work within and across the boundaries of law, jurisprudence, and the visual in various contexts and manifestations. It seeks to bring together a range of diverse and at the same time cumulative research traditions related to these fields to identify fertile avenues for interdisciplinary research.

In our everyday lives, we experience law as a system of signs. Representations of legality are visually manifested in the materiality of things we see and spatially experience. Methodologically, aesthetic texts of legality semiotically emerge as examples of visual jurisprudence and illustrate the constitutive waltz between social governance, formal law, and materiality.

In its tangled relationship to regulation, the visual complexity of law is semiotically articulated as an ongoing process of meaning imbued with symbolism, memory, and cultural markers. Through a legal semiotics framework of symbolic articulation and analysis, the examination of law that happens in conjunction with the visual expands understandings of how law is crafted and takes root. Additionally, such an inquiry challenges the positivist view of law based within the courtroom as disciplinary spatial practices, the observation of everyday phenomenon, and the visible tethering of regulation to cultural understandings of legality generate a framework of visual jurisprudence. The Series seeks to enliven such frameworks as those in which law happens precisely without formal institutions of law and through which a visual-based methodology of law is crafted through everyday instances of ordinariness that contextualize the relationship between law, culture, and banality.

The Series welcomes proposals – be they edited collections or single-authored monographs – emphasizing the contingency and fluidity of legal concepts, stressing the existence of overlapping, competing and coexisting legal discourses, proposing critical approaches to law and the visual, identifying and discussing issues, proposing solutions to problems, offering analyses in areas such as legal semiotics, jurisprudence, and visual approaches to law.

Keywords: Legal Visual Studies, Popular Culture, Everyday Law, Spatiality, Legal Semiotics, Legal Geography, Legal Materiality, Legal Transplant, Bioethics, Cyber Law, Communication, Heritage and Territory, Design, Marketing, Packaging, Digitalization, Arts.

More information about this series at http://www.springer.com/series/16413

Mateusz Stępień • Jan Bazyli Klakla
Editors

Law and Culture

Reconceptualization and Case Studies

Springer

Editors
Mateusz Stępień
Department of Sociology of Law
Jagiellonian University
Cracow, Poland

Jan Bazyli Klakla
Department of Sociology of Law
Jagiellonian University
Cracow, Poland

ISSN 2662-4532 ISSN 2662-4540 (electronic)
Law and Visual Jurisprudence
ISBN 978-3-030-81192-1 ISBN 978-3-030-81193-8 (eBook)
https://doi.org/10.1007/978-3-030-81193-8

This Springer imprint is published by the registered company Springer Nature Switzerland AG.
The registered company address is: Gewerbestrasse 11, 6330 Cham, Switzerland

Acknowledgments

Publication of this book has been made possible thanks to financial support of Faculty of Law and Administration at Jagiellonian University in Cracow, Poland.

Contents

Contributors

Anna Drwal Department of Sociology of Law, Jagiellonian University, Cracow, Poland

Ewa Górska Department of Sociology of Law, Jagiellonian University, Cracow, Poland

Jan Bazyli Klakla Department of Sociology of Law, Jagiellonian University, Cracow, Poland

Joanna Ptak-Chmiel Department of Sociology of Law, Jagiellonian University, Cracow, Poland

Ewa Radomska Department of Sociology of Law, Jagiellonian University, Cracow, Poland

Katarzyna Rużyczka Department of Sociology of Law, Jagiellonian University, Cracow, Poland

Mateusz Stępień Department of Sociology of Law, Jagiellonian University, Cracow, Poland

Magdalena Wojdala Department of Sociology of Law, Jagiellonian University, Cracow, Poland

Part I
Law and Culture Theorizations

Introduction. Drawing on the Legacy of Founding Fathers

Mateusz Stępień and Jan Bazyli Klakla

Abstract The Introduction explains the context, the general aim, and the structure of the book. First, it presents how the idea of publishing the contributed volume was born during periodic seminars on law and culture at Jagiellonian University (Cracow). In this line, the chapter discusses at least a century old tradition of studying the relationships between law and culture at the Jagiellonian University. Second, the Introduction signals that the presented collection consists of a diverse set of chapters that demonstrate how a new generation of legal and social scientists associated with the Jagiellonian University deal with the subject of interest of Cracow-based pioneers of study of law and culture. Third, the Introduction also announces the book structure.

1 Introduction

During periodic informal seminars on law and culture hosted by the Department of Sociology of Law, Jagiellonian University (Cracow), the idea of publishing the presented volume was born. For years, each of the seminar participants has been working separately on various topics and particular subjects of interest (e.g., ranging from migration, modern customary law, and the law in popular culture, to cultural defense, honor-based crimes, and personal law) from which the presented chapters have originated. However, despite their idiosyncratic character, they have been developed under a common umbrella of held assumptions and perspectives. Although the individuals from the seminar group often do not share the same understandings of a particular issue and differ highly when it comes to the methodological standpoints, they mostly agree on some basics about law and culture. The following ideas and attitudes form those basics: displaying sensitivity when approaching culture, which should not be seen as an obvious and intuitive concept; not assuming, at the beginning of the inquiry, that law is inherently embedded in

M. Stępień (✉) · J. B. Klakla
Department of Sociology of Law, Jagiellonian University, Cracow, Poland
e-mail: mateusz.stepien@uj.edu.pl; jan.bazyli.klakla@uj.edu.pl

M. Stępień, J. B. Klakla (eds.), *Law and Culture*, Law and Visual Jurisprudence 5,
https://doi.org/10.1007/978-3-030-81193-8_1

broader culture; and acknowledging the value of case studies in research on the law, associated with directing the "epistemic camera" at the particular, but at the same time praising the need for solid theorization. Those commonalities are not surprising, as participants have joined the group precisely because they initially had something in common. Nevertheless, the tradition of studying the uneasy relationships between law and culture has been strong for at least a century at the Jagiellonian University. The seminar participants have experienced and attempted to elucidate, at least partially, this "native", long-lasting academic thread and intellectual tradition of studying law and culture.

2 Founding Fathers

In this context, it is necessary to mention two outstanding professors of law from Cracow's alma mater. The first is Lothar Dargun (1853–1893). Although he was a professor of constitutional law and German law, he was also interested in ethnography, mainly the cases of property and the kinship systems in the then so-called *Naturvölker*. Dargun is the author of the famous thesis about the primordiality of private ownership over community ownership. He also rejected the concept of primordial patriarchy and criticized the then orthodox vision of the stages of evolutionary development. Among the works of Dargun, the sketch entitled *O zastosowaniu etnografii do historyi prawa* [*On the Application of Ethnography to the History of Law*] (1883) requires special attention. From today's perspective, a large part of his academic achievements can be boldly included in the comparative or ethnographic-focused comparative research on law and culture.

The second outstanding figure is Stanisław Estreicher (1869–1939). After Dargun, he took over as head of the Department of German Law at the Jagiellonian University. He was an exceptional historian of law and an expert in foreign law (especially German and ancient states), who also touched upon the issues close to comparative law and the ethnographic approach to law. His most interesting works include *Początki prawa umownego* [*The Beginnings of Contract Law*] (1901) and *Wypraszanie od kary śmierci w obyczajach naszego ludu* [*Coaxing From the Death Penalty in the History of the Law and Customs*] (1902). Moreover, in the paper titled *Kultura prawnicza w Polsce XVI wieku* [*Legal Culture in 16th Century Poland*] (1932), Estreicher illustrates the cultural factors that formed the specific patterns of actions of lawyers and general attitudes to the law in Poland. Although the paper does not contain any systematic and comprehensive elaborations on the relationships between law and culture or the concept of legal culture, it successfully demonstrates the idea of *longue durée* in the legal sphere and persistence of deeper patterns in the development of Polish law.

Only a few people are aware of the extent to which Dargun and Estreicher's legacy influenced Bronisław Malinowski (1884–1942), who was born in Cracow and was a graduate of the Jagiellonian University. Malinowski's early works confirm that he read and was under the influence of Dargun's views. Moreover, in 1936,

Malinowski recalled that he "was inspired by the teachings and personal guidelines of Professor Stanisław Estreicher". Importantly, it seems that at the time when Malinowski was acquiring his first ethnographic competencies, which related to the first reading of James Frazer's *The Golden Bough*, he already had next to him, at his alma mater, two remarkable scholars who had explored an ethnographic approach to law and dwelled on concrete topics that perfectly fit current law and culture scholarship.

Malinowski's works gained the status of "must-read" in law and culture scholarship. During his career, he devoted much to the study of law through theory-of-culture lenses. Apart from the numerous published and unpublished papers on primitive law and fragments on the functional understanding of law within a broader culture that was included in his monograph—published postmortem—Malinowski conducted a joint seminar for Yale Law School and Yale's Department of Anthropology on "primitive jurisprudence". Since most of the authors dealing with Malinowski's legal thought have focused on the legal threads encapsulated in his reports from field research on the Trobriand Islands, his more theoretical insights on law and culture were not noticed and discussed. In his mature works, the law was part of a much broader theoretical whole: one of five "aspects of culture" or an example of one of several universal "cultural responses" to basic human needs—one of the "many systems of social control".

All of this caused the seminar participants to contemplate the concrete ways in which Dargun and Estreicher's ideas impacted Malinowski. Another intriguing fact is that despite Malinowski's strong links with the Jagiellonian University and his worldwide reputation as the co-founder of anthropological functionalism, the reception of his ideas on law and culture among the scholars from his alma mater was extremely limited. It is striking that not only have the scholars from Jagiellonian University not expanded on the avenues of approaching law established by Malinowski, but they have also found those avenues to be unpopular. One of the reasons behind this is that just before World War II, the adherents of Leo Petrazycki's concept and approach to law found the safe harbor at the Jagiellonian University. It is crucial that in the second part of the twentieth century, authors such as Kazimierz Opałek (1918–1995), Maria Borucka-Arctowa (1921–2018), and Krzysztof Pałecki (1943–), who have from time to time explored the relationships between law and culture, were under the heavy influence of Petrazycian legacy, which was even transformed and expanded in different directions.

More than a century has passed since Frazer's super classic fell into Malinowski's hands during his studies at Jagiellonian University, and nowadays, the participants of the seminar on law and culture believe that this approach, and the earlier traditions on which it is based, must be rediscovered and reanimated in a new sociopolitical context. Much have changed in the legal academy since Dargun, Estreicher, and then Malinowski *et consortes'* approaches to law, which were perceived as a novelty and an insignificant alternative to the dominant paradigm of the understanding of the law. Today, the study of the "cultural face of law", "law as culture", or the "cultural dimension of law" does not have to struggle for legitimacy. Bearing all of this in mind, the presented collection consists of a diverse set of chapters that demonstrate how a new generation of legal and social scientists associated with the Jagiellonian University deal with the subject of interest of Cracow-based pioneers of study of law and culture.

3 Law and Culture. Reconceptualization and Case Studies

In line with the background outlined above, the book you are holding in your hands consists of three parts that explore the relationship between law and culture from various perspectives, both theoretical and empirical. Part I outlines the framework for further considerations and includes new, innovative conceptualizations of two ideas that are important for the subject of law and culture: legal culture and customary law. Both of these appear later in the more empirically oriented chapters in Parts II and III. Part II contains chapters on the relationships between law, customs, and culture, drawing heavily on the tradition and achievements of the anthropology of law and touching on important problems for this discipline—multiculturalism, legal pluralism, and cultural defense. It focuses on the more intangible meaning of culture. Part III, on the other hand, deals with the more material, tangible aspect of culture and the issue of cultural production.

In the opening chapter, Mateusz Stępień aims to explore new avenues for studying the legal culture using Homi Bhabha's theorization of "culture". In Stępień's critical contribution, he shows that the shortcomings of the existing conceptualizations of legal culture are based on the view of culture developed and consolidated in the nineteenth century. The holistic, unitary approach to understanding legal culture is not well suited to the challenges that the legal system faces today. Drawing on Bhabha's understanding of culture as inherently hybrid, Stępień demonstrates the various processes that result in the creation and dissemination of essentialist views about legal culture, and he applies the concept of hybridization to legal culture.

The second chapter in the section on Law and Culture Theorizations is Jan Bazyli Klakla's summary of deliberations on customary law carried out by him in recent years, wherein he proposes a multilayered approach to customary law. Through his chapter, Klakla compares customary law to an onion and unwraps it layer by layer, identifying four main components of customary law: patterns of the expected behavior, predispositions and guidelines for social action, social values, and social identity. That approach aims for greater depth and complexity of possible analysis and reflects a progressive change that occurs in the social order among many communities.

These two chapters constitute the first, theoretically oriented part of the book. Together, they also form the basis for further considerations by other authors in the subsequent parts. It is the rejection of an essentialist, homogeneous, and static understanding of culture in favor of contemporary, heterogeneous, dynamic, and hybrid approaches.

Part II of the book opens with a chapter by Anna Drwal, in which she analyses three judicial opinions issued in the fascinating case of Hadiya concerning "Love Jihad"—a conspiracy theory that Muslims seduce Indian women to convert them to Islam. Using a text analysis embedded in a broader context of traditional Hindu culture, Drwal reconstructs the assumptions in the opinions on categories such as woman, family, marriage, Muslims, and conversion. From the chapter, the image of the inherence of culture in the process of application of the law emerges.

In the next chapter, Ewa Górska presents a case study of customary legal proceedings after a homicide in Hebron, Palestine. Górska comprehensively analyzes customary law in the context of culture, tradition, and sociolegal institutions. Her insightful contribution consists of both (1) a general description of the procedures and institutions used in Palestinian customary law, after a serious crime occurs, and (2) a detailed description of real conflict between two Hebronite clans: al-Jabari vs. al-Haymuni cases from 2014 and 2016 that have raised much attention locally.

Part II of the book ends with the third case study described in Joanna Ptak-Chmiel's chapter on the invocation of cultural defense outside of the system of common law. The subject of this chapter is a case study of an interesting court case, in which arguments based on cultural defense were raised under particular conditions—within the Polish legal system—in a country that is relatively homogeneous and in which judges tend to dominate the proceedings. This multimethod research consisted of an examination of court files, which included the testimony of an expert in culture, a critical analysis of the text of judicial opinions, and an analysis of relevant media publications.

These three case studies combine an empirical, in-depth approach and a critical analysis of the obtained data with the use of the latest achievements of trends such as postcolonial studies, research on multiculturalism, and the feminist perspective. They constitute a valuable methodological addition to case study approaches in research on law and culture.

Part III of the book begins with Ewa Radomska's rich analysis of the relationship between copyright and culture in Poland. The theoretical objective of her chapter is to search for the most important areas of intersection between copyright and culture, including cultural production and participation. Radomska addresses this objective by reconstructing understandings of the interrelations between copyright law and culture, functioning within the Polish public discourse on copyright. The empirical material gathered by Radomska shows that the way in which culture is defined is the most important factor determining the perception of the relationship between copyright and culture.

In the second chapter in Part III of the book, Katarzyna Rużyczka analyzes whether it is possible to find procedural justice in South Korean popular culture. She takes on the radar TV series known as k-drama, which became a tool to promote the culture of this country. Różyczka's goal is to examine the fulfillment of the justice indicators proposed by Tom R. Tyler in selected court hearings presented in the television series *Your Honor*.

The book ends with a chapter by Magdalena Wojdala, who considers whether visual culture poses a threat to law. She refutes the most popular arguments of those who fear the negative impact of visual culture on law. Wojdala addresses the assumptions that (1) the law is affected by sociocultural changes external to it, resulting in the entry of visual culture into law; (2) the impact of visual culture is unfavorable for law, principally because they introduce into law—an area traditionally based on rationality—an element of irrationality and emotionality; and (3) the law is therefore in a state of crisis, and its future is unclear.

4 Conclusions

After eight chapters, we conclude our journey through the world of the complex relationship between law and culture. While our book is not comprehensive, its intention is to present the subject of law and culture from many perspectives, which, although diverse, nevertheless derive from a common source. The book examines the aforementioned achievements of Bronisław Malinowski, Lothar Dargun, and Stanisław Estreicher, as well as the open and in-depth approach to cultural issues in the legal sphere. The editors and authors hope that the book will invigorate the study on law and culture, which is theoretically oriented and at the same time focused on particular and diverse cases.

Mateusz Stępień A Professor of Sociology of Law in the Faculty of Law and Administration at the Jagiellonian University in Cracow (Poland). His research interests focus on exploring the cultural dimension of law. He published papers on Bronislaw Malinowski's concept of law, Confucianism, images in judicial opinions, and power distance in courtroom. He is currently working on the subject of judicial empathy and legal placebo.

Jan Bazyli Klakla A graduate of law, sociology and comparative culture studies at the Jagiellonian University and postgraduate studies in international migrations at the University of Warsaw. Head of the research project "The impact of institutional and legal factors on the choice of a acculturation strategies of foreigners in Poland", expert in security diagnosis in the safety improvement program for the city of Cracow for 2018–2020 entitled "Safe Cracow", associate of the Center for Research on Migration and Intercultural Relations of the University of Almeria and researcher at Holistic Think Tank, part of the Cavatina Holding. He is preparing two doctoral dissertations—in law at the Department of Sociology of Law of the Jagiellonian University and in sociology at the Institute of Sociology of the Jagiellonian University. His interests focus on issues related to migration, education, customary law, restorative justice, as well as the use of social science methodology in research on law.

Exploring New Avenues for Studying the Legal Culture: Drawing on Homi Bhabha's Theorization of "Culture"

Mateusz Stępień

Abstract The chapter begins from the observation of the resurrection of the concept of culture both in biological sciences and social sciences. It argues that legal academia should not ignore these processes that calls for rethinking the idea of legal culture. In this vein, the present chapter aims at identifying the conditions in which the concept of legal culture could be reconceptualized and expanded in a way that extends our understanding of law as a dynamic, embedded, ontologically complex phenomenon. For this purpose, the previous dominant discourse on and main definitions of legal culture are reconstructed and critically examined. The lack of solid theoretical grounds for most of the popular conceptualizations of legal culture constitutes the most striking features of the current discourse on this subject. As a response to this problem, Homi Bhabha's insights on "culture" will be employed in reworking the concept of legal culture. This aim is directed by the need for grounding the use of legal culture in the approach of capturing "culture", which has vast theoretical potential. The chapter intends to stretch the theoretical possibilities of Bhabha's insights, as applied to thinking about legal culture.

1 Introduction

The concept of legal culture (LC) has gained considerable attention in the legal sciences (see Table 1). The term has mainly been utilized by sociologists of law, legal historians, and legal comparatists—described by Anthony Ogus as "obsessed by [that] notion" (2002, p. 419)—as well as advocates of the anthropological approach to law. Moreover, to a considerable extent, LC has entered the common vocabulary of legal dogmatics and even court jurisprudence. Although different authors have often associated different meanings with the term, it remains popular in various professional legal discourses. LC has also been incorporated into more general discussions on political and legal issues: occasionally, lawyers and even

M. Stępień (✉)
Department of Sociology of Law, Jagiellonian University, Cracow, Poland
e-mail: mateusz.stepien@uj.edu.pl

M. Stępień, J. B. Klakla (eds.), *Law and Culture*, Law and Visual Jurisprudence 5,
https://doi.org/10.1007/978-3-030-81193-8_2

Table 1 Most popular definitions of legal culture

No	Author and reference	Definition of legal culture (LC)
1	1a. Friedman and Pérez-Perdomo (2003), p. 193	Popular LC refers to "the cluster of attitudes, ideas, expectations, and values that people hold with regard to their legal system, legal institutions, and legal rules".
	1b. Friedman (1990)	Popular LC is "people's ideas, attitudes and expectations about law and legal process. Out of the legal culture flow lines of force, pressures, and demands that envelope legal institutions and ultimately determine their shape".
	1c. Friedman (1969), p. 34	Popular LC is "the network of values and attitudes relating to law, which determines when and why and where people turn to law or government or turn away".
2	Blankenburg and Bruinsma (1994)	LC includes four components: law in the books; law in action as channeled by the institutional infrastructure; patterns of legally relevant behavior; and legal consciousness, particularly a distinctive attitude toward the law among legal professionals.
3	Bierbrauer (1994), p. 243	LC is "a socially derived product encompassing such interrelated concepts as legitimacy and acceptance of authorities, preferences for and beliefs about dispute arrangements, and authorities' use of discretionary power".
4	Bell (1995), pp. 19–31	LC is "a specific way in which values, practices, and concepts are integrated into the operation of legal institutions and the interpretation of legal texts".
5	Nelken (2004), p. 1	"[L]egal culture, in its most general sense, is one way of describing relatively stable patterns of legally oriented social behavior and attitudes. The identifying elements of legal culture range from facts about institutions such as the number and role of lawyers or the ways judges are appointed and controlled, to various forms of behavior such as litigation or prison rates, and, at the other extreme, more nebulous aspects of ideas, values, aspirations and mentalities".
6	Quinn (2020), p. 19	LC "consists of unstated values and institutional expectations that underpin legal orders and constitute a 'morality' which enables law to be possible".
7	Varga (1995), p. 85	"Legal cultures include ethos, values, conceptual and referential frame related to law, judicial skills and habits, as well as ideology and deontology of legal profession, among others. It is component that gives law a life, makes it dependent from local histories and domestic culture define its orientation, shapes its receptiveness, and, in case of eventual reform, backs of withstands to it".
8	Gibson and Caldeira (1996), p. 59	These operationalize LC through three dimensions: attitudes toward the rule of law, perceptions of the neutrality of law, and relative valuations attached to individual liberty.

(continued)

Table 1 (continued)

No	Author and reference	Definition of legal culture (LC)
9	Merry (2012), pp. 63–68	LC refers to the configuration of "the culture of legal institutions", the "public view of the place of law in social ordering", "legal mobilization", and "legal consciousness".
10	Merryman (1985), p. 2	". . . [A]ll these regimes and legal systems are associated with groups of people, each of which has its legal culture, its deeply rooted, historically conditioned attitudes about the nature of [their regime/system], about [its] role . . . in the society and the polity, about [its] proper organization and operation . . . and about the way [it] is or should be made, applied, studied, perfected, and taught".
11	Van der Walt (2006), pp. 5–6	LC is "a system of meaning that has crystalized, through centuries of legal development and decades of common law adjudication as well as an intellectual tradition, developed on the basis of mostly unarticulated but widely shared assumptions about the sources, the methods, the authority and the development of law".
12	Klare (1998), pp. 146 and 167	By LC "we mean the characteristic legal values, habits of mind, repertoire of arguments, and manners and expressions shared by a group of lawyers at a given, historically situated time and place (. . .) professional sensibilities, habits of mind, and intellectual reflexes that influence professionals and their professional outlook".
13	Van Hoecke and Warrington (1998), pp. 514–515	LC consists of shared understandings of the concept of law, lawmaking and adjudication methodology, theory of argumentation, and theory of legitimatization of law. These elements are viewed as common basic values and as providing the basis for a worldview.

politicians debating in the public sphere refer to LC as part of their argumentative strategies. For example, the recent legal crisis in Poland, which has been ongoing since 2015 (see Sadurski 2019), evoked the claim that some reforms of the judiciary proposed by ruling majority are not congruent with "Western legal culture". Conversely, other participants in this dispute contended that these reforms, in fact, are in line with "Polish legal tradition", which is characterized by vesting political power in legislatures, including broad prerogatives toward the judicial power.

However, some authors who have successfully pictured law in a non-reductive manner have recently placed the concept of LC under critical examination (Cotterrell 1997, 2006; Glenn 2004; von Benda-Beckmann and von Benda-Beckmann 2012). Moreover, even the advocates of cultural studies of law who animated the discussion on LC have expressed some serious objections toward the dominant way of conceptualizing the term (Nelken 2012, pp. 18–46). As can be readily demonstrated, the critical approach toward LC echoes fundamental voices raised against the general concept of "culture" in social anthropology and other social sciences. Since the 1980s increasing numbers of authors have been challenging fundamental assumptions underlying the notions of "culture" and "culture studies"; some scholars have even wondered about the validity or need for the term "culture" in scientific vocabularies (see, e.g., Wolf 1984).

Meanwhile, quite unexpectedly for social scientists, the concept of culture has suddenly been resurrected in neuroscience, biology, evolutionary biology, and primatology (where the sub-discipline of cultural primatology has been established) (see, e.g., Boesch 2012; Henrich 2015). "Hard scientists" have vigorously reanimated broad theoretical and empirical studies on culture. Furthermore, in parallel, some new approaches to culture have been developed and propagated in social sciences broadly understood (e.g., the cultural sociology of Jeffrey Alexander, the concept of cultural models by Giovanniego Bennardo and Victora C. de Muncka). The so-called cultural turn was introduced by Frederic Jameson in his 1998 collection, which has strongly influenced sociology, anthropology, and other fields. Slowly, the concept of culture, understood differently than in the classical period and studied with much more care and self-awareness, has again become the focal point of studying the social realm.

Legal academia should not ignore these processes of the "culturalization" of the "hard sciences" and the rising trend to rework the concept of "culture" in the social sciences. The resurrection of the concept of "culture" calls for, at least, a rethinking the idea of LC. In this vein, the present chapter aims at identifying the conditions in which the concept of LC could be reconceptualized and expanded in a way that extends our understanding of law as a dynamic, embedded, ontologically complex phenomenon. For this purpose, the previous dominant discourse on and main definitions of LC will be reconstructed and critically examined. As will be shown, the lack of solid theoretical grounds for most of the popular conceptualizations of LC constitutes one of the most striking features of the current discourse on this subject. As a response to this problem, Homi Bhabha's insights on "culture" will be employed in reworking the concept of LC. This aim is directed by the need for grounding the use of LC in the approach of capturing "culture", which has vast theoretical potential.

Bhabha's ideas were developed within the field of postcolonial studies, in which many authors criticized the practice of picturing "culture" as something ahistorical, unitary, stable, and reified (see e.g., Ashcroft et al. 1995). Along these lines, Bhabha mostly stresses certain misuses of "culture" and failures in applying cultural analysis. Crucially, Bhabha seeks to refresh the conceptualization of "culture" rather than rejecting the concept completely. Moreover, the reading of Bhabha presented here resembles rather the "hermeneutics of faith", which means that the analysis does not focus on problems, aporias, and inconsistencies in his ideas, but instead rests on those of Bhabha's claims that could invigorate the study of LC. Due to some distinctive features of his writing style and his ideological embeddedness, Bhabha's approach has often been dismissed without much effort to grasp its full content. For some authors (see, e.g., Sangren 1988; Mizutani 2013), Bhabha's views are not acceptable because of his (1) cultivation of a self-indulgent realm of subjectivity across social science, (2) unbalanced emphasis on what is ephemeral in "culture" at the expense of what is more enduring, (3) substitution of one established grand narrative on "culture" with a newer type, and (4) blurring of all difference into indifference, thereby making all hybridity appear identical. In fact, while Bhabha argues convincingly in many of his textual deconstructions, the diffuse reasoning and multiple inconsistencies in his work have led to misunderstandings of his intentions and claims. Nevertheless, some of his thoughts could enable one to explore new ways of looking at "culture". It seems that even the overrepresentation of certain characteristics of "culture" in Bhabha's writings serves well to challenge common conceptualizations of the term. Moreover, he opposes the kind of understanding of "culture" that has received much criticism from those skeptical toward the LC concept in legal academia. This parallel provides another reason to draw on Bhabha's considerations on, invoking the title of his celebrated book, the "location of culture".

The chapter intends to stretch the theoretical possibilities of Bhabha's insights, as applied to thinking about LC. Primarily, it demonstrates how "hybridity" can be productively applied to rework the traditional ways of understanding LC. The presented analysis assumes that we need strong oxygenation of thinking of and about LC, and Bhabha's ideas appear to be ideally suited for this task. More generally, drawing on his thoughts would contribute significantly to delimiting the conditions for utilizing the concept of LC that would generate cognitive benefits. Similarly, Roger Cotterrell has questioned "in what circumstances the concept of legal culture may (...) be valuable in social studies of law" (2006, p. 82). However, the presented approach brings more nuanced guidelines on the fruitful use of the concept than those provided by Cotterrell. Moreover, as opposed to Cotterrell's approach, the recommendations are not exclusively directed to those interested in the comparative sociology of law and close to the sociology of law and similar enterprises. What is more, Cotterrell rejects the possibility of a reconceptualization of LC. Instead, he prefers to radically narrow the scope of the legitimate use of LC only for the purpose of making an overall characterization of the "large aggregates of distinct elements" (2006, p. 88). In contrast, this chapter advocates for a careful and more self-reflexive utilization of the concept but without limiting what it covers to only a simplified approximation of something highly complex, elusive, and complicated.

2 Reconstructing the Current State of Art

2.1 Basic Intuitions Concerning "Culture"

Leaving aside details, let us start from some basic meanings and common-sense views that have been evoked by the term "culture" since its invention (see Kuper 1999). This approach provides needed context for analyzing LC, since many who employ the concept, especially non-professionals, refer to such popular registers of meanings.

First, the term "culture" presupposes the durability and continuity of some elements (values, deeply held assumptions, axioms, general worldviews) or their patterns within some entity (a given society, group). Although "culture" has a tendency toward stableness, it does not preclude dynamism but rather suggests substantial continuity even in the case of rapid societal changes. To put it differently, "culture" as a residual factor, difficult to challenge, remains solid and active even during social transformations. Such connotations are frequently linked with the belief that "culture" encompasses those deeply hidden factors underlying more tangible phenomena, which are not easy to grasp but strongly determine the social realm. The intuitive approach to "culture" focuses on differences between some collective entities in reference to these underlying fundamentals.

Second, in many usages, the term "culture" suggests the limitation of strong voluntarism and total individual autonomy. Mainly, it presupposes the existence of certain co-determining factors beyond the control of individuals. Their existence is constrained by the "cultural filters" that predetermine what they perceive, how they pre-evaluate, and what they see as probable and desirable. Simply put, "culture" filters human experiences. Consequently, it directs agents in a way that is unnoticeable to them. The impact of "culture" could be illustrated by the metaphor of a sailing ship. "Culture" refers to stable ocean currents that impact the movement of the ship, but which do not undermine the roles of the ship's crew, leadership, or construction plan.

Third, from the beginnings of the use of the concept of "culture," it has been utilized to aggregate the elements, traits, or features of a given entity or to indicate the most dominant patterns or tendencies characterizing that entity. Often, "culture" simplifies reality to capture the "essence" (i.e., those deeply submerged culturally determined behavioral triggers) or character of a particular people's, group's, or class's ways of life, viewing these as constituting a systematic whole.

The abovementioned presuppositions commonly associated with "culture" are responsible for the longstanding vitality and popularity of the term. However, at the same time, they are the main reasons for the inflation of meanings associated with "culture." The question here, elaborated in the subsequent sections of the chapter, is whether the most commonly held assumptions about "culture" and cultural explanation have infiltrated the way LC has been problematized and understood.

2.2 *Basic Models of Understanding Legal Culture*

As a starting point, note that even when one refers to the basic intuitions of understanding "culture" (those mentioned above), the notion of LC can be interpreted quite differently. Moreover, the mere phrase "LC" also automatically evokes a set of presuppositions and assumptions concerning the law and its place in the cultural landscape and, as a result, directs attention to different possible registers of meanings. Some basic models of understanding LC are reconstructed below. These models should be treated as mere idealizations to aid in mapping this variability.

First, there are two general models of understanding LC distinguished by the assumed relationship between the legal realm and the other social spheres. According to the **law's culture model**, LC implies that the law, understood as a (semi-)autonomous field or distinctive social machinery, produces its own distinct "culture". Here, "culture" includes meanings, symbolic representations, and ideas, along with the social practices and material features associated with the operation of this machinery. Law produces its "culture", which simultaneously constitutes the environment for its subsequent operations and development. Put another way, LC means "culture" that grows as legal machinery functions. Note that such a way of understanding of LC should not be automatically reduced to the "culture of professionals" or "internal legal culture" (although some definitions stress the internal legal development rather than external influences). In general, this model allows for the study of the relationship between LC and other segments of culture. Importantly, here LC does not faithfully mirror the character of the overall culture.

In contrast, according to the **embeddedness of law model**, LC encompasses the rather unconstrained impact of the wider "culture" on the legal realm. Such a reading emphasizes the embeddedness of law in the broader "culture" of a given community. LC demonstrates the saturation of broader "culture" in the vast operations of law. Simply, "culture" influences "law", which is seen as a deeply culturally situated phenomenon: law reflects the wider "culture" in which it is set. This way of thinking is highly prevalent and typically entertained to denote versatile non-legal embeddings of law. In this vein, Lawrence M. Friedman accentuates that law is "organically related to the culture as a whole" (1975, p. 193).

These two general models of LC provide the framework for making more detailed differentiations. According to the **ideational model** (which is based primarily on the assertion of the durability and continuity of "culture"), the LC means the most basic ideas, values, and aspirations, as developed through long historical processes, related to law that are characterized or shared within some collective entity. Here, LC is usually taken to indicate the collective ideational basics of law that could be also perceived as being located at the deeper, "unconscious" level. In such a case, although they are imperceptible, they in fact determine how the legal machinery works. An ideational reading of LC can be integrated with both models mentioned above: these underlying ideational elements can be seen as (1) existing and working exclusively within the legal sphere or, alternatively, (2) characterizing the wider "culture" in which the law is entrenched.

Next, the **focusing on peoples' mindset model** of LC covers what peoples forming some kind of collective entity think about various legal issues. "Think" is a broad category that denotes different cognitive processes (knowledge, evaluations, aspirations, values, etc.). Such a reading of LC intends to supplement the "black latter" vision of law and focuses on the social processes of constituting the mindsets of the putative addressees of the law. This account generates the problem of conflating the LC with "legal consciousness" and "attitudes toward law". Nevertheless, in the case of the focusing on peoples' mindset model, the stress can be placed on (1) the distinctiveness of thinking about the law (which is in congruence with the law's culture model) or (2) continuity with what people think in general (which satisfies the embeddedness of the law model).

Finally, according to the **law's operations model**, LC is seen as a broad, general, and concise description of how the law functions in a given setting. This model embraces the view that every particular system of legal machinery operates in a distinctive way and stresses that "law in action" must be considered when seeking to grasp the law in a non-reductive fashion. A source of this distinctiveness lies in the scope and the character of the integration between different elements of legal machinery. Peoples' states of mind, institutional settings, legal texts, and practices are, more or less, integrated into a working syndrome. In this vein, the LC, often accompanied by some adjectives, provides a summary of how the law works. In certain cases, only the main feature may be on the radar (e.g., adversarial legal culture). However, referring to this model, more comprehensive attempts at grasping how the law operates are also possible.

2.3 Comments on Current Definitions of LC

When considering the definitions of LC (the most popular are presented in Table 1), their enormous variability is clearly evident. The variety of understandings of LC is reminiscent of the multitude of meanings ascribed to "culture". Each of the selected definitions encompasses one (or multiple) of the different models of possible understanding of LC described above. Thus, the classical approach to LC, developed by Lawrence Friedman (e.g., 1975, 1994, 2006; see Carrillo 2007), clearly refers to the focusing on peoples' mindset model, which is highly debatable for numerous reasons (see def. 1a, 1b, 1c, and 8). Such definitions limit the scope of LC and rest only on the descriptive characteristics of what individuals think about law. Note that focusing on a cluster or network (see def. 1a, 1c) of certain people's thoughts narrows the definition further but also strengthens its exploratory potential. Moreover, some definitions in the literature can be ascribed to the law's operations model. Definition 4 offers the best representation of this model. Here, the process of "integrating" these different elements is stressed. Many approaches try to grasp the LC by referring to distinct aspects or dimensions that function as universal categories of the unifying concept of LC but without tracing the common thread between them (see def. 2, 3, 7, 9, 13). Other authors explore the ideational model. This tradition of capturing LC has long been popular in legal academia (see def. 6, 10, 11), but it also corresponds to how lay users typically utilize the term.

The comprehensive analysis of how the concept of LC has been applied in various fields and contexts constitutes a research agenda of its own. Rather than engaging in this task, only the basic features of the dominant ways of utilizing this concept in legal academia will be pinpointed. This approach will provide hints regarding the basic trends in the use of the concept of LC and the most obvious limitations of those usages.

Let us start from the practice of applying the concept without any self-reflection and carefulness (LC as a self-explanatory concept). Even prestigious journals have published papers that mentioned LC in their titles but lacked any references to what the concept means (see, e.g., Rosenn 1984). Indeed, LC has often been treated as a self-explanatory term that requires no further comment, always ready to be applied to various contexts and in a highly flexible manner (as an elusive independent variable or identity-based category). Such a practice leads to failures in the understanding of culture-related matters.

Moving to those authors who have attempted to elaborate further on the concept, it is not uncommon among this group to formulate the definition of LC without (1) providing its justification, (2) considering the underlying assumptions and adopted reasons for a given understanding of the term under consideration, and (3) dwelling on its potential usefulness as well as its flaws. This practice can be termed an arbitrary approach to LC. Moreover, proposed understandings of LC have often been built on fragile references to social sciences where the discussions on culture still flourish. Certainly, some authors, especially legal anthropologists, have more often referred to external, non-legal literature. But the majority have typically presented only selective references to debates conducted in the social sciences; many have addressed only the legal literature. It is striking that the achievements of the organizational sciences, cultural psychology, and even postcolonial studies, explored in this chapter, have not significantly affected studies on LC.

Next, the reader may be surprised by, as a rule, the atheoretical character of works that refer to LC. This characteristic indicates that most authors who have proposed definitions of LC have not attempted to develop a theory of LC. Providing the theory of a given *X* (here LC) is a far more demanding and challenging task than merely proposing an arbitrary definition of this *X*. However, expanding the definition into a larger theoretical framework can significantly upgrade the concept of LC, at least in three points. First, it would provide a better justification for the concept of LC. Working on such a theory forces its author to be more explicit and transparent about the assumptions held regarding the social world. Second, it would aid in making the concept more suitable for explanatory purposes. Since a theory fulfills an explanatory function, it always uncovers the factors that determine the studied phenomenon. Third, the definition of LC, which is integrated with some broader theoretical assumptions and propositions, assists in posing interesting hypotheses. It is a call to stop employing LC as a basic, dictionary notion and to start seeking to embed it in deeper theoretical thinking, while also relinquishing the idea of building a single universal concept of LC. The next section demonstrates how a more theoretically informed approach can transform the way LC can be understood.

3 Bhabha's Attack on the Classical Concept of "Culture"

Homi Bhabha is a foundational figure in postcolonial studies (see Ashcroft et al. 1995), a thread of the humanities that focuses on various social, political, and psychological processes associated with colonization and decolonization, which are seen as periods of complex and varied cultural contacts and interactions. Postcolonial authors have generally focused on the way the Western discourses on "culture" were formed in colonial settings and on what function they fulfilled for solidifying hegemonic power. Thus, these thinkers find the specific case of colonialism to be an ideal starting point for deconstructing, among other things, the homogenous, essentializing notion of "culture". Edward Said's famous concept of orientalism was already directed against the totalizing views of "oriental" cultures. Certainly, Said laid the foundations for a critical analysis of the discourse on "culture", since the core of the concept of orientalism contests binaries-based European ways of representing cultural differences. What is crucial, as acknowledged below, is that postcolonial authors provide the apparatus and the method for an examination of "culture" in contemporary society. They, and Bhabha especially, have expanded the theoretical possibilities of those categories and processes related to "culture" outside the space of colonial experience. Thus, in the case of "culture", Bhabha recommends "that we learn our most enduring lessons for living and thinking" (1994, pp. 38–39) from those who are subjugated, dominated, and displaced in colonial and postcolonial times.

Bhabha's works provide multiple insights into "culture". In general, his critical approach echoes the way social scientists have been reimagining "culture" over the past five decades. In this sense, Bhabha's thoughts are the product of such a broader critical attitude toward "culture". However, how he formulates his thought is quite idiosyncratic. The highly poetic prose, multivocal narrative, and opaque and nebulous style of writing, which combines metaphors with numerous references to the very broad spectrum of the humanities as well as to historical examples, all make reading Bhabha's works highly demanding. His essays are complex and difficult to comprehend, comprising fragmented mosaics of neologisms and poetry. It is plausible to hold that Bhabha intentionally writes about "culture"-related issues in metaphorical language to avoid constructing a new totalizing and universalizing narrative: he warns against turning his principal concepts such as "ambivalence" or "hybridity" into formulae that appear to capture the nature of "culture" fully (1994, p. 61). The way he presents his ideas seems to be designed to evoke criticism and encourage reflection, but not to provide a highly structured narrative concerning "culture". Frankly, Bhabha does not develop any solid definition of "culture".

These characteristics make the reconstruction and interpretation of Bhabha's ideas a challenging endeavor. With this in mind, some of Bhabha's most fundamental claims can still be presented in an ordered fashion. While this practice may distort certain details, such a strategy can make the presentation more conclusive and aid in examining how his ideas could inform the building of a more theoretically sound concept of LC.

1. For Bhabha, colonial and postcolonial conditions provide a perfect starting point for the revision of the classical notion of "culture". They form laboratories for understanding the discursive process that produces meanings and values (generally that is culture for Bhabha). Bhabha believes that the colonial case can be seen as "the paradigmatic place of departure" (1994, p. 21) from the classical narrative on "culture". Moreover, the colonial conditions constitute a "third space", a strongly ambivalent and indeterminate "location of culture". This fact is a consequence of the most basic circumstances for those subjected to colonial power structures, which consist in "being in at least two [cultural] places at once". In such a context, Bhabha refers to some historical macro-political and micro-psychological processes in colonies interpreted from a critical perspective in order to "learn our most enduring lessons for living and thinking" (1994, p. 39).

2. Bhabha's approach is mainly critical as he aims to demonstrate that specific power dynamics lie at the heart of the traditional, modernistic understanding of "culture", and consequently, "cultural differences". However, what is of major importance, a fundamental critique of the narrative on "culture" does not lead him to reject this notion. Rather, Bhabha seeks to build new sensibilities and make room for more self-reflective and careful discourse on "culture"-related issues. He wants to open up and explode "fissures for critical scrutiny" in this respect (1994, p. 247). Thus, the analysis aimed at deconstructing the dominant view simultaneously helps to propose the frames for further developing a sounder understanding of "culture", free from the totalizing narrative.

3. Moving to more substantial arguments, Bhabha stresses that some social processes that characterized the colonial condition have influenced the production of a certain way of understanding "culture" and, in result, the manner of seeing and articulating differences in terms of "culture". Simply speaking, those processes affected the way communities and peoples perceived (and for Bhabha still do) themselves as part of a particular "culture". Thus, the colonial hegemonic relations, consisting mainly of discriminatory practices, "produced" the dominant understanding of "culture" that lead to the categorization of the differences between people, groups, and political communities in a very particular way.

The discourse of colonizers needed and indeed produced a vision of distinct "cultures", which assisted with managing the colonies. Simply put, introducing differentiations between "solid", "still", and "bounded" "cultures" operated as a means of power (1994, p. 34). This conceptualization has directed colonized peoples' perceptions of identity, belonging, or national community, among other things. But this dynamic does not mean that the colonial authorities possessed total agency over those subjugated. Bhabha insists that, to some extent, the creation of absolute cultural differences was actually a product of the strategies adopted by both sides in this story. However, acknowledging the role of colonial subjects should not be read as neglecting the fact that this classical vision of "culture" was produced to serve the hegemonic domination—rather, it seeks to contest the claim of the absolute agency of colonizers.

Accordingly, Bhabha recognizes that representations of "culture" and "cultural" belonging are not simply received and derived "archaeologically" from the past.

Rather, they are produced here and now, in "the terrifying simultaneity of today". Thus, the way "culture" is understood is more a matter of the present (politics) than the past (history). "Cultures" are always retrospective constructions, meaning that they are consequences of certain diverse historical processes. "Culture", or to be more precise, the discourse on something named "culture", is seen as being constantly "manufactured".

4. This brings us to the following question: What kind of understanding of "culture" was produced under colonial conditions? Bhabha identifies the following features of "culture" imposed by colonial discourse: "purity", "originality", and "fixity" (encapsulated in the phrase "primordial unity or fixity"). Such a way of imaging "culture" denotes that some extra-individual, communal traits have been formed in the past of a given community and are now being reproduced, expanded, and redeveloped. However, such new forms are always the direct continuations of these "original" traits. "Purity" secures and solidifies the differences between "cultures", which facilitates certain aspects of social and psychological engineering by colonizers. Because the sole moment of differentiation between "cultures" creates the feeling of cultural supremacy, this way of thinking also produces the "culture" of the colonial powers. The imposition of the "fixity" into the narrative on "culture" informs the horizon of political goals because it is difficult to alter such "cultures" by normal measures. "Originality" stresses that those systems of meanings had a collective author in the past. It suggests that a certain way of living is deeply rooted in particular collective histories. As was mentioned, colonial discourse developed the idea of "primordial unity or fixity" of "culture" to justify various actions (and the general material inequalities central to colonial rule). Furthermore, the creation of "culture" as pure and original makes the picture of the social world more stable, filled by bounded, entrenched "cultures". This vision of "unity and fixity" worked as a power economizing mechanism because it is easier to rule when assuming (and forcing such claims on others) that the colonized population is divided into several "cultures" with distinctive characteristics rather than consisting of a fluid conglomerate of people with mixed characteristics. Moreover, thinking in terms of separate "cultures" provided the colonial authorities with reasons for collecting or codifying the customary or religious law of "cultural" groups.

5. According to Bhabha, the critical analysis of colonial conditions unmasks what lies beyond the narrative of the "purity and fixity" of "culture". However, drawing on colonial examples can contribute to building a more adequate way of understanding "culture". Against this background, Bhabha's concept of hybridity or hybridization, examined in relation to colonial moments but with potential for much broader application, works as an antidote to a classical reading of "culture" and as a tool for proposing a sounder understanding of "culture". Originally, for Bhabha, this concept encapsulated the paradoxical situations of colonial conditions that demonstrate the "impurity" and "unfixity" of each "culture". Given that the official narrative was designed to cement the opposite view, a paradox is generated. Mainly, the focus on inherent hybridization "challenges our sense of the historical identity of culture as a homogenizing, unifying force, authenticated by the originary Past, kept alive in the national tradition of the People" (Bhabha 1994, p. 37). For Bhabha, the effect of

colonial power is seen to be the production of hybridization rather than the noisy commands of colonialist authority or the silent repression of native traditions (p. 154).

The concept of hybridity has its own history (Young 1995). At its root, *hybrida* has a genetic meaning, signifying the offspring of a tame sow and wild boar that have enhanced traits due to crossbreeding, a characteristic known as heterosis. In the more recent past, hybridity has been used to denote human intervention in the life of plants. Thus, this original sense of hybridity was extended problematically first to concerns of "race science" and subsequently to various cultural interactions (Young 1995, pp. 6–19). Despite such registers, Bhabha has utilized this concept to grasp in an abstract way the various processes, described below, characterizing the colonial condition.

First, colonial authorities often deliberately worked to root their cultural traits in new soil. Second, the reactions of those subjected to the politics of colonial authorities also created new cultural forms. Bhabha emphasizes that even looking from the colonist perspective, the sole binary distinction between colonizers and colonized, as instantiated in the "cultural" differences terminology, produced some unintended consequences. Among them, the borrow ideas or values from the colonizer generated new elements or novel "cultural" constellations. Third, there was inevitably a split between what the colonizers intended and what the subjected appropriated from their attempts. Moving away from the narration of oppression, Bhabha states that hybridity is a necessary attribute of the colonial condition. Fourth, colonial authorities also intentionally created a buffer zone, which is a group of "native" people who were educated and socialized in the mother colony and designated for working as mutual translators and a new power structure. This subtype of the "mimic men", a figure crucial for Bhabha's argument, appear to be "authorized versions of otherness". However, in mimicking the colonizer only in part, they reveal the limits of the colonizer's drive to regulate and control his subjects. Fifth, as mentioned earlier, the colonized experienced "being at least two places at once", which means that they were under the influence of various pressures as well as opportunities. This existential state is another source of hybridization.

Returning for a moment to Bhabha's famous concept of mimicry, it describes a mode of colonial discourse that directed the reactions of colonial subjects toward adopting and adapting to the "culture" of the colonizers. This process should be read as a source of hybridization in a colonial setting. Counter to the colonizers' expectations, as Bhabha observes, the fact that colonial authorities invited colonial subjects to mimic their "culture" in some sense undercuts colonial hegemony because such mimicry blurred carefully constructed differences (between created "cultures"). For Bhabha, ambivalence, another key notion, characterized the workings of colonial authority. It covers unexpected forms of resistance that can be found in the history of the colonized and the equally unexpected anxieties that plagued the colonizers despite their apparent dominance. Moreover, as Bhabha indicates, mimicry is often an exaggerated copying of the colonizer's "culture"—mimicry is repetition with a difference, and so it is not evidence of the total subjugation of those under colonial rule. As Bhabha notes, "mimicry emerges as the representation of a difference that is itself a process of disavowal". In this vein, Bhabha affirms that "the colonial presence is always ambivalent, split between its appearance as original and authoritative and its articulation [by those who mimic it] as repetition and difference" (1994, p. 107). Thus, the results of mimicry are unpredictable, and the dynamics it generates occasionally lead to opposed states—the cracks within a colonial discourse and practice. It plays by the rules of the colonizer but at the same time works against them. As Bhabha observes (1994, p. 86),

> mimicking the colonizer only in part, or selectively colonized reveal the limits of the colonizer's power. Mimicry is, thus, the sign of a double articulation. It could be read as a complex strategy of reform, regulation, and discipline, which <appropriates> the Other as it visualises power. Mimicry is also the sign of the inappropriate, however, a difference or recalcitrance which coheres the dominant strategic function of colonial power, intensifies surveillance, and poses an immanent threat to both <normalized> knowledges and disciplinary powers.

All this inevitably stresses the reality of the ongoing mixing of different elements, identities, meanings, and values in colonial conditions. Accordingly, the construction of a cultural identity always covers over the traces and patches of discrepant cultural meanings produced by that plural, heterogeneous people. In short, for Bhabha, cultural meanings always contain traces of other meanings. Therefore, he argues, "claims to inherent originality or purity of cultures are untenable, even before we resort to empirical historical instances that demonstrate their hybridity" (Bhabha 2006, p. 156). Such hybridity does not correspond to the situation where two then "pure" cultures are hybridizing in certain situations. Rather, those more or less hybrid cultures are still hybridizing with each other. This is an argument against the view that there were cultures already in existence that only later became to some extent hybrid. As Bhabha explains, "for me the importance of hybridity is not to be able to trace two original moments from which the third emerges" (1990, p. 211).

Moreover, Bhabha acknowledges that this production of hybrid cultures, that is, cultures per se, may be consensual or conflictual. This possibility opens up space for searching for the different types of hybridizing. In general, the empirical fact of hybridization, despite all the attempts at concealing it, as Bhabha would add, demonstrates how naive it is to adhere to the "purity and originality" positions. Importantly, stressing such hybridization "moves the question of culture's appropriation beyond the assimilationist's dream, or the racist's nightmare, of a full transmittal of subject matter and toward an encounter with the ambivalent process of splitting and hybridity that marks the identification with culture's difference" (1994, p. 224). Bhabha insists that if cultures are viewed as having stable, discrete identities, then the divisions between cultures can always become antagonistic or potentially antagonistic. Consequently, raising awareness of the culture's hybridization impacts on how we deal with the Other. To blur the fixed boundaries between "they" and "ourselves" could transform our attitudes and policies toward the former. A questioning attitude toward "the authority of cultural synthesis in general" (1994, p. 20) makes possible the discarding of the all-comprising, aggregative notion of "culture". Informed by hybridization, one can better see culture as based on rearticulations, translations of elements that are neither the one nor the other, but something else besides that contests the terms and territories of both sides. Thus, hybridization emphasizes that culture is not a transmission of pre-given contents, but rather an ongoing "grinding" of the elements that travel beyond boundaries.

In Bhabha's writings, the hybridity that occurs in the so-called "third space" also has normative overtones. The concept of the "third space", where the "borderline work of culture" takes place, provides the ethical and political idea advocated by Bhabha. It is an "interruptive, interrogative, and enunciative" (Bhabha 1994, p. 179) space of new forms of cultural meaning and production blurring the limitations of existing boundaries and calling into question established categorizations of "culture". According to Bhabha, this "third space" is a highly ambivalent site where meanings have no "primordial unity or fixity", which "initiates new signs of identity, and innovative sites of collaboration and contestation" (1994, p. 1). The residents of such liminal sites respond to several different cultural narratives simultaneously and may respond paradoxically (for instance) to felt colonial and to felt postcolonial realities at the same time and juncture. This kind of "otherness" is considered a highly productive and inevitable element of human interaction. To be precise, for Bhabha, while some instances of the "third space", where accelerated hybridization occurs, can be tracked in a colonial situation, the idea can also demonstrate the potential of hybridity in present-day societies.

Summing up this line of argument, Bhabha develops the concept of hybridity to describe the nonlinear and non-unidirectional construction of "culture" and identity within conditions of colonial antagonism. However, this argument refers to every society—as he states in some of his interviews—because "all forms of culture are continually in a process of hybridity" (Bhabha 1990, p. 211). Hybridity, simply put, elucidates the fact that cultures are not discrete phenomena; instead, they are always undergoing the process of translating and negotiating "foreign" elements; mixedness is culture's nature.

To reiterate the ideas presented in this section, what matters to Bhabha is how "culture" is dynamically produced and transformed. However, "culture" does not rest on the mechanical reproduction of a set of thoughts and traditions within a given population over time. Rather, it is a lived mixture of elements (ideas, but also postures, movements, and actions) manifested through the ways in which individuals tacitly express themselves. Previously dominant understandings of culture as an all-powerful supra-individual "system", pure in character and originated in the past, are emphatically rejected by Bhabha as an illusory conceptual abstraction that in fact has a strong alliance with power. Instead of viewing culture as a collective prime mover acting on individuals encapsulated within a given society, he shifts attention toward producing certain ways of understanding "culture" and drawing on hybridization as a basic mark of culture. Hybridity helps the postcolonial critic to question the discourse of "culture." It should be stressed once more that hybridity in the Bhabhian sense is not a simple fusion of new and old elements into a crossbreed of ideas, values, or practices. Rather, the accent is put on "translation and negotiation", which makes such hybridization more than merely naïve copying and blending of a one particular culture with the other. The process of hybridity thus (in contrast to creolization or cultural blending) renders the idea of cultures as homogeneous entities inconceivable. In particular, given the rapid pace by which new ideas and thoughts are transmitted across seemingly different societies today, "culture" need no longer have a definitive geographical or pervasive socio-historical context: it is increasingly a creatively disjunctive mix of ideas and practices. Even the same elements are differently and strangely combined. As I will demonstrate below, Bhabha's ideas could substantially improve discussions on "culture" in the legal realm as well as on LC.

4 Bhabha's Lessons Assist in Reworking the Concept of LC

As noted in the introduction, while some details of Bhabha's approach have faced criticisms, the overall argument raised by him and others who question the classical approach to "culture" is slowly beginning to represent a leading voice in the social sciences. If one is willing to recognize Bhabha's core claims as sound, it would considerably influence how she or he would think about LC.

Certainly, the following remarks do not constitute a comprehensive application of Bhabha's thoughts to the new territory, but rather an initial attempt to explore those most evident possibilities that his viewpoint generates for thinking about LC. Moreover, as explained earlier, Bhabha's arguments against the classical way of understanding "culture" partially echo the main critical voices formulated toward LC in the legal academy, which can thus be substantiated and expanded by referring to a Bhabhian approach. Recall that besides providing a broad critique of the simplified notion of "culture", Bhabha does not reject this notion itself, which he still regards as an important category explaining the human condition. All this has significant repercussions for the discourse on LC. Therefore, it is reasonable to raise the following questions: How could Bhabha's approach to culture inform understanding of LC? What new research questions or subject of study related to LC could be proposed after adopting Bhabha's perspective on "culture"? More specifically, how could the concept of "hybrid culture" invigorate discussion and advance the study of culture and law or LC? How could Bhabha's promotion of ideas of ambivalence and hybridity mobilize an analysis of LC? Finally, how does the specificity of the legal sphere appear through Bhabha's conceptual lenses?

1. In general, Bhabha's thought could influence discussions about LC by providing some critically-oriented insight, leading to the deconstruction of the classical understanding of "culture" in legal discourses. Bhabha argues that critical thinking on this issue dissolves certain commonplace oppositions. It also provides tools that make the users of the concept more self-reflective about what the term implies or presupposes. Furthermore, the impact of Bhabha's framework may also be constructive: it would inform attempts to understand "culture" or at least open some new avenues in this regard. As a result, the conceptualization of LC might be profoundly reworked. In light of Bhabha's ideas, some cultures' features might be highlighted, especially those marginalized in dominant conceptualizations. In this case, the

concept of hybridity is the obvious candidate for invigorating the understanding of LC.

2. As explained above, Bhabha examines how a dominant view on "culture" was produced by the dynamic of power structures. Such an approach could be easily extended to LC. To begin with, consider the following difference. Some of the authors who intended to make the law less claustrophobic were clearly aware of various problems with the concept of culture (see especially Nelken 1995, 1997, 2004, 2006, 2007, 2012, 2014). However, the majority of non-professional users unintentionally reproduced the common meanings associated with "culture". With this difference in mind, Bhabha's ideas imply the critical type of questions that commentators on the usages of LC could raise. Among such questions, the most natural are the following: How, in what context, and with what motivations has the concept of LC been used in various types of discourses? What moments and processes are produced in the articulation of the differences between LCs presented as bounded entities? What are the consequences of relying on such conceptualizations? To what extent do older and widely accepted conceptualizations of LC reproduce the images of culture's "purity", "originality", and "fixity"? These aforementioned categories in particular could considerably inform the critical discursive analysis of the practice of employing the concept of LC.

3. In fact, as Bhabha insists, the role of ambiguity and indeterminacy in the cultural realm is far more profound than the dominant discourse stresses—yet the "pure [character] and fixedness" of "culture" are constructed. This issue raises the subject of how unambivalence and coherence (stableness) of a particular LC is manufactured, by what means and with what consequences. That is, how does the legal system produce its picture as fixed and uniform? Informed by Bhabha's ideas, the question is how and why, despite the actual hybridity, is the legal system able to present itself as "stable"? A particular LC can be seen as a consequence of various attempts to still the flux of cultural hybridities. Since Bhabha did not differentiate between different types of such masking processes, one who intends to draw on Bhabha's thought should propose more concrete mechanisms responsible for these activities (e.g., referring to legal realists or Pierre Bourdieu's approach). This is a call for mapping how legal systems mask their operations. In truth, however, certain political strategies might be aimed at the opposite end, that is, a deconstruction of how the law works intended to gain political advantages. Thus, one can see the inherent and external processes that are responsible for creating and contesting the monolithic view of a given LC.

4. As argued above, Bhabha's approach can be applied to substantiate a sounder understanding of "culture" and then LC. The most straightforward way of applying Bhabha's ideas is to examine whether the concept of hybridity facilitates a novel reconceptualization of LC.

Although hybridity has become a master trope across many spheres of cultural analysis, with some reservations, it has hardly been adapted to legal studies. Certainly, some similar ideas of "mixing" between legal systems were introduced in comparative law. For example, the idea of a hybrid legal system at first glance shares some features with hybridization, but its scope is much narrower (e.g., Örücü 2008).

Moreover, some scholars see hybridity as similar to the diffusion that encompasses the mixtures and movements of state law and other norms (Donlan 2011). As Seán Donlan states (2011, p. 13):

> whenever a body of law comes into contact with other systems, it ceases to preserve its native character intact; it takes on new colours of form and content derived from foreign law. In all of the periods of legal history, from early antiquity to the present day, the play of these foreign influences and counter-influences has produced systems of mixed origin; and it would seem, indeed, that no system of civilised law known to history has ever been strictly pure, in the sense of being based solely on indigenous growths.

This approach moves away from the "purity" paradigm but also limits the subject of hybridization to only different types of normative orders or systems of norms. From a different and more abstract perspective, Paul Berman articulates the "normative jurisprudence" that might flow from observations on hybridization in legal systems (2010). For him, "messy interactivity is actually a potentially desirable feature to build into legal and political systems" (2010, p. 12). He calls for "a jurisprudence of hybridity", based on the assumption that people hold multiple community affiliations, which suggests that a conceptualization of the diversity in terms of either universality or separatism seems to be unsound. One can readily find here, at first glance, similar claims to those made by Bhabha. However, Berman's approach is normative (it sketches the shape of a new jurisprudence) and focused on identity politics. Next, Sally E. Merry, referring directly to LC, acknowledges some threads that are quite close to Bhabhian hybridization (2012). But Merry focuses on globalization as a decisive factor responsible for the fact that "legal culture tends to be hybrid" (2012, p. 680). Furthermore, she writes convincingly about the "conditions of hybridity and change" that must be taken into account when seeking to understand LC (2012, p. 69). This approach conflates hybridity as a feature of the LC and its environment. Nevertheless, while Merry as a legal anthropologist is familiar with a critique of the vision of culture as a "fixed" and "bounded" entity, she still refers to the intuitive meaning of hybridity and consequently legal hybridity (which states that there are many legal orders that operate on different levels of organization of society and that globalization strengthens the "mixedness" of any law). Given these limitations, Merry's acknowledgment of hybridity does not translate into a new way of thinking about LC that would address the "hybridity" challenge.

The examples above demonstrate that Bhabha's understanding of culture as inherently hybrid has not yet strongly influenced studies on the legal realm; however, some similar ideas have nevertheless infiltrated the legal sciences.

Moving to the Bhabhian approach and its relevance for studying LC, note that focusing on hybridization already pinpoints certain issues: What could the LC's hybridity mean? Where does hybridization occur within the LC? How would hybridization work within and beyond the LC sphere? Finally, to what extent were particular legal cultures formed by hybridization? However, one seeking to answer these questions must be aware that hybridity is profoundly ambivalent, a phenomenon of many projections. As such, it could be banal, unremarkable, and apparent everywhere. For many authors, hybridity has come to have multiple meanings associated with mixing and combination in the moment of cultural exchange. But such an approach does not bring analytical sharpness to the concept. Although Bhabha views all culture as hybrid, the argument presented in this chapter holds that the concept of hybridity should be substantially upgraded and expanded, for example, through (1) the differentiation between different kinds of hybridization processes and (2) studying this concept in relation to different levels or objects.

Regarding the latter issue, one can notice that legal texts (rules and principles), legal concepts, styles of argumentation, legal institutions, institutional practices, sets of values underlying the law, and actors' thinking about law can all be subjected to hybridization processes. Moreover, one should remember that completely hybrid or pure "LCs" are the ideal models that assist efforts to grasp the real saturation of hybridity/purity. Thus, while hybridity seems to be an inherent feature of each culture, its actual representation oscillates between those two extremes.

Referring to the former issue, for example, Ella Shohat suggests that we should "discriminate between the diverse modalities of hybridity, for example forced assimilation, internalized self-rejection, political co-option, social conformism, cultural mimicry, and creative transcendence" (1992, p. 110). Adjusting such categories to the legal sphere would make the concept of legal hybridity more nuanced and strengthen its explanatory powers. In this line, one can readily propose some basic differentiations of legal hybridization. First, legal hybridization can be unintended. Consider, for example, that certain values or ideas relevant to how law works are propagated by mass media and only slowly, in a long time horizon, enter the legal system. Sometimes the place or institution where the further decision-maker graduated matters. Let us assume that a future minister of justice has earned their degrees in country *X*. While occupying the position and looking for inspiration to reform the judiciary they naturally gravitate toward discussions and imaginaries from country *X*. This situation could initiate the osmosis-like, unintended hybridization process. Certainly, hybridization can be a deliberate effort. This occurs, for example, when the person responsible for reforming or adjusting the legal system refers explicitly to some "foreign" elements. Second, in the case of hybridization by deliberate choice, the fact of adopting a "foreign" legal element could be communicated to the public (publicized/overt deliberate hybridization) or reserved for decision-makers (tacit/concealed deliberate hybridization). Many reasons could explain why the former or latter process happens. Third, different types of hybridization could also be distinguished by referring to the perspective of their results. Hybrid effects could be far from radical and revolutionary and instead consist of small displacements or glitches in the social fabric ("small" hybridization). Most such alterations are only temporary, but in conjunction with others, they can result in an important social change in the long term. Nevertheless, it is necessary to assume the possibility of the existence of legal hybridization that immediately makes a considerable difference ("total" hybridization). The grand historical processes that impact the different levels of law—that simultaneously exert a deep influence on many dimensions—hybridize on many levels, and thus, the "total" change is possible. Fourth, it is useful to distinguish the hybridization that contains the translation and negotiation of what is hybridized (hybridization in a strict sense), where the agents of such hybridization actively search for the new "meanings and values", from the hybridization involving all the different processes in which such direct personal impact does not or only slightly occurs (hybridization in a broad sense). For Bhabha, only the former deserves to be called hybridization.

Applying hybridization to LC undermines the vision of a solid, pure, bounded, and authentic LC in favor of a more unexpected, ambivalent, and fortuitous type. It radically refocuses the points of interest. Moreover, hybridity challenges the practice of the identification of a given LC, its recognition as a distinct LC, only in terms of its difference to other LCs. From Bhabha's perspective, hybridization should be viewed as an aspect of relationships rather than an inherent property of a collective. Thus, researching legal hybridity focuses not only on the exchanges, examining the processes of mutual discovery and influence between different elements related to the operation of law in different places, but also on the ongoing process of translating and negotiating these hybridized parts. Investigating the history of hybridization should not begin with two or more legal cultures, more or less pure, and then tracing their historical movements of hybridization. Rather, it should excavate the ongoing hybridization that transcends the currently existing and stably entrenched cultural forms. The Bhabhian approach calls for something more: imagining the hybridization of the already hybrid. In this context, the centrality of hybridization calls for a rethinking of the link between LC and "legal transplants". It appears that hybridization encompasses Pierre Legrand's claims that the subject of hybridization always needs, in Bhabha's words, "negotiation and translation" as well as Alan Watson's argument that the "transplantation" of law, which is a type of hybridization, is common and is responsible for most of legal developments. This observation calls for focusing on how a particular element has been "negotiated" and "translated" in a given social site (e.g., Ng 2014). This process of implanting or developing the new, hybrid meanings and values needs to be examined on an interactional level.

5. Bhabha explores the "third space" or "liminal space" where, according to him, intensive hybridization occurs, leading to the production and performance of novel meanings and values. Attempting to apply this concept to the legal sphere generates many difficulties. Some result from the substantial variance in how the law was and is understood. Law's historical variability makes such speculation about the relationship between the "third space" and the law highly demanding. However, narrowing the scope of interest to vaguely stretched so-called Western law—characterized by its strong connection with the state organization, articulated mostly in texts, and operated by professionals and distinguishable from other ordering tools—enables one to consider the basic interactions between the law and the "third space".

First, the law, considered as a well-structured domain, highly professionalized and characterized by numerous procedural requirements, leaves little room for legal liminality. It does not directly constitute the space "beyond" and "between" dominant discourses where the new meaning and values (both those related directly to the law and those secured by law) can easily flourish. Moreover, at first glance, the law can be seen as a sphere opposite to the "third space"—in most cases it secures certain established social values rather than facilitating the emergence of radically new ones. In this reading, the law works as a homogenizing factor, responsible for minimizing social hybridizations by imposing unifying standards. It is focused on balancing, distinguishing, and securing rather than opening, enabling, and stimulating.

Second, one can argue that in a democratic society, the law provides and secures the necessary freedoms (civil rights) that enable citizens to collectively undertake various types of hybridizing. These mass movements could create the incipient "third space", where the new values are growing. Thus, from this perspective, the living fabric of society may generate the various "third spaces" that are in fact secured by legal provisions.

Third, it is possible to claim that even law in itself, to some degree, possesses some potential for enabling the "third space". This scenario can occur in cases where deliberative processes based on free and open communication are, to the largest possible extent, implemented during legal decision-making. Admittedly, the procedural rules regulate what happens in deliberative arenas. Nevertheless, certain elements of liminality can occur there. The existence of different versions of alternative dispute resolution ADR-like processes also opens up a potential space for legal liminality. Frankly, however, the potential for installing such "third spaces" into law should not be overstated. If so, the conditions most conducive to hybridization lie outside the legal domain.

5 Conclusions

The ideas of Homi Bhabha encourage one to look at the discourse on "culture" and LC from new angles. His concepts of hybridity, ambivalence, third space, and mimicry provide some initial tools for cultural analysis and for rethinking LC. The latter effort is important because studies on LC have become mired in what could be perceived as unproductive discussions regarding the seriously flawed conceptualizations. Furthermore, the dominance of the intuitive understandings of the term under consideration has not stimulated more sound theoretical use of the concept. Moreover, those authors seriously interested in LC have not kept up with the broad stream of research on culture produced not only in evolutionary sciences but also in cultural psychology, cultural neurobiology, and organizational sciences. The majority of authors concerned with culture have moved on from mere "criticism of what is now obvious" toward searching for more nuanced and sound paradigms, frameworks, and theories of culture. In this vein, as discussed above, Bhabha's insight provides a new space for reimagining the concept of LC. As was demonstrated, the concept of "hybrid culture" can invigorate discussions and studies of LC in this respect. In particular, the promotion of the ideas of ambivalence and hybridity opens new themes and accentuates what typically is marginalized when one refers to "culture" or LC. Nevertheless, Bhabha's approach also assists with tracking the particular characteristic of the legal sphere—the lack of wide "third spaces" of law (i.e., the only marginal importance of legal liminality).

Bhabha's critical remarks on the classical understanding of culture and his constructive propositions, together with the research on various aspects of culture conducted after the "turn against culture" (Abu-Lughod 1991), allow for delimiting the conditions for utilizing the concept of LC that would bring important cognitive benefits. To put it differently, the LC could be still a useful, productive, and inspiring concept, but this outcome is possible only under certain conditions sketched below. Since using "culture" and "culture"-related arguments in legal settings is more prominent than ever, the sociologically oriented researchers within the legal academy are destined to provide some constructive guidelines, general pieces of advice for laypersons as well as professionals who seek to refer to LC. The following are the most basic recommendations.

1. General care with utilizing the concept is needed: certainly, "culture" and consequently LC are not the primary concepts. They require further explanations. Many problems result not only from the variety of approaches to culture in academia but also, more importantly, from the multitude of meanings and preconceptions toward it held by lay users.

2. When utilizing the concept of LC, one needs to be aware of the various flaws associated with typical usage of the term "culture", which clearly influences the intuitive understanding of LC. The mapping and addressing of those flaws (essentialism, stigmatization, tautological character, conflation of causes and consequences, homogenization) constitute the common heritage of the social sciences and humanities. All this critical insight needs to be taken into account by those wishing to absorb the term. A myriad of papers and books warns against the riskiness of certain ways of utilizing culture and thus LC. Such awareness translates into more active reactions to those who employ the concept of LC incorrectly.

Note here that using the concept of LC brings one important challenge. The relations between law and culture can be variously problematized. However, the term LC suggests the possibility or even the necessity of isolating the legal elements from the rest. However, such separation might be grossly inadequate in cases where social normativity works differently than is suggested by the picture of different, separate types of social norms, the law included. Thus, the term LC either cuts off the normative reality to distract from what is distinctively legal (according to the law's culture model) or prioritizes looking from the law's internal perspective at other social domains (in line with the epiphenomenal character of the law model). Either way, the legal realm is placed in a hegemonic position.

3. Among major flaws in the popular understanding of culture, those stressed by Bhabha are especially important for those studying or referring to LC because of the vast and important ethical and political consequences of thinking in terms of "purity and fixity". Bhabha's insistence on avoiding assumptions about the "purity", "fixity", and "originality" of culture is readily extendable and applicable to LC.

4. Any attempts at utilizing the term "culture" demand greater awareness about the history of this term and its connection with both power and genuine interest in the Other. This issue raises the fundamental question of why the concept of culture has been developed, and what functions it has fulfilled. Thus, the potential user should be aware of what the authors as well as non-professionals utilizing the concept of LC have intended to gain by employing this notion. The most important reasons for appealing to LC are as follows: acknowledging the differences, facilitating the

reinvigoration of the study of law, taking into account the deep embeddedness of law, and institutionalizing the research directed at the law's contextual factors. Referring to non-professionals, the use of the concept is driven by the needs for acknowledging the "soft" elements that are necessary for law to function well, stressing certain axiological aspirations, and providing the *longue durée* narrative on a particular legal issue. Each potential user should ask the simplest question: What is the concept of LC for, and why do I need the term under consideration? Those self-reflexive considerations on the place of LC enable one to clarify, first for themselves, and later for the audiences, what role the concept plays in one's overall argument.

5. Unfolding the potential of the term, one needs to indicate strictly where culture is located. This requirement is due to the abstract character of the notion of "culture" and, therefore, LC. First, the potential user needs to realize whether they invoke "culture" as a determining factor (ultimate or proximate) or rather as a consequence of particular social processes. In reality, social processes could be located in both registers simultaneously ("causes", "results"), but the good practice is to indicate at the beginning from where the inquiries begin. Second, from a different angle, the potential user should decide whether they are referring to culture as covering (1) the specific content (culture as a specific thing, object, type of reality), (2) the mechanism (culture as a mechanism of transmission or social memorizing), or (3) the consequences of processing certain content by a given operational mechanism (the repertoire of attitudes and behavior shared by a given group of people). This is clearly an oversimplified map of possibilities, but the gold standard of utilizing LC consists in acknowledging what in fact LC encompasses. It can evoke (1) certain meanings and values (or other elements classified as the content of the culture) related to the working of the legal system, (2) the specific operational syndrome that produces and transforms those contents, or (3) the descriptive characteristic of a given community in reference to how its members think on legal issues (which is a result of varied processes) or how the legally relevant actions are patterned. The concepts of culture and LC cannot simultaneously encompass so many spheres and aspects—the user must delimit the intended points of reference and provide a more rigorous specification of the used concept. Third, the potential users should clarify whether they are seeking to utilize the concept to grasp (1) the more or less wide tendencies considered in the *longue durée* perspective (this reading is closer to comparative law) or (2) the actual ethnographic socio-legal reality with its real density at the grassroots level (this is an anthropological reading). The difference between these two broad registers of meanings needs to be strongly acknowledged. Rather than stretching the concept in different directions, one should directly indicate the basic reference context.

References

Abu-Lughod L (1991) Writing against culture. In: Fox RG (ed) Recapturing anthropology: working in the present. School of American Research Press, Santa Fe
Ashcroft B, Griffiths G, Tiffin H (eds) (1995) The post-colonial studies reader. Routledge, London
Bell J (1995) Comparative law and legal theory. In: Krawietz W, Maccormick N, von Wright H (eds) Prescriptive formality and normative rationality in modern legal systems. Duncker & Humblot, Berlin, pp 19–31
Berman PS (2010) Towards a jurisprudence of hybridity. Utah Law Rev 1:11–29
Bhabha HK (1990) The third space: an interview with Homi Bhabha. In: Rutherford J (ed) Identity, community, culture, difference. Lawrence and Wishart, London, pp 201–213
Bhabha HK (1994) Location of culture. Routledge, London
Bhabha HK (2006) Cultural diversity and cultural differences. In: Ashcroft B, Griffiths G, Tiffin H (eds) The post-colonial studies reader. Routledge, New York
Bierbrauer G (1994) Toward an understanding of legal culture: variations in individualism and collectivism between Kurds, Lebanese and Germans. Law Soc Rev 29(2):243–264
Blankenburg E, Bruinsma F (1994) Dutch legal culture. Kluwer Law and Taxation Publishers, Deventer
Boesch C (2012) Wild cultures: a comparison between chimpanzee and human. Cambridge University Press, Cambridge
Carrillo JJ (2007) Links and choices: popular legal culture in the work of Lawrence M. Friedman. South Calif Interdiscip Law J 17(1):1–22
Cotterrell R (1997) The concept of legal culture. In: Nelken D (ed) Comparing legal cultures. Dartmouth, Aldershot, pp 13–32
Cotterrell R (2006) Law, culture and society. Legal ideas in the mirror of social theory. Ashgate, Aldershot
Donlan SP (2011) The Mediterranean Hybridity Project: crossing the boundaries of law and culture. J Civ Law Stud (4):355–396
Friedman LM (1969) Legal culture and social development. Law Soc Rev 1(1):29–44
Friedman LM (1975) The legal system: a social science perspective. Russell Sage Foundation, New York
Friedman LM (1990) The republic of choice: law, authority, and culture. Harvard University Press, Cambridge Mass
Friedman LM (1994) Is there a modern legal culture? Ratio Juris 7(2):117–131
Friedman LM (2006) The place of legal culture and its position in the sociology of law. In: Freeman M (ed) Law and sociology. Oxford University Press, Oxford
Friedman LM, Pérez-Perdomo R (2003) Legal culture in the age of globalization: Latin America and Latin Europe. Stanford University Press, Palo Alto
Gibson JL, Caldeira GA (1996) The legal cultures of Europe. Law Soc Rev 30(1):55–85
Glenn PH (2004) Legal cultures and legal traditions. In: Van Hoeck M (ed) Epistemology and methodology of comparative law. Oxford University Press, Oxford
Henrich J (2015) The secret of our success: how culture is driving human evolution, domesticating our species, and making us smarter. Princeton University Press, Princeton
Klare KE (1998) Legal culture and transformative constitutionalism. South Afr J Hum Rights 14 (1):146–188
Kuper A (1999) Culture. The anthropologist's account. Harvard University Press, Cambridge
Merry SE (2012) What is legal culture? An anthropological perspective. In: Nelken D (ed) Using legal culture. Wildy, London
Merryman JH (1985) The civil law tradition: an introduction to the legal systems of Western Europe and Latin America. Stanford University Press, Stanford
Mizutani S (2013) Hybridity and history: a critical reflection on Homi K. Bhabha's post-historical thoughts. Ab Imperio 4:27–48
Nelken D (1995) Understanding/invoking legal culture. Soc Leg Stud 4(4):435–452

Nelken D (1997) Puzzling out legal culture. In: Nelken D (ed) Comparing legal cultures. Dartmouth, Aldershot

Nelken D (2004) Using the concept of legal culture. Aust J Leg Philos 29:1–28

Nelken D (2006) Rethinking legal culture. In: Freeman M (ed) Law and sociology. Oxford University Press, Oxford, pp 200–224

Nelken D (2007) Defining and using the concept of legal culture. In: Orucu E, Nelken D (eds) Comparative law: a handbook. Hart, Oxford, pp 109–132

Nelken D (2012) Using legal culture: purposes and problems. In: Nelken D (ed) Using legal culture. Wildy, London

Nelken D (2014) Thinking about legal culture. Asian J Law Soc 1(2):255–274

Ng M (2014) Legal transplantation in early 20th century China – practicing law in Republican Beijing (1910s–1930s). Routledge, London

Ogus A (2002) The economic basis of legal culture: networks and monopolization. Oxf J Leg Stud 22(3):419–434

Örücü E (2008) What is a mixed legal system: exclusion or expansion? J Comp Law 3(1):34–52

Quinn G (2020) Legal culture and the CRPD. In: Kakoullis EJ, Johnson K (eds) Recognising human rights in different cultural contexts: the United Nations Convention on the rights of persons with disabilities (CRPD). Palgrave Macmillan, London, pp 19–44

Rosenn KS (1984) Brazil's legal culture: The Jeito revisited. Fla. Int'l L.J. 1(1):1–44

Sadurski W (2019) Poland's constitutional breakdown. Oxford University Press, Oxford

Sangren PS (1988) Rhetoric and authority of ethnography: "Postmodernism" and the social reproduction of texts. Curr Anthropol 29:405–435

Shohat E (1992) Notes on the "Post-Colonial". Soc Text 31(32):99–113

Van der Walt AJ (2006) Legal history, legal culture and transformation in a constitutional democracy. Fundamina 12(1):1–47

van Hoecke M, Warrington M (1998) Legal cultures, legal paradigms and legal doctrine: towards a new model for comparative law. Int Comp Law Q 47:495–636

Varga C (1995) Transition to rule of law: on the democratic transformation in Hungary. Philosophiae iuris, Budapest

von Benda-Beckmann F, von Benda-Beckmann K (2012) Why not legal culture. In: Nelken D (ed) Using legal culture. Wildy, London

Wolf ER (1984) Culture: panacea or problem? Am Antiq 49(2):393–400

Young RJC (1995) Colonial desire: hybridity in theory, culture, and race. Routledge, London

Mateusz Stępień A Professor of Sociology of Law in the Faculty of Law and Administration at the Jagiellonian University in Cracow (Poland). His research interests focus on exploring the cultural dimension of law. He published papers on Bronislaw Malinowski's concept of law, Confucianism, images in judicial opinions, and power distance in courtroom. He is currently working on the subject of judicial empathy and legal placebo.

Customary Law Is Like an Onion: A Multilayered Approach to Customary Law and Its Status in the Contemporary World

Jan Bazyli Klakla

Abstract In this chapter a new, original conceptualization of customary law is presented, suitable and adequate for the role it may play in the contemporary world. The concept that is proposed is a multi-layered approach applied by distinguishing several dimensions within the phenomenon of customary law that vary in terms of their normative character. Through his chapter Klakla compares customary law to an onion and unwraps it layer by layer, identifying four main components of customary law. Firstly, he refers to the behavioral aspect of this system containing patterns of the expected behavior. The second layer, still closely connected with actual human behavior, is constituted of predispositions and guidelines for social action. Then, Klakla moves toward layers that have more symbolic meaning, are connected with human behavior in more indirect ways and constitute a cognitive-cultural component of customary law: the layer of social values and the layer of social identity. That approach aims for greater depth and complexity of possible analysis and reflects a progressive change that happens in the social order among many communities.

1 Introduction

Customary law, as a phenomenon residing at the intersection of law and culture, is a concept particularly relevant to this book. In Part II of the book, devoted to the case study, this issue is most strongly touched upon by Górska's chapter on homicide in modern Palestinian customary law, but it is also important for the issues raised by Ptak-Chmiel in her "Case Study of the Invocation of Cultural Defense Outside of the Common Law" or Drwal in the chapter about "Love Jihad" in India. Here, in Part I of the book, which is oriented more theoretically, I attempt an original reconceptualization of customary law in order to get closer to an approach that allows deep understanding of this phenomenon within the conditions of the

J. B. Klakla (✉)
Department of Sociology of Law, Jagiellonian University, Cracow, Poland
e-mail: jan.bazyli.klakla@uj.edu.pl

M. Stępień, J. B. Klakla (eds.), *Law and Culture*, Law and Visual Jurisprudence 5,
https://doi.org/10.1007/978-3-030-81193-8_3

contemporary world. Theorization in the field of customary law is tricky, as one has to avoid attracting criticism for being ignorant of cultural issues on one hand and being ignorant of legal issues on the other.

Thus, my goal is to combine the legal and anthropological sensibilities in such a way as to offer a nuanced approach to customary law. At the same time, I aim for it to be compact enough to be flexible and applicable in future empirical research. To facilitate the understanding of my argument by lawyers and anthropologists as well as representatives of other sciences who may find it interesting, I use the metaphor of an onion, an object everyone knows regardless of their field of studies. The issue of customary law is important not only from the perspective of those societies that are studied in this context but also for the science of law in a more general sense, as it is an inspiration for "enlarging the realm of legal studies to embrace formerly 'suppressed discourses of non-state law'" (Roberts 1994, p. 963).

2 Law and Culture

I will start my considerations with a few remarks on the relationship of law—not limited to customary law—and culture. Stępień writes on this subject in his chapter on redefining the concept of legal culture. As I see my chapter as part of a larger whole that this book is, I would like to avoid repeating at this point what has already been raised by other authors. Therefore, I only highlight those assumptions that are necessary for the understanding of my further arguments.

First and foremost, for me, law is a part of culture, not a separate entity. The image of law as an element of culture, one of its interrelated aspects, was emphasized in the earliest definitions of culture. Tylor, on the front page of his work "Primitive Culture" (1871, p. 1), lists law as part of a larger whole that co-creates culture, alongside knowledge, beliefs, art, morality, custom and all other abilities acquired by man as a member of society. Geertz (1983, p. 218) writes that "law, rather than a mere technical add-on to a morally (or immorally) finished society, is, along of course with a whole range of other cultural realities from the symbolics of faith to the means of production, an active part of it". In other words, law is simply one of the social practices of giving meaning that make up the culture. As has been a bit harshly, but accurately, pointed out by Mezey (2001, p. 46), this means that despite the best efforts, law cannot be separated from culture, and culture cannot be separated from law. The legal realm is an integral part of culture (Rosen 2006).

Such an understanding of law obviously raises questions about the relationship between law and other social structures (Baier 2016, p. 2). If, as many anthropologists recognize, the complexity of social life consists of many aspects—for example, economic, technical, political, aesthetic or legal—then we cannot fully understand any of them in isolation from the rest (see Levi-Strauss 1963, p. 358).

The adoption of this assumption has very specific consequences for the further course of my thinking about customary law. Firstly, it distances us from the question of whether or not customary law is in fact properly law. Regardless of the answer given, customary law and other kinds of law are all elements of the same cultural apparatus. A similar criticism of excessive concentration on issues of defining the law has been made by Llewellyn, for whom such enquiry is associated with an excessive narrowing of the legal field. He expresses his position as follows: "So I am not going to attempt a definition of law. (...) A definition both expands and includes (...) and the exclusion is almost always rather arbitrary. I have no desire to exclude anything from matters legal. In one aspect law is as broad as life" (Twining 1973, p. 591). Hence, issues of definition will not bother me in this chapter, and I will return to them at the end only to emphasize once again the futility of the disputes that arise on their basis.

Therefore, in this approach, which I also adopt for the purposes of this chapter, the differences between legal norms and other social norms are not strongly emphasized (Johansson 2016, p. 113). Rather, the emphasis is on their coexistence, the interdependencies and complementary relations that exist between them (Baier 2016, p. 6). Woodman, in the context of theorizing about customary law, puts it in the following way (2001, pp. 29–30):

> The claim advanced here is not merely that the word "law" should be applied to some non-state normative orders. That claim might be answered by arguing that it is worthwhile to use terminology that distinguishes between the normative orders of states and other normative orders. Or it could be said that it is preferable to adhere to the traditional terminology which, it is sometimes alleged (although, I believe, mistakenly), uses the term "law" only for the state's normative order. The claim is that there is no clear distinction in fact between the social phenomena referred to as state laws and other social normative orders.

Hence a large number of seemingly extra-legal elements and concepts present in my proposal for the understanding of customary law. The normativity is only—to use the second of the metaphors that I considered when writing this chapter—the tip of the iceberg when it comes to customary law understood as a social phenomenon. What is hidden underwater many would probably not call a "berg" in the strict sense of the word—after all, it lies below sea level and it would be difficult to climb. However, this is an immanent and in many ways fundamental part of what an iceberg is. The same applies to customary law, and I will attempt to show it on the following pages of this chapter.

Finally, such an assumption requires the adoption of an adequate concept of culture as a specific meta-basis for further considerations. If customary law is to be treated as a phenomenon that is still alive, changing and adapting to the reality of the contemporary world—and this is the approach I will present on the following pages—then the "adequate" conceptualization of culture will be the one that shares these features. Therefore I reject in advance, as highly inadequate, the conceptualization of culture as a single, homogeneous set of knowledge or beliefs that are relatively seamlessly passed down from generation to generation, as well as any notion of a both limited and geographically located culture, as suggested by such expressions as, for example, "Albanian culture", "Polish culture", and so on (for more detailed consideration of this aspect of culture see, e.g., the review of the concept of culture in cultural geography by Mitchell [1995]). The important note is that I see a concept of "national" culture as an overly unified one, one that ignores significant cultural differences within the country. In my proposal for the conceptualization of customary law, while opposing the notion of culture as static, homogeneous or unchanging, I will instead be using the concept of culture as a heteronomous and dynamic process.

Undoubtedly, this is an approach much better suited to this conceptualization than the approach to culture that may initially be associated with the onion metaphor. It was Hofstede who used this metaphor to describe culture itself. In his opinion, culture consists of different layers and therefore can be compared with an onion. On the outer layer of the onion are symbols, such as food, logos or monuments. The next layer is made up of heroes, and may include real-life public figures such as politicians, athletes or entrepreneurs, and characters derived from popular culture, such as Superman. On the third layer, closest to the core, there are rituals such as the sauna, karaoke and social gatherings (see Hofstede et al. 2005). However, the similarity of this approach to the conceptualization of customary law proposed in this chapter is only apparent. Although Hofstede tries to perceive culture as not static but rather dynamically changing, he is not able to escape far-reaching generalizations that force an approach to culture as a homogeneous whole in the name of the "one country–one culture" paradigm.

3 Customary Law

Scientific honesty requires me not to start immediately with the explanation of the thesis proposed in the title—that customary law is like an onion—but rather to outline the context in which reflection on this phenomenon has been shaped. For many years, considerations concerning customary law were based on disputes over definitions. In fact, they were focused on conceptualizing the law itself in such a way that this concept would contain the phenomenon they were studying. The underlying question was: do the communities we study have law if they do not have a developed legal system in the modern sense? Gluckman notes that it is a pointless and barren discussion (1965, pp. 180–181):

> Radcliffe-Brown and others have defined "law" on occasion by the sanctions behind it, basing themselves on one of Roscoe Pound's remarks, that law is "social control through the systematic application of the force of politically organized society". Further, if "politically organized" implies the existence of courts, then there are societies without law. Thus Evans-Pritchard stated that "in the strict sense of the word, the Nuer have no law". Yet in another work on them published in the same year he spoke of Nuer law and of legal relations, and he described how people might recognize that justice lay on the other side in a dispute. His pupil Howell (an administrative officer) followed him here in his Manual of Nuer Law (1954), stating that "on this strict definition, the Nuer had no law". He adds immediately: " (…) but it is clear that in a less exact sense they were not lawless", and he states that he therefore uses the term law "rather loosely".

Those conceptualizations of law that are in fact positivist in nature seem inadequate to research focused on law in the sense of a social phenomenon. Putting a strong emphasis on institutional features, such as the regulatory authority, the judiciary and law enforcement agencies, they take as their framework a centralized state organization and distinguish the presence of provisions, courts or sanctions as necessary legal attributes (Roberts 2013, p. 27).

Moving away from binding the law with state power—which in research practice has turned out to be a dangerous trap, as research is often focused on communities without such power—anthropologists have long understood law, and therefore customary law, as a set of norms with certain specific characteristics. For example, Elias in "The Nature of African Customary Law" (1956) suggests, albeit cautiously, that customary law is what is considered obligatory by members of the community (Gluckman 1965, p. 182). Similar thinking—with emphasis on the role of sanctions—is demonstrated, for example, by the previously mentioned Llewellyn and Hoebel in their famous work "The Cheyenne Way" (1941). As Hoebel summarizes in another book, "The Law of Primitive Man" (1954), a social norm is a legal norm when its ignoring or breaking is threatened or faced by the actual use of physical force by a person or group with a socially recognized privilege to do so (Burke 2011, p. 17; Gluckman 1965, p. 181). In this context the words of Llewellyn that I have already quoted (p. 46) seem prophetic—those approaches are both too narrow (including only norms in their scope) and too broad (because non-legal norms may also be considered obligatory or sanctioned by force). Hence, I would be inclined to the thesis put forward by, for example, Roberts (1994, p. 970) that early studies on customary law were often conducted using definitions and a priori categories specific to the culture and legal systems of the researchers, not of the subjects. This observation then raises the question of how individual cultures withstand attempts to cram them into these tight frames.

By proposing a multi-layered approach to customary law, I am trying to avoid this type of error. As far as possible, the approach is created by me from the bottom up. It is true that it is not based on my own empirical research but rather the ethnographic material collected by other researchers; however, when constructing the categories of this conceptualization, I have tried to reject those proposed a priori by others in favor of those that are based on data.

At the same time I also refrain from adopting too many assumptions, especially those with an ethnocentric overtone, as such practice is especially dangerous in research on customary law. An example of how far astray this can lead our thinking about this phenomenon and how many harmful judgments it can generate is given by Walley (1997, p. 421):

> A recent front-page article in the New York Times concerning Fauziya Kasinga highlights the assumption of the oppressive nature of "tradition" (Dugger 1996). Despite information in the article suggesting Kasinga's elite and "modern" background (for example, Kasinga's father owned a successful trucking business in Togo, and she attended boarding school in Ghana), the language of the article stresses the exotic, relying on such terms as tribal law, bloody rite, banish[ment], and family patriarchs in their tribe (Dugger 1996). Rhetorically, the article suggests the ironic parallels between the alleged fetters of "tribal customs" and actual fetters in a Pennsylvania prison, where Kasinga was detained while seeking political asylum; here, the irony emerges as Dugger challenges the assumption of "freedom" in the United States by suggesting parallels with the (unquestioned) oppression of "tradition" in

> African countries. Similarly, Kasinga's televised response to a surprised Ted Koppel, informing him that most young women in Togo are happy to have the procedure done and "think it is something very great", could not dislodge the program's implicit assumption that these women are coerced and would gladly flee their own countries to escape such practices (…). Thus, rather than acknowledging Kasinga as a young woman who had dared to resist social norms of which she disapproved (in part because she was raised in a liberal household that offered alternative life choices), the media accounts instead emphasized the allegedly coercive and oppressive nature of African cultures and societies as a whole.

Cheater suggests that this is the result of an evolutionary approach that dominated anthropological research years ago, which left its mark on thinking about customary law, but also on general beliefs about societies different from ours. Hence the view that "primitive" societies had a very different kind of law than "advanced" societies, and were "enslaved" by their habitual, automatic, mindless obedience to this "custom" (Cheater 1989, p. 155). It can also be seen as an effect of the orientalist and colonial approach toward non-Western, non-European cultures (see, e.g., Chanock 1985; Diala 2017).

On top of this, there is a problem of an overly simplifying approach to customary law, which was noticed by Geertz (1983, p. 208), among others. This is what he wrote in the context of research on *adat*—customary law—in Malaysia and Indonesia (1983, p. 208):

> The mischief done by the word "custom" in anthropology, where it reduced thought to habit, is perhaps only exceeded by that which it has done in legal history, where it reduced thought to practice. And when, as in the study of *adat*, the two mischiefs have been combined, the result has been to generate a view of the workings of popular justice perhaps best characterized as conventionalistic: usage is all. As *adat* was "custom", it was, for the legist-ethnographers who gave their attention to it, by definition at best quasi-legal, a set of traditional rules traditionally applied to traditional problems.

Hence, my proposal, which equates customary law to an onion, goes in the opposite direction—it broadens rather than narrows its definition, and it will sooner contain elements that some will argue do not belong to the onion (although I will try to convince you that they do) than reject elements that undoubtedly do belong to it.

4 Customary Law Is Like an Onion

So what does it mean to say that customary law is like an onion? It can be said that it has layers, that it is a complex, multi-element structure whose individual parts differ from one another and constitute an identifiable separate quality but also an essential element of a larger whole.

The idea of treating law and customary law as a multi-element complex structure is not new. Comaroff and Roberts (1981) describe the way in which communities deal with the inconsistency of the content of legal norms (both in terms of the contradiction of customary law and state law, as well as within the framework of customary law itself). It is solved by the implied elevation of certain categories of norms from the level of literally treated directives to the level of symbolic features. This allows them to accommodate to each other, as they exist within two separate orders, or two layers. Geertz (1983, pp. 214–215) recognizes customary law as a pragmatically ordered set of social tools for the realization of interests and the management of conflicts of power that cannot be distinguished from one another analytically. And these tools, in his opinion, are of a very different nature. Cheater writes (1989, p. 155):

> Society, as we have seen, comprises both rules and behaviour which deviates from these rules. In one sense, instead of defining "law" as a set of binding rights and obligations, we might regard it as the relationship between these rules and actual behaviour, and how this relationship is managed. Here we are including within the definition of law not merely explicitly legal institutions, but also the broader field of the "customary" resolution of conflict.

I myself started my reflection on customary law by separating its two components—directival–behavioral, containing patterns of due behavior, and cognitive-cultural, or legally relevant assumptions about the social world which in the course of socialization are acquired by people living in certain areas. In this sense, customary law combines elements of both a directival and a symbolic meaning. However, the proposal that I present below goes a bit further. The separation of two components would correspond to the distinction of the onion bulb and its leaves, which, although they are two of its most characteristic elements, are, firstly, not the only ones and, secondly, are also internally differentiated.

As you can see in Fig. 1, the individual parts of the onion differ significantly—it has roots, a so-called heel, leaf sheaths arranged in layers, which are also different depending on whether they are in the outer or inner layer, and green assimilation leaves growing out of it—and characteristics of each element depend on the degree of onion development and the environment in which it grows (Brickell 1992, p. 345). Each of these elements both "is" in itself an onion and forms the onion as one of its constituent parts. When an onion is stripped of some of these elements, it does not cease to be an onion, but its properties to some extent change.

In next sections of this chapter I unwrap the onion layer by layer, identifying four main components of customary law. Firstly, I refer to the behavioral aspect of this system containing patterns of the expected behavior. The second layer, still closely connected with actual human behavior, is constituted of predispositions and guidelines for social action. Then, I move toward layers that have more symbolic meaning, are connected with human behavior in more indirect ways and constitute a cognitive-cultural component of customary law: the layer of social values and the layer of social identity (see Fig. 2).

4.1 Layer I: Patterns of the Expected Behavior

If we were to find an onion in its natural environment, we would probably look for its most visible element: long, green, spiny leaves. In the case of customary law, such a

Fig. 1 Wellcome Library, London. An onion, coloured woodcut, Ortus sanitatis Arnaldus de Villanova, Published: 1491. Licence CC BY 4.0

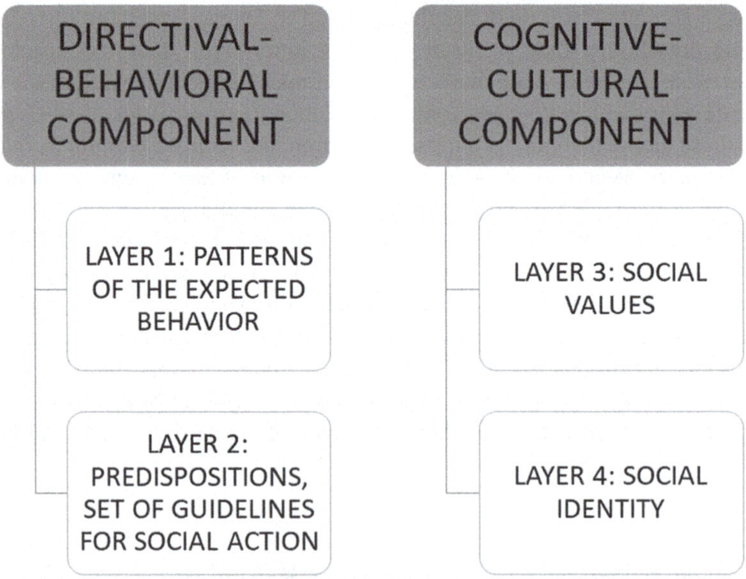

Fig. 2 Graphic diagram of customary law layers

layer is visible to the naked eye in the form of the socialized patterns of behavior people are expected to follow as well as their actual behavior. An example of such expected patterns of behavior may be regulations related to forest management in the Albanian customary law known as *Kanun* (see de Waal 2004; Klakla 2017). These regulations were very precisely described and based on the recognition of certain areas as the property of a specific group of brothers (*vllazni*) and areas further away as the property of a specific clan (*fis*); then, at a certain distance, the forest was the common property (*kujrit*) of the village and, finally, beyond this distance, it belonged to the district (*bajrak*). There were several levels of management: clan chiefs, village elders, lesser elders and the people themselves (de Waal 2004, p. 32). By recognizing certain areas as the property of a specific group, a model of decentralized forest management was introduced. The duties of each group, the scope of its responsibilities, and the consequences of not fulfilling them were precisely defined. As Hasluck writes (1954, p. 162):

> Village Assemblies dealt with matters of exclusively village interest. They regulated wood-cutting and irrigation rights, for example. They fixed the date at which beasts might be sent up to their summer pasturage on the high mountains. They stipulated the number of beasts that might be sent up by each family. They took steps to see that no one appropriated more than his fair share of forest, irrigation water or grazing. In so doing they made a valuable contribution to the public peace.

As can be seen in the above example, such a customary norm shares some similarities—in structure or degree of detail—with legal norms. Another example from the same customary law corpus are the strict rules governing the prohibition of extra-marital relationships. Customary law makes it clear that children born of such unions do not enter the family and do not inherit property. Meanwhile, the wife and her lover (as there is no marital or gender equality in *Kanun*), when they are caught in the course of a sexual act, may be killed. However, this right is also regulated by law—the husband can fire only one shot at each of them. During the wedding, the bride's parents provide ammunition for the husband to use if the wife turns out to be unfaithful. In this way, they sanction their daughter's death as a punishment for adultery and it does not become the basis for initiating blood feud (Trnavci 2008, p. 21; Klakla 2015a, b, p. 77).

It is not without reason that in the onion metaphor which I have described this layer of customary law corresponds to the leaves. Not only, as I have already mentioned, are these the easiest part to observe in the natural environment; also, because of the way the onion is shaped, the protruding leaves in the planted vegetable can give the illusion that only a small part of the plant remains outside. Meanwhile, the reality is quite the opposite. And it is similar in customary law: in my proposal, the patterns of behavior visible to the naked eye are only one, "outer" layer of a complicated system.

Secondly, the excessive growth of onion leaves has consequences for the other elements—what is inside begins to disappear in favor of what is outside. With this comparison, I would like to draw your attention to the problem of codification of customary law. When customary law is written down and thus necessarily becomes a static set of directival statements, it loses many of its key characteristics. Customary law as a social phenomenon is no longer flexible, it may no longer be a valid guideline for social action, it loses its correspondence with socially shared values and it may also lose its status as an element of social identity. A warning in this context is the truth known to anyone who has ever grown an onion—when we let the leaves grow too much, it does not benefit the plant as a whole.

The examples cited are based on the assumption that customary law has a specific status in the community. They make sense when we are talking about customary law as a normative system that is the actual regulator of a part of social life falling within its competence. We assume that the norms of customary law are actually "fully" in force—people know their regulating content and the pattern of appropriate behavior they propose, they find it desirable and their behavior reflects this at least to some extent. However, this is not always the case. And when these conditions are not met, when there are no implemented and observable patterns of behavior and the knowledge of the exact regulating content of norms in communities decreases, I still do not think that it is adequate to speak about the disappearance of customary law—just as the onion after its leaves have been cut does not cease to be an onion, although it is probably less visible in the field.

4.2 Layer II: Predispositions, Set of Guidelines for Social Action

Customary law is a complex system that for centuries has been the foundation and main regulator of the social order within societies that currently function in significantly different social and political conditions from those that existed during the formation of the system. The situation of Roma groups in Central Europe is a good example. In Romani customary law, we find material norms, commands and prohibitions, as well as procedures for imposing the consequences of breaking the applicable rules and resolving conflicts within the community—very similar to the *Kanun* I already mentioned above. Currently, the isolation of Roma groups is gradually fading away; in Poland such a process has been taking place since the 1950s, when the authorities started programs of forced settlement combating the itinerant and independent lifestyle of the Roma people. It is obvious that customary law in the form described above is no longer the only normative guideline for Roma, who do not currently live in such extreme isolation from the non-Romani environment and who enter into relations with state institutions as citizens who have both rights and obligations (Klakla 2015a, b, p. 91; Leeson 2013). Similarly, societies and local communities in Albania, the Middle East, the Caucasus, Central Africa and other regions in which customary law has played an important role for centuries are undergoing or have gone through intensive social processes that change, sometimes radically, the shape of those societies.

So what to do in the situation in which many of these communities find themselves? On the one hand, the knowledge of specific norms and patterns of behavior rooted in customary law disappears. However, on the other hand, the reference to customs and traditions deriving from this law, as well as the values on which it was based and the internalization of which it facilitates, is still an essential part of the social life of these communities. To understand this, we have to reach a little deeper, closer to the ground, to discover the layers of the onion that have hitherto been obscured by green leaves—to look for those elements of customary law that lie beyond the directives and behaviors that are visible to the naked eye. For the purposes of this chapter, let's call this process "unpacking" the onion, or customary law.

The first stage of unpacking is looking beyond the normative layer in the strict sense. When we do this, we will see that customary law is more than just norms—it is also embodied dispositions to act and evaluate the behavior of others in a certain way, which some researchers in this context conceptualize as a *habitus* (see Voell 2003).

An example in which this layer of customary law is visible is the situation described by Voell, who studies how Albanian customary law is implemented under different socio-cultural conditions—specifically, after the migration of people from the sparsely populated north of the country to the suburbs of the capital. He describes *Kanun* as a *habitus* associated with a specific social and economic environment (2003, p. 85). *Habitus* is "a whole of internalized tendencies and attitudes that shape human perceptions, thoughts, preferences, expressed in everyday behavior, (...) a principle that generates practices that can be objectively classified, as well as a system for classifying these practices" (Bourdieu 2006, p. 216) or, in other words, a set of underlying patterns of behavior and response, of acquired dispositions to act and evaluate in a certain way (Voell 2003, p. 90).

According to Voell, the social field that structures the *habitus* associated with *Kanun* is characterized by geographic and social isolation and patriarchal tribal organization. A similar social field, and thus the basic components of the customary *habitus*, can also be found on the outskirts of Tirana. Voell therefore claims that "if the *Kanun* is regarded as *habitus* (...) and not just as a book of rules that has been forgotten in the course of history, its practice does still exist, even in an urban area like Bathore, in central Albania" (2003, p. 86). Thus, in order to find out how customary law is realized in these new conditions, it must be "unpacked" from the strictly normative layer. Then *Kanun* can be described as *habitus* in the sense of Pierre Bourdieu; the internalization of the constituting structures of a given social field. This process provides for a system of predispositions, a kind of framework and set of guidelines for social action, which in turn again structures the social field (Voell 2003, p. 89).

Voell speaks of social organization in Bathore, a suburb of Tirana, as an example of this layer of customary law. The migrants from the Albanian north took clan organization based on *Kanun* with them to a new territory (Voell 2003, pp. 95–96). It was not a direct equivalent of the structure known from the mountainous, inaccessible and loosely populated north, but rather a response to new living conditions based on a *habitus*. For Voell this *habitus* is derived from customary law, but in my proposition, I see it as an inherent layer of a wider phenomenon called customary law.

The aforementioned guidelines for social action, which for me constitute a second layer of customary law, are also behind the interesting phenomenon of the revival of this law in the periods of weakening of state power caused, inter alia, by political transformation (see Voell 2003; de Waal 2004; Klakla 2017). It takes place when the above-mentioned social field underlying the formation of a specific *habitus* related to customary law does not change radically. This revival, however, does not mean a direct return to a normative layer identical to that which functioned decades or centuries ago.

To explain this relation I will refer to the context of post-socialist Albania, as the practice of blood feud is a model example of a gap between the original normative layer of customary law and the actual social behavior during the times of customary law re-emergence (Klakla 2015a, b). Yes, the notion of the *Kanun* as a general cultural concept is present in northern Albanian society, but its practice is closely interwoven with everyday social action (Voell 2003, p. 90). Hence, the revival of customary law in post-socialist Albania is, rather, a situation in which our onion produces new leaves in place of the dried—up old ones—they are apparently similar, growing from the same core, but they are not the same.

The *Kanun* describes blood revenge as an acceptable reaction to a crime or insult to the honor of a family but specifies that only a perpetrator can be a target. The contemporary understanding developed after 1991 widens the group of potential targets by adding all male or even female relatives of the perpetrator. Sometimes it also includes minors in the family. Gjin Marku of the National Reconciliation Committee in Albania (an non-governmental organization that works to mediate and prevent blood feud conflicts) states that "the problem with blood feuds today is that people are using their own personal interpretation of the *Kanun* to suit their needs (. . .) They are abusing the laws instead of following the original script, and this is why you see young women (. . .) becoming targets" (Cohen 2012). It is against the rules of customary law (which can be seen as its first layer) written down by Gjecov, as they state: "Fathers shall not be killed in place of their sons, nor sons in place of their fathers, but each shall die for his own sin" (Fox and Gjeçov 1989, p. 172). Using the *Kanun* to justify blood revenge was certainly the most negative aspect of the rebirth of customary law that happened in Albania in the times of transition.

4.3 Layer III: Social Values

Going further in an "unpacking" process, even closer to the ground, we tear off another layer of our metaphorical onion. Behind the guidelines for social actions (which may be conceptualized as *habitus*), and thus indirectly also behind the specific patterns of expected behavior, there are values associated with this law. At this point, it does not seem advisable to consider the adopted theory of values in depth. Sufficient for understanding further considerations is a declaration of rejection of the existence of objective values (because it is always an object or state of affairs desired by someone), but at the same time a willingness to empirically research whether a given object or state of affairs is a value in a given social group (see Pałecki 2013a, b).

In order to offer an example of these values, which constitute the third layer of customary law, I refer once again to the procedures used in resolving individual and inter-clan disputes. It is possible to extract certain values, which can then be applied in other areas of social life—in conflict resolution procedures based on state law, but also in everyday life—from the instruments and norms related to the customary resolution of conflicts.

An example of such a value is impartiality. Customary mediation is based on a specific understanding of this value. Cultures whose main category of thinking is a group are forced to make a very strong, clear definition of who belongs to this group, who is the designate of the term "we". Hence, there is a very strong distinction between theirs and others. In order to maintain the rules of impartiality, the mediator should come from outside this environment, but in reality this is impossible. For the very initiation of mediation, the parties reporting to the mediator, the most important thing is his social position within the group. Customary mediators most often come from well-known families with a long tradition of community service. Therefore, the mediator entering the case will always be connected with both parties by a network of relations, which for us would be an absolute basis for considering him biased. Here, on the contrary, they determine the possibility of mediation by him. One of the usual mechanisms in the procedures to ensure balance in the process conducted by conciliators involved in relations with the parties is to provide participants with, on the one hand, the possibility of a veto over specific persons, and, on the other, the right to appoint their representatives to the group coordinating the conflict resolution process (Pely 2011a, pp. 437–438; Offiong 1997, p. 433; Çelik and Shkreli 2010, p. 897).

Another value that exceeds the specific regulations of customary law is honor. Describing in detail what honor is neither easy nor necessary for the purpose of this chapter (for more detailed considerations regarding honor see my conceptualization of this phenomenon developed using the metaphor of panopticon (Klakla 2017)). It is however important to note that honor is often one of the key values associated with (or in my opinion making up) customary law. It can act as a rationale for both layers mentioned in previous sections of this chapter. Let's take as an example the concept of the blood feud, present in many customary law bodies (see Mangalakova 2004; Mustafa and Young 2008; Pely 2008, 2011b; Gendron 2009; Phillips 2011).

Being guided by honor and—for example—the initiative of deep involvement in a blood feud (a conflict with huge costs known in advance) is a rational behavior. To illustrate this, one can use an example which, due to its popularity, will clearly present this problem—the pyramid of needs (Maslow 2016, pp. 115–119). Greatly simplifying this theory, it can be stated that, in the long run, a person should satisfy first his physiological needs, then the needs of security, belonging, respect and recognition, and self-realization. The inability to meet more basic needs prevents the realization of those higher in the pyramid. For people brought up in certain cultures, engaging in armed conflict, fighting to the death for the sake of honor alone, is irrational, because doing so places a sense of security much higher than honor, which they consider more basic. However, one has to accept the fact that for others, when a flaw appears in someone's honor, its restoration takes a place among the most basic needs. From this point of view, the actions undertaken by such individuals should be considered as wholly rational, although within a hierarchy of values different from ours (Pely 2011b).

The layer of values in customary law is an extremely important one, although so abstract and sometimes seemingly invisible that it may escape the attention of researchers and practitioners. It affects the relationship between customary law and state law—a key topic in this context, to which I will return later in the chapter. It can be observed that certain values are ascribed to conciliators both in customary proceedings and in restorative justice institutions implemented under state law systems—victim–offender mediation, conferences and others—but the process of implementing these values differs in these cases. It is like the impartiality and neutrality of the conciliator, which I described as an example, but also other values, such as confidentiality or responsibility (see Klakla 2014). It is important not to assume that these terms mean the same thing regardless of the cultural context in which they are used.

4.4 Layer IV: Social Identity

Thus, through the unpacking process, we have reached the fourth layer of customary law, which is an element of social identity. Social identity is part of people's identity derived from the groups to which they belong, a person's sense of who they are based on their group membership (Scheepers and Ellemers 2019, p. 129) and also the way "in which individuals and collectivities are distinguished in their social relations with other individuals and collectivities" (Jenkins 2014, p. 5). In other words, identity is "a matter of knowing who's who" (Jenkins 2014, p. 5). And customary law can play a significant role in that process.

To give an example, I will refer again to Albanian customary law. Although the *Kanun* was written down in the 1930s by Franciscan priest Gjeçov and its copies have been widely available since then, what the *Kanun* says is not as important as what people think it says (Joireman 2014, p. 10). It was (and still is) the ultimate authority on Albanian tradition, although few have read it (Reineck 1993, p. 40). Joireman (2014, p. 10) writes that "the *Kanun* is used as a totem, much in the fashion that the constitution is used by some Americans who may refer to their 'Constitutional Rights', but never have seriously read or studied the Constitution". It is also compared to knowledge of the Bible in Western culture, in as much as certain metaphors and references are a part of common knowledge and are known even by those who have not read the Bible (see Arsovska 2006). Even Gjeçov himself claims that during his studies he had not found the "original *Kanun*". At the same time Voell writes about *Kanun* as the basis of Albanianness (2003, p. 89):

> The *Kanun* and the blood feuds in the north are presently considered as one of the biggest problems in Albania, but are also seen as a monument of Albanian identity. In socialist times the *Kanun* had been used by researchers from both linguistics and archaeology as an argument to legitimise and foster a distinct Albanian identity. The different versions of the customary law were considered to have been derived from a single *Kanun* observed in all of Albania. This was proof that Albanians had never been assimilated by foreigners and, even after centuries of foreign rule, still maintained this distinct identity (Elezi 1975, p. 35: Zojzi 1967, p. 118). (...) [T]he *Kanun* is recognised as a crucial element in Albanian history (...). This rhetoric is still valid today in some speeches of politicians and scholars. The *Kanun* is not only an important element in the identity discourse of the state, it is part of the northern Albanian's self-portrayal. It is presented as an icon of their perpetual resistance, of their cultural identity, and—as confirmed by scholars and travellers, who are frequently cited by name (Durham, Hahn, Nopcsa)—a major cultural achievement.

Of course, it is not only for Albanians that customary law is an important element of identity. An example of such a role played by other bodies of customary law is the unifying power of the Romanipen for Roma groups. It has always been something that binds dispersed Roma groups together and builds a common Roma identity, but the way it does so has changed over the centuries with the changing status of customary law in this community. While Roma customary law formed the basis of informal social control within this group—that is, where the normative layer was still intact—the most severe sanctions were largely based on group ostracism. As Leeson (2013, p. 279) writes, for social ostracism to be an effective form of social control, several conditions must be met. First of all, the control of the individual by members of the community must be as continuous as possible and the flow of information within the community must function smoothly. In other words, a misdemeanor must be noticed by others, and then information about the offense must be distributed effectively among the whole group. The exclusion of the offender from the community must also be viewed as desirable by the majority of the community and at the same time undesirable to a potential perpetrator.

For centuries, it has not been possible for Roma to pass on information quickly due to their itinerant lifestyle. Communication between groups, although it obviously did exist, was not efficient enough to ensure an effective flow of information about persons who had committed offenses against the group and should be ostracized. Moreover, the lifestyle of the Roma community, which is subject to many customary regulations, does not appear at first glance to be more desirable than a settled life. The answer to these conditions was the institution of "pollution" present in Romani customary law—in the multi-layered model discussed here, it would be located in the vicinity of external layers, specific patterns of behavior, but also guidelines for social action or *habitus*. Pollution, just like a taboo, is a metaphysical concept referring to the division into the sacred and the profane, and therefore to religious or magical beliefs. Without going into a detailed description of what pollution is, let me just mention that thanks to this concept, the Romani customary law is to some extent self-enforcing. By going against the rules, the individual becomes tainted by the mere fact of it. This can be compared, as Gropper (1975,

p. 90) says, to the equation of transgression and sin, which makes pollution inevitable when the rules are broken. This, of course, requires a deep faith in the legitimacy of these regulations as well as their presence in all the layers of customary law.

For centuries, what united the dispersed Roma groups was the fear of exclusion, and thus condemnation to a life of eternal pollution. Nowadays quite often knowledge of specific regulations is lost, or even the *habitus* common for Roma communities are lost due to sometimes radical change in the environmental and cultural conditions in which the Roma function in modern countries. Nevertheless, *Romanipen* is still what connects them, although it does so in a different way. The identity function that binds the group together is performed not so much by the specific regulations of this law as by the reference to the body of customary law itself. Being a Roma means respecting and valuing heritage and customary law—even if it doesn't provide valid regulations helpful in the everyday life of modern Romani communities, it does help to provide an answer for one of the most important questions a man can ask—who am I?

5 Conclusions

In this chapter I have presented my understanding of customary law based on the idea of its multi-layered nature. In my opinion, customary law is like an onion—it has many layers that differ significantly from one another. Patterns of due behavior are only the outermost manifestation of customary law; underneath them lie predispositions and guidelines for social actions, social values and social identity.

I started my deliberations by criticizing attempts in research on customary law to strictly define the law, with the promise to return to this topic in the summary, which I do now. Geertz in his published lectures for law students writes about how such attempts can be restrictive when we talk about customary law (1983, pp. 214–215):

> So much, then, for distant ideas. Not that there isn't more to be said about them; there is virtually everything. But my intent has not been, as I mentioned earlier, to compress Islamic, Indic, and Malaysian notions about the interconnections of norms and happenings into some handbook for ex patria litigants but to demonstrate that they are notions. The main approaches to comparative law—that which sees its task as one of contrasting rule structures one to the next and that which sees it as one of contrasting different processes of dispute resolution in different societies—both seem to me rather to miss this point: the first through an overautonomous view of law as a separate and self-contained "legal system" struggling to defend its analytic integrity in the face of the conceptual and moral sloppiness of ordinary life; the second through an overpolitical view of it as an undifferentiated, pragmatically ordered collection of social devices for advancing interests and managing power conflicts. Whether the adjudicative styles that gather around the Anschauungen projected by ~aqq, dharma, and adat are properly to be called "law" or not (the rule buffs will find them too informal, the dispute buffs too abstract) is of minor importance; though I, myself, would want to do so. What matters is that their imaginative power not be obscured. They do not just regulate behavior, they construe it.

I have the impression that an attempt to squeeze the concept I have presented into the framework of rigid definitions would turn out to be destructive for it. Instead of a definition, I would like to draw your attention to the fragment of Geertz's lecture that I highlight, which seems to correspond well with what I present in the previous pages—customary law (just like state law, but this is a topic for a different paper) is something more than just a simple regulator of the behavior of members of a given community.

Therefore, I would like to return once again to Gluckman and his criticism of defining law. Writing about this topic, he notes that (1965, p. 178):

> many volumes have been written on this subject, and it may seem a sweeping impertinence if I say, somewhat categorically, that much of this controversy has arisen from arguments about the word "law," apparently based on the assumption that it must have one meaning, and one meaning only. But the contrary is obviously true. Indeed, in any language most words which refer to important social phenomena—as "law" obviously does—are likely to have several referents and to cover a wide range of meanings.

Gluckman argues that since all words that refer to important social phenomena are by their nature ambiguous, if we want to use them in scientific discourse, we must accept this ambiguity. Thus, there is no point disputing the superiority of one meaning over another. We can agree to a kind of mutual semantic tolerance in order to be able to deal with complex sets of facts, such as those involved in the entire process of social control, and thus the law and its institutions (Gluckman 1965, p. XXIII).

The above considerations apply to both law and custom and, consequently, customary law. Gluckman (1965, p. 199) states that "use of more than one word to cover the same rules, and of one word to cover more than one type of rule, is not due to inability (...) to differentiate between types of rules. Our own words (...) serve multiple purposes. 'Custom' in the Concise Oxford Dictionary is given as both 'usual practice' and as 'established usage having the force of law', aside from meaning duty on imports". From this perspective, it does not seem to me that the multi-layered concept of customary law goes far beyond the semantic tolerance mentioned above, incorporating elements such as *habitus*, values or social identity.

This multi-layered approach has certain consequences, and I would like to devote the last few paragraphs to one, which I consider perhaps the most important. Adoption of the multi-layered concept of customary law determines that this law is not inherently contradictory to state law. In the literature, both in those works concerning customary law and in those for which it is a side topic, an opinion can be found that customary law is a relic of the past and should be analyzed mostly in a historical context. Societies that still follow customary law are seen in the best case as anthropological curiosities. It happens frequently that one faces the assumption that in order to modernize a community in which customary law is still present it is necessary to completely eradicate customary law as a regulator of interpersonal relations, as it is a backward legal system. This is noted, inter alia, by Voell when he writes (2003, pp. 88–89):

> There are scholars from Tirana who rarely travel to the north. In their publications the Kanun is discussed exclusively on a historical level. Others, also speaking without actual field experience, refuse to admit that the Kanun exists today. It is considered a degraded version of the ancient law, which at the time made sense but is not suited to modem conditions. From this perspective, current practice is considered a primitive survival. Thus, the discourse on the Kanun and the people who are observing it appear to be not very different from that of the socialist period.

Meanwhile, the contradiction in the patterns of expected behavior required by the two corpora of law—the customary and the state—can occur only (although it does not prejudge it!) when both of them are characterized by a directival–behavioral component, especially a layer that consists of patterns of expected social behavior. However, when one of them is limited by social conditions to the other layers mentioned in this chapter, the situation is quite different. Of course, this reduced body will most often be customary law, even though I am not saying that the multi-layered construction is unique to it. State law may also be like an onion, but it is much more difficult to observe empirically, as we deal less often with the disappearance of certain of its layers (especially the first). The situation is different in the case of customary law, mainly due to the social processes which often result in its subsidiary character. Adopting the multi-layered concept of common law requires a deeper reflection on the relation between customary and state law, as well as the relation of their individual layers to one another. Then we can analyze much more complicated relations than the direct contradiction of the required patterns of behavior.

References

Arsovska J (2006) Understanding a 'Culture of Violence and Crime': the Kanun of Lek Dukagjini and the rise of the Albanian sexual-slavery rackets. Eur J Crime Crim Law Crim Just 14:161–184

Baier M (2016) Introduction. In: Baier M (ed) Social and legal norms: towards a socio-legal understanding of normativity. Routledge, New York, pp 1–14

Bourdieu P (2006) Habitus i przestrzeń stylów życia. In: Bourdieu P (ed) Dystynkcja. Społeczna krytyka władzy sądzenia. Scholar, Warszawa, pp 215–278

Brickell C (ed) (1992) The royal horticultural society encyclopedia of gardening. Dorling Kindersley, London

Burke P (2011) Law's anthropology: from ethnography to expert testimony in native title. ANU Press, Canberra

Çelik AB, Shkreli A (2010) An analysis of reconciliatory mediation in Northern Albania: the role of customary mediators. Europe-Asia Stud 62(6):885–914

Chanock M (1985) Law, custom, and social order: the colonial experience in Malawi and Zambia. Cambridge University Press, Cambridge

Cheater AP (1989) Social anthropology: an alternative introduction. Routledge, New York

Cohen NS (2012) Blood feuds still boiling in Albania. USA Today, July 29

Comaroff JL, Roberts S (1981) Rules and processes: the cultural logic of dispute in an African context. Chicago University Press, Chicago

De Waal C (2004) Post-socialist property rights and wrongs in Albania: an ethnography of agrarian change. Conserv Soc:19–50

Diala AC (2017) The concept of living customary law: a critique. J Leg Pluralism Unofficial Law 49 (2):143–165
Dugger CW (1996) Women's pleas for asylum puts tribal ritual on trial. New York Times, April 15
Elezi I (1975) La lutte contre les survivances du droit coutumier. Studia Albanica 12(2):31–46
Elias TO (1956) The nature of African customary law. Manchester University Press, Manchester
Fox L, Gjeçov S (1989) The code of Leke Dukagjini. Gjonlekaj Publishing Company, New York
Geertz C (1983) Local knowledge. Further essays in interpretive anthropology. Basic Books, New York
Gendron R (2009) Alternative dispute resolution in the North Caucasus. Caucasian Rev Int Aff 3 (4):333–341
Gluckman M (1965) Politics, law and ritual in tribal society. Basil Blackwell, Oxford
Gropper RC (1975) Gypsies in the city: culture patterns and survival. Darwin Press Incorporated, New Jersey
Hasluck M (1954) The unwritten law in Albania. Cambridge University Press, Cambridge
Hoebel EA (1954) The law of primitive man: a study in comparative legal dynamics. Harvard University Press, Cambridge
Hofstede GH, Hofstede GJ, Minkov M (2005) Cultures and organizations: software of the mind. McGraw-Hill, New York
Jenkins R (2014) Social identity. Routledge, London
Johansson S (2016) Institutions and norms in collaboration: towards a framework for analysing law and normativity in inter-organizational collaboration. In: Baier M (ed) Social and legal norms: towards a socio-legal understanding of normativity. Routledge, New York, pp 107–120
Joireman SF (2014) Aiming for certainty: the Kanun, blood feuds and the ascertainment of customary law. J Leg Pluralism Unofficial Law 46(2):235–248
Klakla JB (2014) Mediacje w albańskim prawie zwyczajowym. In: Czapska J, Szeląg-Dylewski M (eds) Mediacje w prawie. Wydawnictwo Uniwersytetu Jagiellońskiego, Cracow, pp 71–82
Klakla JB (2015a) Kanun–albańskie prawo zwyczajowe. Główne założenia oraz wpływ na społeczeństwo albańskie w XXI wieku. In: Średnicka E (ed) Wzajemne relacje prawa i kultury. Wydawnictwo Kasper, Cracow, pp 71–95
Klakla JB (2015b) The attitudes towards the customary law within Roma Groups in Central Europe. Polish J Arts Cult 14:83–100
Klakla JB (2017) The rebirth of customary law in a time of transition. The case of Albania. In: Fekete B, Gárdos-Orosz F (eds) Central and Eastern European socio-political and legal transition revisited. Peter Lang, Frankfurt am Main, pp 75–88
Leeson PT (2013) Gypsy law. Public Choice 155(3-4):273–292
Levi-Strauss C (1963) Structural anthropology. Basic Books, New York
Llewellyn KN, Hoebel EA (1941) The Cheyenne way: conflict and case law in primitive jurisprudence. University of Oklahoma Press, Norman
Mangalakova, T (2004) The Kanun in present-day Albania, Kosovo, and Montenegro. International Center for Minority Studies and Intercultural Relations, Sophia, pp 1–15
Maslow A (2016) Motywacja i osobowość. Wydawnictwo Naukowe PWN, Warszawa
Mezey N (2001) Law as culture. Yale J Law Hum 13:35–67
Mitchell D (1995) There's no such thing as culture: towards a reconceptualization of the idea of culture in geography. Trans Inst Br Geogr 20(1):02–116
Mustafa M, Young A (2008) Feud narratives: contemporary deployments of kanun in Shala Valley, northern Albania. Anthropol Notebooks 14(2):87–107
Offiong DA (1997) Conflict resolution among the Ibibio of Nigeria. J Anthropol Res 53(4):423–441
Pałecki K (2013a) Neutralization of values in law–main concepts. In: Pałecki K (ed) Neutralization of values in law. Wolters Kluwer, Warszawa, pp 22–58
Pałecki K (2013b) Aksjologia prawa. In: Kociołek-Pęksa A, Stępień M (eds) . Leksykon socjologii prawa, Beck, Warszawa, pp 1–7
Pely D (2008) Resolving clan-based disputes using the Sulha, the traditional dispute resolution process of the Middle East. Dispute Resolut J 63(4):80–88

Pely D (2011a) Where east not always meets west: comparing the Sulha process to western-style mediation and arbitration. Confl Resolut Q 28(4):427–440

Pely D (2011b) When honor trumps basic needs: the role of honor in deadly disputes within Israel's Arab community. Negot J 27(2):205–225

Phillips FP (2011) There is a world elsewhere: preliminary studies on alternatives to interest-based bargaining. Cardozo J Confl Resolut 13:413–436

Reineck JS (1993) The past as refuge: gender, migration, and ideology among the Kosova Albanians. Ann Arbor, Berkeley

Roberts S (1994) Law and dispute processes. In: Ingold T (ed) Companion encyclopedia of anthropology. Humanity, culture and social life. Routledge, London, pp 962–982

Roberts S (2013) Order and dispute: an introduction to legal anthropology. Quid Pro Books, New Orleans

Rosen L (2006) Law as culture: an invitation. Princeton University Press, New Jersey

Scheepers D, Ellemers N (2019) Social identity theory. In: Sassenberg K, Vliek MLW (eds) Social psychology in action. Evidence-based interventions from theory to practice. Springer, New York, pp 129–143

Trnavci G (2008) The Albanian customary law and the canon of Lekë Dukagjini: a clash or synergy with modern law. http://works.bepress.com/genc_trnavci/1. Accessed 3 Dec 2020

Twining W (1973) Law and anthropology: a case study in inter-disciplinary collaboration. Law Soc Rev 7(4):561–583

Tylor EB (1871) Primitive culture: researches into the development of mythology, philosophy, religion, art and custom. J Murray

Voell S (2003) The Kanun in the city. Albanian customary law as a habitus and its persistence in the suburb of Tirana, Bathore. Anthropos, 85–101

Walley CJ (1997) Searching for "voices": feminism, anthropology, and the global debate over female genital operations. Cult Anthropol 12(3):405–438

Woodman GR (2001) Customary law in common law systems. IDS Bull 32(1):28–34

Zojzi R (1967) Questions concernant le droit coutumier albanais. Studia Albanica 4(2):117–126

Jan Bazyli Klakla A graduate of law, sociology and comparative culture studies at the Jagiellonian University and postgraduate studies in international migrations at the University of Warsaw. Head of the research project "The impact of institutional and legal factors on the choice of a acculturation strategies of foreigners in Poland", expert in security diagnosis in the safety improvement program for the city of Cracow for 2018–2020 entitled "Safe Cracow", associate of the Center for Research on Migration and Intercultural Relations of the University of Almeria and researcher at Holistic Think Tank, part of the Cavatina Holding. He is preparing two doctoral dissertations—in law at the Department of Sociology of Law of the Jagiellonian University and in sociology at the Institute of Sociology of the Jagiellonian University. His interests focus on issues related to migration, education, customary law, restorative justice, as well as the use of social science methodology in research on law.

Part II
Law, Custom and Culture

Part II

[illegible]

Indian "Love Jihad" Goes to Court

Anna Juzaszek

Abstract In the chapter, the author address the problem of "Love Jihad", a conspiracy theory suggesting that Indian Muslims, to take control of India, seduce non-Muslim women to force them to convert to Islam. Focus is put on a case study of three judicial decisions (from 2016 to 2018) in the case of Hadiya, a young woman who converted from Hinduism to Islam and who had to fight in court for her freedom to do so, against her father. The phenomenon of "Love Jihad", its background, and the reasons underlying its discussion in India are explained. Main aim is to reveal what arguments were used and what assumptions concerning selected social issues can be drawn from them. It is relevant especially from the point of view of culture-forming and educational functions of judicial opinions. Culture-forming function concern the contribution of judicial opinions to the culture and the relation between the justice system and society, whereas educational function concern the communication of proper behaviour, which is reinforced by the fact the court in principle acts as an impartial entity in the trial.

1 Introduction

Between 2016 and 2018 in India, one particular case attracted the media's attention. It concerned a girl in her twenties called Akhila Asokan (at some point she changed her name to an Islamic name, Hadiya, which I use in this chapter) who converted from Hinduism to Islam against her parents' will and refused to return to her family home. The father could not believe that she independently made such a decision and began a court battle to release her from the alleged detention. The case became famous for two reasons. First, it was associated with the phenomenon called "Love Jihad". Second, the case ended up in the Supreme Court of India.

The term "Love Jihad", also known as "Romeo Jihad", refers to rumors that concern Muslim men luring Hindu women into marriage by promising them great,

A. Juzaszek (✉)
Department of Sociology of Law, Jagiellonian University, Cracow, Poland
e-mail: anna.drwal@doctoral.uj.edu.pl

M. Stępień, J. B. Klakla (eds.), *Law and Culture*, Law and Visual Jurisprudence 5,
https://doi.org/10.1007/978-3-030-81193-8_4

romantic love. The next step is to convince the women to convert to Islam. The main aims of such an activity are supposedly to Islamize India, to reduce the number of Hindu people, and to take control of the country for Muslims. At least this is how it is portrayed by the propagators of these rumors. However, there is no evidence of such activities.

Hadiya's case consists of two separate cases. The first one ended with the judgement of the first instance, whereas the second went through two instances (this is elaborated in detail later in the chapter). Therefore, three verdicts were issued concerning the life of the Indian girl. Two of them had similar resolutions, whereas the third differed entirely in its conclusion. Twice (in the first and third verdict) the judges ruled that the girl was not under any illegal detention and once (in the second verdict) that she was under the duress of third parties, and therefore, should have been returned to her parents even though it was against her will.

The following questions arise: How were these verdicts justified in the judicial opinions? What kind of arguments were used, and consequently, what kind of assumptions concerning selected social issues can be drawn from them? The assumptions contained in the judicial opinions may be a consequence of the convictions, presuppositions, and beliefs of the judges who issued the verdict and prepared the opinion, after all, "none of us lives a value-free life" (Davids 2017, p. 740). Therefore, the judges' understanding of the law and the facts of the case, among other factors, can be "shaped by the judges' values, their sense of good society, and just order" (Davids 2017, p. 741). This can be perceived as an example of how the culture understood here as "a description of a particular way of life, which expresses certain meanings and values not only in art and learning but also in institutions and ordinary behaviour" (Williams 1998, p. 48), influences judges' decision-making process.

At the same time, the analysis of judicial opinions has its limitations especially when it comes to discovering personal beliefs of judges. To name a few, judges may not always present the real reasons behind a given conclusion (see Cohen 2015), which could be because they want to avoid any negative consequences (e.g., disciplinary action); alternatively, it could be because they want their decision to be upheld by the higher court, and therefore, they will stick to some proven convention (Stępień 2019, p. 8). Moreover, judicial opinions are often made by more than one judge. In the Hadiya case, in the first instance (High Court of Kerala) two judges were making a conclusion, and in the second instance (Supreme Court of India) three judges were. Each of them might have different assumptions, beliefs, and reasons even though they all came to the same conclusion (Stępień 2019, p. 8). Just by reading the judicial opinion, we do not know exactly how it was constructed (e.g., some parts could have been copied from a different judicial opinion), who actually wrote it (e.g., it could be a judge assistant), and why certain arguments were included (e.g., we do not have access to the judges' discussions).

Due to the above, I predominantly focus on what was revealed in the judicial opinion without drawing far-reaching conclusions on the judges themselves. I believe that even such limited research is relevant, especially taking into consideration the functions of the judicial opinions, particularly culture-forming and educational ones. The culture-forming function of the judicial opinions concerns *inter alia* their contribution to the culture and the relation between the justice system and society (Rzucidło 2020, pp. 117–118). In this regard, judicial opinions serve to promote a specific vision of justice and have their axiological, ideological, and legal-political dimensions. The educational function concerns inter alia the communication of a proper manner of behavior, which is reinforced by the fact that the court in principle acts as an impartial entity in the trial (Rzucidło 2020, p. 119). There are of course other functions; however, in this chapter, I am interested mostly in the relationship between society, culture, and the judicial system.

I attempt to answer the abovementioned questions, using instrumental case study in its evaluative type (McDonough and McDonough 2014, pp. 206–207; Zainal 2007, pp. 3–4) of assumptions concerning woman, family, marriage, Muslims, "Love Jihad", and conversion, which can be reconstructed from the judicial opinions issued in the Hadiya case. The main reason for choosing this method is that it allows one to focus on a smaller part of the reality and to analyze not only the judicial case but also its social and cultural context. The background of the case is particularly interesting and helps to understand what happened and why. Additionally, it reveals how the verdicts may fit into certain cultural and social narratives and consequently support them. On the other hand, those narratives may also have an impact on the judges' decision-making process, or at least equip them with arguments to justify their final conclusion. However, taking into consideration the limitations associated with the above-mentioned judicial opinions, comments in this chapter on the possible influence of certain social narrations on the judges must be treated purely speculatively and require further research.

The first part of the chapter is devoted to an introduction to a particular social context of the Hadiya case, namely the phenomenon of "Love Jihad". I present how it is portrayed and who the propagators of its existence are. In the next part, I focus on the broader cultural background of "Love Jihad" to show what this theory is based on. In the third and main part, I return to the Hadiya case to examine the judicial opinions issued in this case. The analysis is divided into three parts: (1) women, family, and marriage; (2) Muslims and "Love Jihad"; and (3) conversion. Lastly, in the conclusion, I summarize and offer answers to the aforementioned questions.

2 "Love Jihad"

"Love Jihad" is a conspiracy theory that assumes that Indian Muslims, to take control of India, seduce non-Muslim women (mainly Hindus, although it is sometimes suggested that Christian women are also targets), persuade them to marry, and force them to convert to Islam and eventually bear many children (Iwanek 2016, p. 358). However, what should be implied once again is that no evidence—at least for now—exists of such activities (Strohl 2018, p. 4), even though the discussion of "Love Jihad" has already lasted more than 10 years.

The main actors spreading the rumors concerning the subject are Hindu nationalists and right-wing Hindu organizations, including the Bharatiya Janata Party (Indian People's Party) the ruling party in India since 2014 (Gupta 2009, p. 13; Hossain et al. 2016, p. 670). Therefore, in the description of "Love Jihad", we can find traces of the shape of the Indian society desired by Hindu nationalists, who have centered their ideology around the concept of Hindutva (see Strohl 2018, p. 4; Rajeshwar and Amore 2019, p. 1; Gupta, p. 13). Hindutva can be roughly explained as Hindu nationalism, an ideology of religious right for which only Hindus are the true patriots, true Indians, while Muslims and Christians are foreigners to the Indian land (Ludden 1996, pp. 22, 23, 274). The theory of "Love Jihad" is one of the manifestations of this ideology.

One of the Hindu right-wing organizations, Hindu Janjagruthi Samiti (HJS), runs a website that is a mine of information about the discussed theory of "Love Jihad". HJS also publishes a book on the subject in English, Hindi, Marathi, Gujarati, Bengali, Kannad, and Telugu. The following is how they define "Love Jihad" (Hindu Janjagruthi Samiti 2020):

> "Love Jihad" is a war declared by Jihadis against Hindus and Christians through the medium of deceptive love. Today it has become need of the hour for Hindus to take proper precautions so that Hindu women should not fall prey to this demon of Love Jihad. Unite and come forward to thwart the conspiracy of "Love Jihad" and save our cultural heritage by preserving the valuable treasure of Hindu girls.
>
> Morality and culture of Bharat is preserved because of the Hindu woman. Hindu girls are the gene-banks of Hindu culture. Allowing them to marry boys from other sects amounts to surrendering the invaluable genes of Hindu lineage to them. Do not allow this to happen. Save our cultural heritage (...) O Hindus! Take an oath that you will not allow any Hindu girl you know to become a victim of "Love Jihad"!

These quotes effectively summarize the atmosphere around "Love Jihad". It is presented as a battle, a war against Hindu culture and tradition. Hindus must therefore unite and oppose this act of aggression. Within this discussion, a woman is not a subject but merely an object. Women are the carrier of Hindu culture. In this thinking, it is unacceptable for a Hindu woman to undergo conversion and thus leave her familial religion because it would equal the destruction of the Hindu culture genes she carries. Women are portrayed here as weak, easily manipulatable, and unable to take care of themselves (Gupta 2016, p. 297). They are depicted as an easy target for Muslim men who can impress them with expensive gifts, designer clothes, and fancy cars (Gupta 2016, p. 295). Acquaintance with a Muslim is also perceived as dangerous for woman's chastity, which is said to be the most valuable thing she owns (Hindu Janjagruthi Samiti 2020). In particular, premarital sex is supposed to be one of the modus operandi of followers of Islam (Iwanek 2016, p. 365). Therefore, the Hindu Janjagruthi Samiti suggested that parents should keep an eye on their daughters' activities, check their mobile phones, and not let them have unrestrained freedom or follow the Western style of life (2020). They should teach their daughters about Hindu tradition, culture, religion, and the importance of Dharma (i.e. "the privileges, duties and obligations of a man, his standard of conduct as a member of the Aryan community, as a member of one of the castes, as a person in a particular stage of life" [Kane 1962–1975, p. 3, after Davis 2010, p. 16]), and make them proud of their origins (Hindu Janjagruthi Samiti 2020).

Therefore, there is a reference to so-called Western culture, which in "Love Jihad" discourse manifests itself in the celebration of Valentine's Day (Hindu Janjagruthi Samiti 2020) and New Year, eating cake on one's birthday, believing that all religions are equal (Pandey 2020), and dating or participation in meetings without parental control (Iwanek 2016, p. 373). Parents who let their children, especially daughters, act according to the Western way of life are said to be raising them improperly (Pandey 2020). What is more, it is supposedly easier for Muslims to seduce a girl who deviates from traditional Hindu behavior (Iwanek 2016, p. 373). Therefore, collectivism, social control and adherence to the customs are praised, whereas individualism and liberalism are not considered desirable ideas for Hindu society by the supporters of the discussed conspiracy theory.

Iwanek (2016, p. 373) indicated that in the "Love Jihad" narrative, the fight against Westernization is combined with the fight against Islam. This is even confirmed by the name "Love Jihad", where the word "love" exemplifies Western modernism, whereas "jihad" symbolizes radical Islam. The word "jihad" is understood here in negative terms as a battle, a holy war against non-Muslims, the aim of which is to eradicate other religions (in India mostly through forced conversions) (Hindu Janjagruthi Samiti 2020). It is worth mentioning that this word also has a different meaning and can be understood as an internal struggle to be a better Muslim (Khan et al. 2018, pp. 1–2). The term love refers in the discussed context to making marriage decisions based on romantic feelings (Sharma et al. 2014, pp. 1–2). The term "Romeo" is even more suggestive. It is associated with passionate affection, which may occur in secret without taking into consideration the established social boundaries and the opinions of parents or the community. Therefore, it is the sole decision of a couple to be together. This is controversial in traditional Hindu society, which is elaborated later in the chapter.

How then are the Muslims (the main culprits), and their culture portrayed in the "Love Jihad" discourse? First of all, they supposedly pretend to be modern and liberal and to believe in personal freedom to seduce Hindu girls, but after the wedding, they reveal their true, radical (to be understood as religious fanaticism) selves (Iwanek 2016, p. 373). It is claimed that a woman will never be happy having a Muslim husband because she will be either treated as a servant, sold to Islamic countries, or used for prostitution (Hindu Janjagruthi Samiti 2020). Additionally, Muslims are believed to be full of lust, with much sexual desire and high potency, traits that are supposed to attract Hindu women (Hindu Janjagruthi Samiti 2020). As Iwanek (2016, p. 357) wrote, Muslims are presented as almost half-wild people who do not have any culture, lead uncivilised lives, and are guided only by their lusts.

An excellent graphic summary (available online) of what was said in this chapter is on the cover of the book "Love Jihad" published by Hindu Janjagruthi Samiti

(2000). An in-depth discourse analysis of the graphic is performed below from the perspective of the views of those who proclaim the existence of "Love Jihad".

First of all, we see an inter-faith couple. The woman is a Hindu, which is indicated by the traditional clothing she is wearing, whereas the man is a Muslim, which is indicated by his thoughts of conversion. The heart symbolizes the romantic involvement of the woman. She looks dreamy and unaware of the risks she is supposedly heading toward; she does not perceive the situation rationally but rather emotionally. The man has an unpleasant expression of anger and determination. He could be said to look obsessed with the idea of converting the girl from Hinduism to Islam. They are alone driving on a motorbike to some place private, and therefore, we can assume they are on a date. This (i.e., feelings and date) relates to Western style of life and a deviation from the traditional Hindu behavior. Additionally, a Hindu temple in rays of sunlight is behind them in the distance; the way it is portrayed (i.e., bright, luminous colors) suggests positive inclinations. It looks like a safe and happy place from which the girl is taken by a Muslim boy. The further from the temple the couple drives, the closer to the abyss they venture. This could be read as danger awaits in places where the Hindu community is absent and where social control is nonexistent. According to the graphic in the dark gulf, suicide due to depression, prostitution, and terrorist activities await. Those are the things that are supposed to happen to a girl who fraternizes with Muslims.

3 Reasons Underlying the Ongoing Debate About "Love Jihad"

It is said that the term "Love Jihad" was first used in India around 2007–2009 (Gupta 2016, p. 300; Hossain et al. 2016, p. 678); however, the idea of jihad through love and the pornosexualization of Muslims (Anand 2011, pp. 49–50) is not a new concept. Stories of Hindu girls being kidnapped by Muslim men have been constantly vivid in Indian society (Anand 2011, p. 65). For example, in the 1920s there was an uproar in British India due to allegations that Muslims were abducting Hindu women, raping them, and forcing them to marry and convert (Gupta 2009, pp. 13–14). In 1947, there were suggestions that the partitioning of British India into India and Pakistan (a Muslim state) was just the beginning, and that Muslims were going to take control of the whole Indian subcontinent through an information war (e.g., by buying the media), demographic war (e.g., by seducing Hindu girls), and proxy war (by spreading terror) (Krishnaswami n.d., p. 41, after Anand 2011, p. 50). As we can see, the idea is not new and has constantly returned in public discussion.

Even during the preparation of this chapter, an event occurred in India that was related to this topic. In October 2020, the Indian jewelry company Tanishq released a commercial (DW News 2020) in which a Muslim mother-in-law was organizing a baby shower for her Hindu daughter-in-law. Therefore, we can assume that it was an inter-religious marriage between a Muslim man and a Hindu woman. The advertisement showed a peaceful gathering of Muslims and Hindus and a happy Hindu woman who had a good relationship with her Muslim mother-in-law. The daughter-in-law was in a traditional Hindu outfit, and therefore, she probably did not change her religion after marriage. The mother-in-law says at the end: "If we unite, what can't we do?" (DW News 2020). The description of the commercial on YouTube was as follows: "She is married into a family that loves her like their own child. Only for her, they go out of their way to celebrate an occasion that they usually don't. A beautiful confluence of two different religions, traditions and cultures" (BBC 2020a).

This advertisement provoked such a negative reaction that the company decided to withdraw it after only 2–3 days of being online. On their Facebook profile, Tanishq (Facebook 2020) stated that the idea behind this campaign was to "celebrate the coming together of people from different walks of life", but it caused such a severe response that they decided to remove it "keeping in mind the hurt sentiments and well being of our employees, partners and store staff". Why did this campaign receive such a reaction? The company was accused of supporting "Love Jihad" by presenting a false image of reality in the advertisement, namely a happy Hindu woman in a marriage with a Muslim. Some Twitter and Facebook users called for a boycott of Tanishq (cf. Tanishq Facebook 2020; Tanishq Twitter 2020).

The social response to rumours concerning "Love Jihad" may be perceived as an example of moral panic (Strohl 2018; Gupta 2016, p. 296; Anand 2011, p. 67). It refers to a time in which society (or its part) is scared of a certain group of people (but not exclusively)—so-called folk devils—because those people are perceived to be a threat to the established values and way of life of a given community (Cohen 2002, p. 1). Moral panic often has little to do with real danger, or at least there is disproportion in the perception of what the possible threat is and what it looks like in reality. The actors of this phenomenon exaggerate the scale of the supposed danger, repercussions to society, and inevitability of the consequences (Goode 2017, pp. 2–3). Moral panic may be planned, controlled, and triggered for a specific purpose (Herdt 2009, p. 5). To be successful, there must be some points of resonance with already existed concerns (Garland 2008, p. 12). Therefore, it exposes the ideologies and hierarchies functioning in the society and reproduces the rules and roles established for years through fear, disgust, and social exclusion of those who do not fit into the existing order (Herdt 2009, p. 18). As a consequence of societal fear, expectations exist that something should be done to overcome the threat. Hence moral panic may initiate changes in the law and social policies, and may lead to a strengthening of the control apparatus, harsher police actions, or stricter sentences (Goode and Ben-Yehuda 2009, p. 35).

Thus, the following question arises: Why is this theory of Muslims being the seducers of Hindu girls so alive in India? I briefly outline possible reasons for why this country is such a fertile ground for this concept. However, it should be underlined that this is not an exhaustive explanation because it is not the aim of this chapter nor is there enough space for it. At the same time, I believe this background is crucial for an enhanced understanding of supporters of the existence of "Love Jihad" and the course of the Hadiya case.

3.1 Some Aspects of Hindu Tradition

As was already indicated in the previous section, in the "Love Jihad" discourse it is possible to see some desirable traits of Indian society, especially its Hindu part. Those traits are connected mostly to Hindu tradition, which we can safely assume is still crucial for many Indian citizens (of course not for all). One of the important social institutions is marriage. Traditionally in India, it is not a union between two people but between two families (Hossain et al. 2016, p. 677). The understanding and similarities of opinions and values should be between the parents of future spouses. Therefore, in the ideal situation, the families that are supposed to be connected by marital ties should have a similar background, religion, social status, and economic situation, and also be from the same varna or caste (there are thousands of castes, that are segregated into four varnas: Brahmin, Kshatriya, Vaishya and Shudra [Lodhi and Bala 2016, p. 100]; the system was officially abolished in India but still functions in the society). Marriage is also associated with prestige. Consequently, a mixed marriage, such as an inter-religious relationship, may not be treated as prestigious by the communities from which the spouses come (Hossain et al. 2016, p. 678; Tyagi and Sen 2020, p. 8). For example, marriage outside the cast may even lead to so-called honor killings (Kashyap 2020, p. 75; Ahmed 2020). Even Muslim families do not want their child, especially their daughter, to get married to a non-Muslim (Gupta 2016, p. 298). Inter-faith marriages complicate the reality, confuse the long-sanctioned order, violate boundaries between communities, and propose different values from those traditionally held (Gupta 2009, p. 15). Therefore, inter-faith marriages are controversial and attract negative attention not only due to the "Love Jihad" conspiracy theory.

Consequently, in India, approximately 90% of marriages (the number is even higher among the Hindu community) are arranged, which means that parents (and other adults in the family) look for and choose a partner for their children (Edathumparambil 2017, p. XIV). Mostly the future spouses can say no to the proposed candidate, which leads to a further search. At the same time, not many would decide to marry someone who has not received their parents' approval (Kashyap 2020, p. 76). This is why romantic feelings and love are for some part of Indian society controversial. They may occur regardless of religion and social affiliation of the parties, against the established rules and parental preferences (Sharma et al. 2014, p. 2). Therefore, love marriage is associated with manifestations of individualism (see Donner 2016; Heitmeyer 2016). A woman's love is perceived as especially dangerous for Hindu patriarchal society because as male property, she should not be taught that she can choose something on her own (Gupta 2016, pp. 293 and 297). At the same time, there is a place for love in the relationship, but it should develop after the marriage, not before. Simply put, love is not considered to be a proper argument for the selection of one's future spouse (Kashyap 2020, pp. 74–76).

Another point of resonance between "Love Jihad" theory and the traditional Hindu worldview is the perception of family and a woman. As previously mentioned, traditional Hindu society is patriarchal. Kashyap (2020, pp. 73–76) indicated that it is the eldest man (mostly the father) who has the highest authority in the family. Parents are legitimated to make decisions for their children, as was seen in the example of marriage arrangements. Finding a good spouse is even perceived as a parental duty. Traditionally, a woman is viewed as inferior to a man, and her prime role is to be a wife and mother. In consequence girls are socialized to be submissive (Natarajan 2016, p. 2). Moreover, female sexuality is an important issue. A woman who loses her chastity brings dishonor to her family, and also reduces her marriage prospects (Tandon and Luthra 2016, p. 1). Therefore, she must be protected and controlled mostly by imposing additional restrictions on her. Losing one's chastity in the eyes of traditional Indian society is relatively easy, and being a victim of sexual assault may already reduce a woman's value even though it was not her doing (Natarajan 2016, p. 6). Topics such as women's sexuality, the need to exercise control over women to protect them, or the importance of parental involvement in the decision-making process of their grown-up offspring are also touched on in the "Love Jihad" discourse.

3.2 *Muslims and the Demographic War*

Another issue is the ongoing distrust of Muslims in India. This aversion to the believers of Islam is grounded in the long history of conflicts between Hindu and Muslim communities: for example, the Mughal government on the Indian peninsula for over 300 years (sixteenth to nineteenth centuries) (see Richards 1995); the division of British India into India and Pakistan and the tense political situation between those countries (Akhter 2016, p. 208); the unresolved situation in Jammu and Kashmir, where the majority of residents are Muslims (see Zia 2019; Tavares 2008; Census of India 2011); and accusations that Muslims are legally privileged (Austin 2001, pp. 15–23). Note that in India Hindus, Muslims, Christians, Parsis and Jews have their own sets of rules called personal laws which regulates private and family life of those five religious communities, such as marriage, divorce, adoption but also inheritance, succession and religious matters (Subramanian 2014, p. 4) and Muslims are the only ones who still have the right to polygamy due to the existence of the personal law system. Furthermore, Muslims are often linked with terrorist activities in the media or movies (see Bhat et al. 2017; Umber et al. 2018), and "Love Jihad" is supposed to be just one of the examples of such activities financed by Arab countries (Hindu Janjagruthi Samiti 2020; Gupta 2009, p. 15).

The accusations towards Muslims of conducting a demographic war (Krishnaswami n.d., p. 41, after Anand 2011, p. 50) in India are particularly crucial because they are directly linked to "Love Jihad", the main goal of which is supposed to be increasing the number of Muslims to take control of India. Already during colonial times, there were voices saying that Hindu is a dying race (Sethi 2002, p. 1546). Where did this fear come from? It is partly from the results of the census conducted on the Indian subcontinent. The percentage of the Muslim population is constantly increasing, whereas the percentage of the Hindu population is decreasing. In 1951 (the first census in independent India), the mosaic of the Indian population was 84.9% Hindus and 9.9% Muslims (Anand 2011, p. 52). In 1991, Hindus accounted for 82.4% of Indian citizens, whereas Muslims accounted for 11.7% (however, this census was not conducted in Jammu and Kashmir where Muslims are the majority, so it is possible that the actual number of Muslims was higher depending on how the final results were counted) (Business Standard 2015). In 2001, Hindus accounted for 80.5% and Muslims 13.4% (Census of India 2001). The last census from 2011 (the next is planned for 2021) again revealed an increase in the proportion of Muslims—to 14.23%—and a decrease in the number of Hindus—to 79.8% (Census of India 2011). However, the rate of the Muslim population's growth has been slowly decreasing since 1991, possibly due to the constant increase in education and literacy, but it is still slightly higher than the rate of the Hindu population's growth (Business Standard 2015). What is important, the literacy rate among Muslims (64.2%) is still lower than that in the Hindu community (68.3%) (NFHS-4 2015–2016, p. 63). However, to Hindu nationalists, there are only two explanations for the increase in the number of Muslims: (1) the high fertility and potent sexuality of Muslims, which are supposedly sanctioned by their religion and culture but not by factors of socioeconomic delay or poverty, and (2) their desire to take control of the Indian subcontinent by overpopulation (Anand 2011, pp. 52–54).

The recent Citizenship (Amendment) Act may serve as an example of the negative perception of the Muslim community. The act facilitates the acquisition of citizenship for illegal immigrants but only for non-Muslims fleeing Muslim-majority countries, namely Pakistan, Afghanistan, and Bangladesh (BBC 2020b). The controversies mainly focus on the fact that religion becomes a relevant factor in the process of obtaining Indian citizenship (HRW 2020).

3.3 Conversion Laws

Conversion is another interesting subject from the perspective of "Love Jihad". Abandoning the Hindu religion has for a long time been perceived as a dangerous and undesirable phenomenon. This is even manifested in Indian law. Literature stated that the first anti-conversion legal regulations were enacted during the British period (first in the 1930s) (Jain 2019, p. 2). Those laws were not introduced by British authorities but by Indians in the Princely States (Coleman 2007–2008, p. 23). The reason behind them was the activity of Christian missionaries in the subcontinent, which was seen as a threat to the religious identity of Indians (Huff 2009, p. 4), especially considering the British support the missionaries received (Stubbs 1993, p. 366).

After independence, some Indian states (8 out of 29) enacted Freedom of Religion Acts, which aimed to regulate the phenomenon of conversion from one religion to another (Ahmad 2018, p. 1). In every act, the idea is similar (however, the details of the laws differ). The states wanted to eliminate conversion by force, fraud, and inducement or allurement (Jain 2019, pp. 2–3). To be more precise, in Odisha (formerly Orissa), for example: "No person shall convert or attempt to convert, either directly or otherwise, any person from one religious faith to another by the use of force or by inducement or by any fraudulent means nor shall any person abet such conversion" (section 3 of Orissa Freedom of Religion Act, 1967). Moreover, the understanding of force or deception is very broad. Force "shall include a show of force or a threat of injury of any kind including threat of divine displeasure or social ex-communication" (section 2b of Orissa Freedom of Religion Act, 1967). Fraud "shall include misrepresentation or any other fraudulent contrivance" (section 2c of Orissa Freedom of Religion Act, 1967). Therefore, saying that unbelievers may face the wrath of God may already be perceived as persuading someone by force to change his/her religion. If the person who changes religion because of forcible conversion is a minor or belongs to the Scheduled Castes or Scheduled Tribes or is a woman, the punishment is often more severe (cf. section 4 of Orissa Freedom of Religion Act, 1967). As we can see, converting a woman is viewed as a more reprehensible behavior than converting a man. This fits the narrative of "Love Jihad" in which 'losing' women is considered an enormous tragedy for the Hindu nation.

The anti-conversion laws were contested as unconstitutional because of the wording of Article 25 of the Indian Constitution, according to which "all persons are equally entitled to freedom of conscience and the right freely to profess, practise and propagate religion" (The Constitution of India 1949). Especially crucial is the right to propagate, understood by some as the right to convert (Ahmad 2018, p. 19). However, the Supreme Court of India in the judgement *Rev Stainislaus v. State of Madhya Pradesh* did not agree with this understanding and ruled that propagation means to spread religion by exposing the believers (not to convert people); therefore, the discussed acts do not violate the Constitution (Claerhout and De Roover 2019, p. 13). In addition, the laws have been criticized for being unnecessary, because in the Indian Penal Code there are provisions that could be used in case of forced conversion (Jain 2019, p. 5). For example, Article 153A forbidding the promotion of enmity between distinct groups (also religious), or Article 295A concerning behavior that aims to outrage religious feelings or insult religious behavior (Indian Penal Code 1860). As we will see, they were used in such a situation in the state of Kerala where the case of Hadiya occurred and where special regulations concerning conversion have not been passed.

Notably, while accusations and arrests have been made based on the discussed anti-conversion law, there have been no convictions (Ahmad 2018, p. 21). Furthermore, there are no official reports that show the scale of the phenomenon. Despite this, the discussion of forced conversion in India has not ceased to exist. Especially active in this domain are Hindutva groups and people linked to the BJP—*Bharatiya*

Janata Party (USCIRS 2018, p. 4). Moreover, while abandoning Hinduism is presented as a negative thing, converting to Hinduism is highly praised. For Hindu nationalists, this is solely considered coming back home, returning to the religion of one's ancestors, and correcting a mistake, not conversion. Some nationalist Hindu organizations have claimed to lead a Ghar Wapsi (returning home, homecoming) campaign, the aim of which is to reconvert Indians back to Hinduism on a massive scale (Rajeshwar and Amore 2019, pp. 1–2, 6 and 10). Therefore, Ghar Wapsi is often perceived as outside the scope of anti-conversion laws (USCIRS 2018, p. 4; Ahmad 2018, p. 21; Mustafa and Sohi 2017, p. 941). Thus, the anti-conversion laws are in reality directed (although not openly) against Christianity and Islam. Even though there are probably no convictions under these laws, various reports suggest that they have an impact on the growth of hate crimes against religious minorities and distrust between different communities (USCIRS 2018, p. 4; Ahmad 2018, p. 20; Jain 2019, p. 2).

The topic of "Love Jihad" is strictly entangled with the topic of anti-conversions laws. After all, the main aim behind it is supposed to be the conversion of Hindu women. Currently, in Uttar Pradesh, the government is considering the introduction of anti-conversion laws similar to those in force in other states. The main reason behind such a decision is suspicion of the existence of forced conversions in the name of "Love Jihad" (Mishra 2020).

4 Hadiya Case

Under the abovementioned circumstances in 2016, the case of Hadiya was brought to the High Court of Kerala and became mixed up with "Love Jihad" discourse. When Hadiya was 23–24 years old and studying in Salem (Tamil Nadu), she decided to openly manifest her change of faith (according to her statement, she had already been following Islam unofficially for 3 years [SvA-cf, p. 151]) and go to college wearing a veil. When her parents found out they tried to bring her back home, which was unsuccessful due to her actions. Eventually, when reporting it to the police did not help, her father decided to file a writ petition of habeas corpus under Article 226 of the Constitution of India[1] to the High Court of Kerala (hereinafter "the Court"). The purpose of this procedure is to bring a person under alleged captivity before the court, and if the person is actually under detention without legal grounds, to secure the release of that person (Johari and Mishra 2019, p. 123).

[1]226. (1) Notwithstanding anything in article 32 every High Court shall have power, throughout the territories in relation to which it exercises jurisdiction, to issue to any person or authority, including in appropriate cases, any Government, within those territories directions, orders or writs, including writs in the nature of habeas corpus, mandamus, prohibition, quo warranto and certiorari, or any of them, for the enforcement of any of the rights conferred by Part III and for any other purpose (Constitution of India 1949).

Anticipating the facts of the case, to make the rest of the chapter easier to understand, allow me to briefly summarise all three judgements. The first proceeding ended quickly; the Court ruled that Hadiya, regardless of what her father said, was not under any illegal detention (AvS-fj, p. 9). The father did not accept this decision and a few months later filed a second writ petition of habeas corpus with new allegations. This initiated a second, separate procedure. This time, after the longer procedure (almost 9 months), the Court agreed with the father of Hadiya and ruled that (1) custody of Hadiya was granted to her father, she should be escorted by the police to her parental home, and the whole family would have police protection; (2) the marriage of Hadiya to her husband Shafin Jahan was declared null and void (marriage was concluded during the pending court case); (3) the Director General of Police should carry on the investigation concerning the matter; and (4) the Director General of Police should enquire into the mistakes of the previous Investigating Officer (AvS-s, pp. 93–95). In response, Shafin Jahan decided to file an appeal from the verdict of the High Court of Kerala to the Supreme Court of India. The Supreme Court of India did not agree with the reasoning of the lower court and set aside the verdict, and simultaneously allowed the police investigation to continue but without encroaching on the marital status of Hadiya and Shafin Jahan (SvA-sc, pp. 40–41). After this judgement, Hadiya returned to her husband.

Before I begin the analysis of the content of the judicial opinions, it is worthwhile explaining how this kind of decision is structured. Most of the verdict is a chronological report of what happened during the case. Some of the statements and writings of individual participants are paraphrased. The court also explains what happened during the hearings and what decisions (not a final judgement) were issued after each one. Sometimes the court quotes passages of the middle orders in a final judgement. At the end of the judicial opinion, there is a resolution of the case and the summary of motives behind it. However, the parts are not clearly separated. Additionally, it is worth mentioning that the judges who issue the final verdict are not always present on every hearing that takes place in a given case.

The analysis of the judgement is divided into several previously discussed topics. First, the issues that I raised in the context of the Hindu tradition are analyzed: women, family, and marriage (marriage will not be analyzed in the first judgement due to the fact that Hadiya was not married until the second procedure). Next, I present what appeared in the judgements about Muslims and "Love Jihad" itself. Lastly, I focus on the phenomenon of conversion.

4.1 First Judgement (the High Court of Kerala, Asokan K.M. v. The State of Kerala, from 25th of January 2016, WP(Crl.)/25/2016)

The first court procedure concerned the allegation raised by the father, according to which Hadiya was illegally kept by people mentioned in the writ petition (the significant actors are introduced later in the chapter), whose aim was to force her to convert for unknown reasons. The emphasis of the father's writ petition was on the fact that it is forbidden in India to force or allure people into religious conversion (SvA-cf, pp. 142 and 144). In addition, the father stressed that parents are entitled to "advise their children and mould their career" (SvA-cf, p. 145) and "protect the future of children" (SvA-cf, p. 146), even if those children are grown up. He added that the "laws in our country are aimed at protecting the rights of our citizens and protecting culture and tradition of our citizens" (SvA-cf, p. 146).

To support his claim, the father appealed to the anti-conversion laws as well as the traditional role of parents in Indian society. In Kerala, there are no special anti-conversion laws; however, as mentioned previously, provisions exist in the Indian Penal Code that can be used against forced conversion.

The procedure itself was mainly focused on Hadiya's explanations concerning the circumstances of her change of faith. She stated that it was her own conscious decision and she was helped by other people only because she asked them to (SvA-cf, pp. 150–155). The case was resolved at a second hearing by declaring that Hadiya was not under any illegal detention (SvA-cf, p. 182).

4.1.1 Women and Family

Not much was said in the first judgement. The Court only wrote the following: "Under the above mentioned circumstances [mostly Hadiya's and Smt Sainaba's (the social worker who helped Hadiya during the case and with whom Hadiya lived for some time) explanations] (...) She is at present staying in the above said institution [Sathyasarani — the institution which provides Islamic courses in which Hadiya was admitted] on her own wish and will" (AvS-fj, p. 9). The Court listened to Hadiya and did not contest her words, which were not overthrown despite the opposition of her father. There was no questioning of her voice solely for being a woman. It was said that she was firm and strong while communicating her will ("the alleged detenue had taken an adamant stand" [AvS-fj, p. 7]).

Although not paraphrased in the final judicial opinion, the words of the Court from the middle order, issued after the first hearing, seemed to accurately summarize the arguments that were considered decisive in resolving the court procedure. "We are of the opinion that the alleged detenue [Hadiya] needs to be given liberty to take her own decision with respect to her future life. (...) we are inclined to let her go along with the said lady" [Smt Sainaba] (SvA-cf, p. 168).

There are some suggestions in the judgement that a better solution in the Court's opinion would be if Hadiya reconciles with her father and returns home. "Despite much persuasion made by this court, the alleged detenue is not willing to go along with the petitioner [the father] to her parental house" (AvS-fj, p. 7). As the Court stated, it actively attempted to convince her to return home ("persuasion made by this court"), but in the end, she was not forced to act in a manner she did not want to. Therefore, even though the Court admitted that familial consent is an important value, the free choice of an individual was considered more important.

4.1.2 Muslims, "Love Jihad", and Conversion

There was no discussion in the written judicial opinion about Muslims, Islam, or "Love Jihad". Moreover, not much has been said about conversion. The Court only reported in the verdict with no additional comment about a parallel criminal procedure underway concerning Mr Aboobacker, who was accused of instigating and motivating Hadiya's conversion (AvS-fj, p. 4). This has been prequalified as a punishable offence under Section 153A (promotion of enmity between e.g. religious groups), 295A (offending religious feelings), and 107 (abetment) of the Indian Penal Code (AvS-fj, p. 4). As for his role in Hadiya's conversion, Aboobacker was a father of one of her Muslim roommates. As Hadiya claimed, she asked him for help when she did not want to return home because in her opinion her parents would not let her practice Islam. From what we know, he helped her for a few days mostly by looking for an institution that runs Islamic courses and would admit her (SvA-cf, pp. 150–151). Unfortunately, there is no information on how this investigation ended. In addition, the Court did not comment on the issue of conversion in India, even though it was mentioned in the father's petition.

4.2 Second Judgement (the High Court of Kerala, Asokan K.M. v. The Superintendent of Police, from 24th of May 2017, WP (Crl.).No. 297 of 2016 (S))

As previously mentioned, a few months later Hadiya's father filed a new writ petition of habeas corpus to the High Court of Kerala. This time the case took approximately 9 months and became far more complicated. The judgement itself has around 100 pages.

The case could be divided into two parts: before and after Hadiya's wedding. In the middle of the trial, Hadiya got married to a Muslim man—Shafin Jahan. She did this without informing the Court about her plans, which did not meet with a positive reaction (AvS-sj, pp. 19–20). The Court immediately changed its attitude towards Hadiya and her situation, which is elaborated later in the chapter. The marriage was probably one of the primary reasons the case was classified by some media as an example of "Love Jihad". The Court seemed at least alerted if not convinced of the merit of father's allegations. Additionally, it ordered a police investigation to check the background of people who had helped Hadiya and her husband. The results revealed no evidence of illegal activities (SvA-cf, pp. 486–489). Regardless of that, the Court decided that Hadiya was under illegal detention and should be under parental custody (AvS-sj, p. 93).

Moving on to the details of the case, this time the father's writ petition was much more extensive in its allegations against Indian Muslims. According to him, some people wanted to take Hadiya out of the country to Syria to join ISIS and fabricate a false marriage. He claimed that not only was his daughter in danger but also the whole of India. The Social Democratic Party of India (SDPI) and Popular Front of India have been accused of having terrorist connections and conducting anti-national activities to Islamize India and implement Sharia law. The goal of the SDPI is supposedly the complete eradication of the non-Muslim population. Allegedly, there exists a plan to expel Hindu people from Kerala. Hundreds of girls are supposed to be detained in the institution where Hadiya was studying Islam (Sathyasarani), where, as the Hadiya's father claimed, they are regularly raped (SvA-cf, pp. 184, 187–188, 190, and 210).

There is no place in this chapter to analyze the father's position in detail; however, the several examples from the 30-page text already reveal the tone of his writ petition. He presented the case as if the Hindu people were under imminent threat from the Islamic, anti-national, terrorist organizations operating in India or even generally from the whole Muslim population. One of their main activities is supposedly luring people (also under the pretext of love) into conversion and threatening them later that if they try to reconvert, they will be beheaded as on the videos they are allegedly forced to watch (SvA-cf, pp. 199, and 220–221). His daughter's behavior, conversion, and refusal to return home are said to be the consequences of the above-described Muslim endeavors.

4.2.1 Woman, Family, and Marriage

The Court indicates what characterizes a woman, such as "a female in her twenties is at a vulnerable stage" (AvS-sj, p. 29), and a "girl aged 24 years is weak and vulnerable, capable of being exploited" (AvS-sj, p. 91). According to it, a young woman is not able to independently take care of herself even when she is no longer a minor. She cannot distinguish what is right or wrong for her because she is from her female nature, highly susceptible to the influences of others. This is stated by the Court as a general and obvious truth about women. This type of thinking may have far-reaching consequences. In such an approach, ensuring women's safety is practically possible only by restricting her freedom. This rhetoric of safety is often used as an excuse to deprive a woman of her autonomy, especially in patriarchal societies.

It is moreover directly said by the Court that "as per Indian tradition, the custody of an unmarried daughter is with the parents, until she is properly married" (AvS-sj, p. 29); "Her marriage being the most important decision in her life, can also be taken only with the active involvement of her parents" (AvS-sj, p. 93). This is presented not only as a part of tradition but as the correct structure of a society wishing to protect the welfare of women. Her agency is restricted because it is believed that she should be constantly guided by proper caregivers, meaning her parents and later on her husband. They should be the ones who are making the decisions for her or at least be controlling whether her decisions are the proper ones. Since this societal rule exists to ensure a good life for a woman, it is suspicious if she does something against her 'natural' guardians. It can be for example assumed that she is under the impact of someone else due to her supposed defenselessness and naivety.

The Court even went a step further and invoked a *Parens Patriae* doctrine, which can be described as a symbolic acquisition of parental control by the Court. In its opinion, it is the Court's duty to protect women not only from threats but even from exposure to danger. It was stressed that all the Court's actions were done to ensure safety and were in the best interests of the girl (AvS-sj, pp. 19, and 28–29). The Supreme Court of India later explained that this doctrine can be used in exceptional situations concerning most of all mentally ill persons or minors who don't have a parent or legal guardian or the parent/legal guardian is not suitable (abusive, negligent etc.)

Additionally, the Court perceived Hadiya herself as having only moderate intellectual abilities and as a naive person not capable of making her own decisions (AvS-sj, p. 74). Consequently, the Court said that it is not "safe to let Ms. Akhila [Hadiya] free to decide what she wants in her life" (AvS-sj, p. 90). To be clear, no psychological evaluation of Hadiya was conducted during the trial. It was all based on the Court's impression of her and her behavior. A portrait of Hadiya drawn by her father probably also had an impact on the Court's perception. He said that inter alia "she, being a fragile girl both mentally and physically, is not expected to express her real will and wish" (SvA-cf, p. 199); "weak, foolish and fragile girls like detenue" (SvA-cf, p. 200); "a hapless, foolish and imprudent girl" (SvA-cf, p. 206); and "mentally weak and prone to mental disease" (SvA-cf, p. 357).

With this in mind, it is not surprising that even though Hadiya during the whole trial repeated that it is her own choice to be a Muslim and not live with her parents because she was convinced they would not respect her choice of religion (SvA-cf, p. 282), she was ignored by the Court. Credibility was given to the father when he promised that he would let Hadiya practice Islam under his roof despite his strongly negative attitude towards Muslims and Islam. The Court even stated that the father's words led to the conclusion that Hadiya "can have no complaint against her parents" (AvS-sj, p. 91).

From the above, a certain picture of the family already emerges. Continuing this thread, the Court, as in the previous proceedings, tried "to persuade her to accompany her parents" (AvS-sj, p. 12). It was also said by the Court that "we place on record our dissatisfaction at the continued residence of the detenue with the 7th respondent [Smt Sainaba], who is a stranger" (AvS-sj, p. 17). The Court assumed from the very first hearing that it would be better for Hadiya if she chose to live with her parents rather than with someone with whom she does not have any familial relation, "a stranger" as the Court described. The family house was considered the safest and most suitable place for Hadiya. The genetic ties were seen as more important than her personal choice with whom she felt more comfortable. It was even presented as the laws of nature with which it is difficult to argue: "There are no other persons in this world, who would consider the welfare and wellbeing of their daughter to be of paramount importance than her parents. The nature provides numerous examples of even animals taking care of and protecting their progeny sacrificing their very lives for the purpose. The Homo sapiens is no exception" (AvS-sj, p. 90).

Moving on to the topic of marriage, as was previously mentioned, in the middle of the case Hadiya got married to a Muslim man. She met her husband on the matrimonial site "Way to *Nikah*" (*nikah*—ar. marriage) and they decided to get married (AvS-sj, p. 48). According to the Indian division on love and arranged marriages, this would fall more into the arranged category. "Way to *Nikah*" (2020) is a matrimonial website focused above all on facilitating the finding of a future spouse. Furthermore, Hadiya and Shafin Jahan decided to get married after only one meeting (SvA-cf, p. 465), which is similar to how the process may look when parents are arranging the marriage. It was perceived similarly by the Court (AvS-sj, p. 78); however, it still caused a disturbance in a social reality like those described above when it comes to a love marriage. As already indicated, according to what the verdict contained, it is beyond comprehension that a child can make this decision without his or her parents involved. Therefore, it could be said that Hadiya getting married without even informing her father and mother broke from the established social order. Notably, the Court stated that if it is a love marriage then the Court would accept the choice of a girl (AvS-sj, p. 78). This is slightly contradictory to what the Court stated about parents' involvement in their children's choice of partner.

In addition, an issue of power existed. If the marriage had been considered valid, then the parents would have lost control over their daughter because the husband would have been her new guardian, and he was not chosen by them. The Court even stated that the rights of parents were trampled on by the people who were helping Hadiya with arranging a marriage (AvS-sj, p. 81). The Court agreed with a different verdict in which it was stated that parental authority also exists over a woman who is no longer a minor (AvS-sj, p. 92).

Remarkably, the Court also perceived marriage as an attempt to deprive not only parents but also the Court of control over Hadiya: "It is clear that the alleged marriage is only a make-believe, intended to take the detenue out of reach of the hands of this Court" (AvS-sj, p. 80); "The question that crops up now is whether the marriage that has been allegedly performed is not a device to transport her out of this country" (AvS-sj, p. 28); "Sri. Shafin Jahan is only a stooge who has been assigned to play the role of going through a marriage ceremony. The alleged marriage is only a sham and is of no consequence. The same was intended only to force the hands of this court and to scuttle the proceedings in this case that were progressing" (AvS-sj, p. 85).

The Court expressed its dissatisfaction with the fact that no one asked it for permission to solemnize this marriage; no one informed the Court about that. The Court indicated that it all happened when Hadiya knew that, in the Court's opinion, she needed to finish her degree as everything had been arranged to get her admitted to the college. Instead, she came to the court with a husband who was called "a stranger" by the Court. The Court did not even want to interact with Hadiya that day, even though she was in court and her lawyer proposed that she could personally explain everything. The Court just dismissed her by saying that it was not necessary and it was the decision of the Court when would be appropriate time to listen her (AvS-sj, pp. 19–20, and 26).

The Court did not stop at verbally expressing its dissatisfaction. It was decided that Hadiya had to be sent to a ladies hostel, where she would be under strict control: only her parents would be allowed to interact with her and it would be prohibited for her to use or possess a mobile phone (SvA-cf, p. 400). She stayed in the hostel until the end of the court procedure—approximately half a year. It was not the first time the Court had done that; the first time had been after the first hearing (SvA-cf, pp. 229–230), but after 1 month the Court changed its mind and Hadiya returned to Smt Sainaba.

The Court's actions and statements revealed that power over the life of Hadiya during the court procedure was fully up to its decisions. The Court would not have let Hadiya undermine it by taking actions contrary to it. Taking into account how the Court perceived the parental authority and the fact that it invoked the *Parens Patriae* doctrine, we could say that the Court acted as a traditional father figure; that is, the head of the family with whom in particular a daughter should consult for all decisions regardless of age. At the same time, it said that this was all done in the best interest of a child—here a grown woman.

The image of the desired vision of society (in the discussed scope) that emerges from the judgement is patriarchal and traditional. There are visible similarities in the perception of women, family, and marriage between the verdict, the "Love Jihad" discourse, and the traditional Hindu worldview. The female sex is said to be weak, easily manipulated, and therefore in need of protection from the male part of society. Parental control has almost no limits, especially for matrimonial decisions. It is even the parents' right to take part in it. Consequently, the voice of the man, the father, is considered here to be stronger, more reliable than the voice of a young woman. Whereas she is perceived as someone unable to know what is right for her, he is pictured as all-knowing in this regard. In this vision of a society, not much space exists for a woman's individuality and agency because it is considered dangerous for her.

4.2.2 Muslims and "Love Jihad"

As previously mentioned, in the father's opinion, his daughter was forcefully converted to Islam and soon would be exported from the country for terrorist purposes. Moreover, it was supposed to be an example of the wider operation of Muslim radical organizations in India whose plan is to eradicate Hindus and take control of the country.

The Court did not comment on every allegation made by the father; however, at the very beginning it ordered the police to investigate the background of the case: the reasons underlying Hadiya's conversion, the activities of Sathyasarani, the financial situation of Hadiya and people helping her, and later on, how the marriage came about, who Shafin Jahan is, and whether he has any terrorist connections, among other things. There were some suspicions concerning, for example, the source from which Hadiya received money for a lawyer or her husband's Facebook posts, his political connection to the SDPI, and the fact he had an ongoing criminal case concerning his probable participation in a fight because of a political dispute. However, as it was already mentioned, the investigation did not reveal any hard evidence against any of the people involved in the case (SvA-cf, pp. 440–463 and 486–489).

The reaction of the Court to these findings was that the investigation was simply not done properly. "Either he [the Deputy Superintendent of Police] has been influenced and subjugated into studied inaction or he lacks the alertness and competence that is expected of an Investigating Officer probing an issue of such seriousness. (…) [T]he seriousness of the issues involved, the widespread allegations of forcible conversion that were coming up and the national interest that is at stake" (AvS-sj, p. 60). Those statements suggest that the Court considered the threats (concerning the existence of an Islamic, terrorist, anti-national, and organized movement, one of the goals of which is to lure Hindus, especially women, into converting to Islam) to be real and that the allegations against Muslims were not exaggerated. It was treated as a serious matter with possible consequences for the entire nation.

The Court seemed to accept that the "Love Jihad" movement was involved in the conversion of Hadiya. It claimed that (AvS-sj, pp. 73–92):

> (…) nor has he made any attempt to probe the activities of the said organizations and antecedents. Since it is clear that, there are other players behind the scenes controlling Ms. Akhila, her case that everything has been at her instance, cannot be accepted. (…) at any rate, there are sufficient materials available to justify a conclusion that there are forces acting from behind the curtains controlling Ms. Akhila and extending all necessary support to her. (…) there are reports of girls taken out of the country after such conversions, having become untraceable. (…) taken note of the functioning of radical organizations pursuing activities of converting young girls of Hindu religion to Islam on the pretext of love. The fact remains that such activities are going on around us in our society.

The question remains why the Court was so certain about it. As has already been noted, the police found no convincing evidence about it during the investigation. Furthermore, to strengthen its conclusion, the Court recalled the case of *Shahan Sha A* v. *State of Kerala*, but in this case, the investigators clearly stated there was no evidence of the existence of the "Love Jihad" movement regarding compulsive conversions (SvS). The Director General of Police informed the Court that there were three reports from the investigation that suggested the existence of the "Love Jihad" movement; however, again there was no evidence to support these statements (SvS). However, the High Court of Kerala, after reviewing the police reports in the *Shahan Sha A v. State of Kerala*, decided that it was clear from the reports that the efforts were made in India to convert Hindu girls to Islam on the pretext of love (SvS). Therefore, the Court in *Shahan Sha A v. State of Kerala* ignored the opinion of the Director General of Police. It then relied on that case in the Hadiya case.

The Court had no doubts about the truthfulness of the accusations towards Muslims despite the lack of any clear evidence. The threat was considered to be real enough to order the police to escort Hadiya after the verdict from the ladies hostel to her parents' house, and to provide protection and maintain surveillance over the whole family (AvS-sj, p. 93). Moreover, the Court never questioned the allegations raised by the father. It agreed with him or was silent about some of the topics he raised. Belief in the threat from Muslims was so great that the Court even grossly exceeded his authority granted to him in a habeas corpus procedure and dissolved the marriage of Hadiya and Shafin Jahan by declaring it null and void.

4.2.3 Conversion

The content of the judgement indicates that in the Court's opinion, Hadiya was forced into a change of faith. "Ms. Akhila [Hadiya] only gives a vague statement in her affidavit that she had acquired knowledge about Islam by 'reading Islamic books and also viewing interesting videos'. What are the materials on the basis of which she had developed an interest in Islam religion is unavailable. Are there any radical organizations involved, are questions that plague an inquisitive mind" (AvS-sj, p. 63). It was not believable to the Court that it was Hadiya's own choice to convert to Islam. It was apparently not even "normal human conduct of a girl aged 20 years" (AvS-sj, p. 75) to abandon studies and become interested in religion.

Additionally, the Court indicated in a verdict that, "she appeared to be repeating verses and quotations in Arabic that she has apparently memorised. According to the Police, and the Senior Government Pleader, she has been made to believe that she would go to hell if she did not accept Islam and is under such a belief. She also appears to be a gullible person" (AvS-sj, p. 74). Adding to this the general conviction of the Court that young women are easily exploited (especially Hadiya) and the belief concerning the existence of "Love Jihad", it is not that surprising that forcible conversion was discussed in this case.

At the same time, the Court stressed in the judgement that, "[b]e that as it may, it is not our concern or attempt to decide whether Ms. Akhila should follow Islamic faith or the Hindu faith. The question of faith and religion are matters of personal conviction and this court does not consider it necessary to interfere in such matters that are personal to Ms. Akhila" (AvS-sj, p. 74). Despite that, there was visible distrust in the concept of conversion. It seems that it had to be properly proven to be believable. A simple statement was not sufficient for the Court. Moreover, the fact that the convert was convinced that there may be repercussion after death if she did not follow a specific religion was considered suspicious. This may be because threatening someone with eternal suffering is treated as conversion by force by anti-conversion laws in India.

4.3 *The Third Judgement (the Supreme Court of India, Shafin Jahan v. Asokan K.M. & Ors., from 9th of April 2018, Criminal Appeal No. 366 of 2018)*

Shafin Jahan filed a special leave petition to the Supreme Court of India (hereinafter "the Supreme Court") to overturn the verdict of the High Court of Kerala. He raised the objection that the order contradicts the independence of women by limit Hadiya's right to decide for herself and unnecessary uses the religious arguments. He also claimed that it was not an example of "Love Jihad" because Hadyia's decision to convert was not related to the marriage with Shafin because she met him already being a Muslim. Finally, he accused the Court of Islamophobia and stated that it "has erroneously given in to the hysteria created by Respondent No. 1 [the father]" (SvA-cf, pp. 113–117).

The reaction of the Supreme Court was different from the one presented by the High Court of Kerala in its second judgement. One of the first sentences was as follows: "…it can be said that when the liberty of a person is illegally smothered and strangulated and his/her choice is throttled by the State or a private person, the signature of life melts and living becomes a bare subsistence" (SvA-sc, p. 1). Additionally, one of the three judges of the Supreme Court, while agreeing with the verdict, decided to write his own opinion to "express my anguish with the grievous miscarriage of justice which took place in the present case and to formulate principles in the expectation that such an injustice shall not again be visited either on Hadiya or any other citizen" (SvA-sc, p. 42). I do not provide a separate analysis of the main judicial opinion and the additional voice of the third judge. In the chapter, those two parts are treated as one due to the similarities between the two.

4.3.1 Woman, Family, and Marriage

The Supreme Court did not generalize about the characteristics that women were supposed to have due to the very fact of being a woman. Considerations are underway about adult individuals and their rights without making a distinction between men and women. It was indicated that the Constitution of India "(…) protects personal liberty from disapproving audiences" (SvA-sc, p. 56); "the essence of this personal liberty is the right to choice in the matter of a life partner or religion" (SvA-sc, p. 56). Those are the central issues for someone's identity and "society has no role to play in determining our choice of partners" (SvA-sc, p. 57). Moreover, the paternalism the Court displayed towards an adult woman was criticized: "the High Court has lost sight of the fact that she is a major, capable of taking her own decisions and is entitled to the right recognised by the Constitution to lead her life exactly as she pleases" (SvA-sc, p. 59); "the schism between Hadiya and her father may be unfortunate. But it was no part of the jurisdiction of the High Court to decide what is considered to be a 'just' way of life or 'correct' course of living for Hadiya. She has absolute autonomy over her person" (SvA-sc, p. 54).

The emphasis was placed on the personal freedom of every person, especially a major. An adult woman is first and foremost an independent human being who does not need a guardian and has every right and capability to make her own decisions, even if they are against her parents' wishes. Even the courts are not entitled to dictate what is a correct way of life for an individual (in case of religion, partner, dressing habits and so on).

This narration automatically influences the perception of the family, and especially parental authority, over adult children. The Supreme Court indicated that the submission of Hadiya's right to choose over the father's right to choose life for his daughter by the High Court of Kerala was "(. . .) a manifestation of the idea of patriarchal autocracy and possibly self-obsession with the feeling that a female is a chattel" (SvA-sc, p. 2). According to the Supreme Court, it was crucial to remind of the right of choice to keep "at bay the patriarchal supremacy" (SvA-sc, p. 39). The High Court of Kerala, according to the Supreme Court, forgot "(. . .) that parental love or concern cannot be allowed to fluster the right of choice of an adult in choosing a man to whom she gets married" (SvA-sc, p. 25); "(. . .) his [father's] viewpoint or position cannot be allowed to curtail the fundamental rights of his daughter (. . .)" (SvA-sc, p. 40).

The Supreme Court of India underlined "(. . .) obeisance to the societal will destroy the individualistic entity of a person" (SvA-sc, p. 39); "[t]he social values and morals have their space but they are not above the constitutionally guaranteed freedom" (SvA-sc, p. 39). Therefore, in the considerations of the Supreme Court, the will of the individual is placed above the will of the community. The Supreme Court of India portrayed Indian society as an individualistic instead of a collectivist one: "[s]ans lawful sanction, the centripodal value of liberty should allow an individual to write his/her script. The individual signature is the insignia of the concept" (SvA-sc, p. 40). Freedom to choose faith is understood as "(. . .) essential to personal autonomy" (SvA-sc, p. 39); "(. . .) the substratum of individuality and sans it, the right of choice becomes a shadow" (SvA-sc, p. 39).

The Supreme Court in its judgement presented a different perception of how a just and proper society should look in India. First of all, there is an individual, their happiness, and the right to live according to their wishes. Despite traditional approach to family, still practiced by many members of the Indian society, family subordination, especially over women, cannot prevail over the agency of a human being. The Supreme Court strongly claimed that the approach of the Court was wrong, unacceptable, and based on incorrect assumptions.

A choice of a partner outside one's social group is not considered a threat by the Supreme Court, or as something undesirable that breaks the boundaries and disrupts the established order. It is just an emanation of the unfettered choice of an individual, and this is the value that should be protected and propagated. In the verdict, the Supreme Court evoked another judgement—*Lata Singh v State of U P*, 5 SCC 475 from 2006, in which it stated that if parents are not happy about a choice of their child to marry outside their caste or religion, the only thing they can do is cut-off social relations (SvA-sc, p. 52). This is no doubt a more liberal approach and distant from the traditional process of choosing the right spouse. Parents can of course be involved, but it is not their right anymore.

4.3.2 Muslims and "Love Jihad"

Nothing was said directly about Muslims or Islam in the verdict. However, plurality and diversity were pictured as important values in Indian society. "The strength of our Constitution lies in its acceptance of the plurality and diversity of our culture" (SvA-sc, p. 59); "[t]he cohesion and stability of our society depend on our syncretic culture" (SvA-sc, p. 59); "[c]ourts are duty bound not to swerve from the path of upholding our pluralism and diversity as a nation" (SvA-sc, p. 59). It is not precisely explained what the Supreme Court has in mind here. However, we can assume that it still refers to respect for someone's choice: in what to believe, with whom to spend a life, and how to spend it. In India, there are many diverse possibilities and one should not be perceived as better than others, especially by state authorities. From a broad perspective, those words of the Supreme Court could be read as a defense that the Muslim way of living is not worse than the Hindu way. Moreover, the maintenance of clear societal groups (religious, economical, caste), not mixed with others, is not portrayed as something desirable.

Apart from that, the judges of the Supreme Court did not comment on the allegations of possible terrorist threats and the radicalization of some Muslims organizations. It just mentioned that it was not the job of the Court to pass any judgements considering these subjects. Police were obliged to find out if any criminal activities were going on and act upon them. As the Supreme Court indicated, the goal of the habeas corpus procedure is to meet the alleged detenue, find out about the independent choice of that person, and if necessary make sure that person is released from any illegal restraint (SvA-sc, pp. 24–26). Therefore, the Supreme Court decided that it was not part of this procedure and thus avoided the discussion. The Supreme Court only mentioned at the end that the National Investigation Agency may continue its investigation but without interfering in the married life of Hadiya and Shafin Jahan (SvA-sc, pp. 60–61).

4.3.3 Conversion

The Supreme Court declared the following: "faith of a person is intrinsic to his/her meaningful existence. To have the freedom of faith is essential to his/her autonomy; and it strengthens the core norms of the Constitution. Choosing a faith is the substratum of individuality and sans it, the right of choice becomes a shadow" (SvA-sc, p. 39). Notably, the Court put similar assurances in its second judgement, but the result was entirely different. It seems that for the Supreme Court, Hadiya's statement concerning her religious choice was enough. We can speculate the reasons behind this. It could be greater confidence in women's capabilities to make their own decisions or unwillingness to believe in the rumors of "Love Jihad". It is also possible that the Supreme Court did not treat the conversion itself (especially from Hinduism) as undesirable and dangerous.

5 Conclusions

The main aim of this chapter was to analyze judicial opinions in the Hadiya case to reveal what kind of assumptions can be found in them concerning the characteristics of women and their position in Indian society, the role of the family and marriage, and a portrait of Muslim, "Love Jihad", and conversion. These issues were chosen due to their connection to the "Love Jihad" discourse, an example of which was said to be (e.g., in the media) the Hadiya case.

In the first judicial opinion issued by the Court, not much information is provided. However, we do know that the Court focused predominantly on Hadiya's choice and her explanations of the matter. The father's opinion and the reconciliation of the family were not treated as more important than the right of an adult woman to independently make decisions concerning her life: where to live, whom to be, in what to believe. There are no points of reference to the traditional Hindu perception of a woman and her place in the family. Therefore, the assumptions that emerge from this judicial opinion are that a woman's voice is equal to that of other members of society and there is no need for her to be under parental control once she is already an adult. The change of religion from Hinduism to Islam was not seen as a threat. The approach of the Court was mainly liberal as opposed to conservative.

The second judicial opinion discussed in this chapter is much richer in this regard. The assumptions presented by the Court are mostly of a traditional and patriarchal nature. There are also many similarities with the narrative around the "Love Jihad" theory. Women are portrayed as generally weak, gullible, and unable to make wise decisions. Consequently, they need to be protected by males. In this vision, the institution of a family is of the utmost importance, especially for women who need guardians. First, it is the father, who then actively chooses his replacement—the husband. It is not only a parental obligation to help with selecting life partners for their children, it is also their right. While the father's assurances and opinions were not contested by the Court, Hadiya's were rejected as unreliable, or sometimes the Court even refused to hear them. The threat from Muslims was perceived as real and fairly close. There were also no doubts about the existence of "Love Jihad". Consequently, the conversion of a person, especially when it concerns a woman and marriage, looks at least suspicious.

While the Court in a second proceeding mostly discussed freedom from danger, coercion, influence, and manipulation, the Supreme Court focused on the freedom to choose: one's own way of life, religion, and a life partner. From the judicial opinion of the last verdict emerges a picture of society in which individuality and variety are seen as advantages. Inter-caste and inter-religious marriages are not considered a problem, as long as it is an independent decision of spouses. The influence of the family on adult persons is limited. It can advise and support but not have full control.

This description does not fit with the traditional and patriarchal society, which is openly criticized in the verdict.

If we look at the culture-forming and educational function of judicial opinions, the second judgement may be perceived or used by some as proof that "Love Jihad" exists. Consequently, it may increase the sense of threat from Muslims regardless of whether it is real or not. Even in the judgement, the Court relied on a different verdict while commenting on this conspiracy theory. Moreover, it perpetuated an image of an incompetent woman and praised the traditional social arrangement (especially concerning family and marriage).

On the other hand, the judicial opinion issued by the Supreme Court (and to some extent the first verdict of the High Court of Kerala), which promoted a more liberal vision of society and critiqued the one draw in the second verdict by the Court, may be an impulse for change in the society or at least for a discussion on the suitability of the traditional societal order. This verdict also has the strongest impact on the other courts among the three discussed, and consequently on the citizens whose cases shall be resolved by those courts. It can also be perceived as a sign that the changes in Indian society are already happening. The assumptions presented by the Supreme Court do not come from nowhere.

As previously mentioned, the institution of the court has been assigned the attribute of impartiality, which makes the theses spoken by it generally stronger and more credible. Through this, judicial opinions influence to some extent the culture of the society by sanctioning certain solutions or propagating a change or new perspective. Taking into consideration the media attention that Hadiya's case received, it can even be assumed that the impact of those judicial opinions was stronger than in regular cases.

On the other hand, this process goes both ways. Certain cultural narratives functioning in society may have an impact on the final result of the case and how the case is perceived, among other things. A specific vision of society allows a rational and acceptable (at least for a part of society) judicial opinion of the verdict to be prepared, even though the conclusion may be based in reality on different reasoning. Moreover, the personal beliefs of judges are not indifferent to the decision-making process. This seems especially visible in the second judgement of the Court. The Court went as far as (1) making a decision to confine Hadiya for many months in a ladies' hostel and cut her off from the world, except her parents; (2) deciding also on the annulment of her marriage even though it had no authority to do so in this proceeding; (3) invoking the *Parens Patriae* doctrine, which is used mostly on minors or mentally disabled people, not on healthy adults. All of that was done in Court opinion to save Hadiya from the danger in which she supposedly found herself. It seems that this type of involvement might suggest a certain deeper belief of the judges issuing the verdict in the rightness of the assumptions emerging from the judical opinion. Especially, that the Court did not have any clear evidence in this case and therefore, relied heavily just on his own observations and convictions.

The narrative of "Love Jihad" might also have had an additional impact on the judges in Hadiya case, especially taking into account moral panic theory. According to research by Miriam Gur-Arye (2018), judges are not fully immune to it and it may provoke them to, for example, demonize the accused (the author investigated cases involving people who fled the scene of an accident in Israel) and impose more severe penalties for the same crimes. The narrative of the Court in the second case was clear: "Love Jihad" really do exists, the threat is real and decisive steps must be taken to defend women. However, it is of course impossible to answer definitely whether "Love Jihad" theory or the personal preferences and convictions of the judges actually had an impact in this case due to the limitations in research on judicial opinions or the lack of additional data in this regard (for example, interviews with judges). Therefore, it is said with caution and would require further research.

References

Ahmad T (2018) State Anti-conversion Laws in India. https://www.loc.gov/law/help/anti-conversion-laws/india-anti-conversion-laws.pdf. Accessed 11 Dec 2020

Ahmed S (2020) Love Jihad: victimization of women through media; violation of their basic human rights. In: Women's world; epitome of victimization and emancipation. https://doi.org/10.2139/ssrn.3576061

Akhter Z (2016) India–Pakistan relations: efficacy of culture. Millennial Asia 7(2):207–229

Anand D (2011) Hindu nationalism in India and the politics of fear. Palgrave, New York

Austin G (2001) Religion, personal law, and identity in India. In: Larson GJ (ed) Religion and personal law in secular India: a call to judgment. Indiana University Press, Bloomington, pp 15–23

BBC (2020a) Tanishq: Jewellery ad on interfaith couple withdrawn after outrage. https://www.bbc.com/news/world-asia-india-54520390. Accessed 3 Dec 2020

BBC (2020b) Citizenship Amendment Act: court refuses to put controversial law on hold. https://www.bbc.com/news/world-asia-india-51203104. Accessed 20 Aug 2020

Bhat MR, Iqbal K, Akhtar S (2017) Portrayal of Muslims as threat to society by the media—an overview In Indian context. Int J Innov Res Adv Stud 4(7):450–455

Business Standard (2015) India's population at 1.21 billion; Hindus 79.8%, Muslims 14.2%. https://www.business-standard.com/article/current-affairs/india-s-population-at-1-21-billion-hindus-79-8-muslims-14-2-115082600038_1.html. Accessed 11 Dec 2020

Census of India (2001). https://censusindia.gov.in/census_data_2001/india_at_glance/religion.aspx. Accessed 11 Dec 2020

Census of India (2011). https://censusindia.gov.in/2011census/C-01.html. Accessed 11 Dec 2020

Claerhout S, De Roover J (2019) Religious freedom and the limits of propagation: conversion in the constituent assembly of India. Religions 10(3)

Cohen S (2002) Folk devils and moral panics: the creation of the mods and rockers. Routledge, London

Cohen M (2015) When judges have reasons not to give reasons: a comparative law approach. Wash Lee Law Rev 72:483–571

Coleman JR (2007–2008) Authoring (in)authenticity, regulating religious tolerance: the legal and political implications of anti-conversion legislation for Indian Secularism. Cult Dyn 20 (3):245–277

Davids JA (2017) The role of worldview in the judicial decisions of justice Paul Stevens. Liberty Univ Law Rev 11(3):723–764

Davis DR Jr (2010) The spirit of Hindu law. Cambridge University Press

Donner H (2016) Doing it our way: love and marriage in Kolkata middle-class families. Mod Asian Stud 50(4):1147–1189

DW News (2020) India: Tanishq Jewellery ad pulled after "Love Jihad" uproar. https://www.youtube.com/watch?v=ZjKc7EtvvcU. Accessed 11 Dec 2020

Edathumparambil B (2017) Strangers to spouses: a study of the relationship quality in arranged marriages in India. Wipf and Stock Publishers, Eugene

Garland D (2008) On the concept of moral panic. Crime Media Cult Int J 4(1):9–30

Goode E (2017) Moral panic. The encyclopedia of juvenile delinquency and justice. Wiley, New Jersey, pp 1–3

Goode E, Ben-Yehuda N (2009) Moral panics. The social construction of deviance. Wiley-Blackwell, Singapore

Gupta C (2009) Hindu women, Muslim men: Love Jihad and conversions. Econ Polit Weekly 44 (51):13–15

Gupta C (2016) Allegories of "Love Jihad" and Ghar Vāpasī: interlocking the socio-religious with the political. Archiv Orientalni 84(2):291–316

Gur-Arye M (2018) The legitimacy of judicial responses to moral panic: perceived vs. normative legitimacy. Crim Just Ethics 37(2):141–163

Heitmeyer C (2016) Intimate transgressions and communalist narratives: inter-religious romance in a divided Gujarat. Mod Asian Stud 50(4):1277–1297

Herdt G (ed) (2009) Moral panics, sex panics: fear and the fight over sexual rights. NYU Pres, New York

Hindu Janjagruthi Samiti (2000). https://sanatanshop.com/wp-content/uploads/2019/11/Love_Jihad_E-510x646.png. Accessed 12 Dec 2020

Hindu Janjagruthi Samiti (2020) Signature campaign: need for the Union Govt. to pass a law against 'Love Jihad' to avoid repetition of cases alike killing of 'Nikita Tomar'! https://www.hindujagruti.org/hindu-issues/love-jihad. Accessed 20 Aug 2020

Hossain SMD, Ladsaria SK, Singh R (2016) 'Love-Jihad'; protection of religious proximity: an Indian situation. Int J Human Cult Stud 2(4):669–690

HRW (2020) "Shoot the Traitors". Discrimination against Muslims under India's New Citizenship Policy. Human Rights Watch. https://www.hrw.org/report/2020/04/09/shoot-traitors/discrimination-against-muslims-under-indias-new-citizenship-policy. Accessed 20 Aug 2020

Huff JA (2009) Religious freedom in India and analysis of the constitutionality of anti-conversion laws. Rutgers J Law Relig 10:3–7

Iwanek K (2016) "Love Jihad" and the stereotypes of Muslims in Hindu nationalism. J Altern Perspect Soc Sci 7(3):355–399

Jain M (2019) Anti-conversion law: critical analysis in India. J Hum Rights Law Pract 2(1):1–8

Johari A, Mishra AK (2019) The constitutional law of India: dispenser of India's destiny. Cyberlekh Publications, New Delhi

Kane PV (1962–1975) History of Dharmaśāstra, vol 1. Bhandarkar Oriental Research Institute, Poona

Kashyap L (2020) Changing couple relationships in India. In: Abela A, Vella S, Piscopo S (eds) Couple relationships in a global context. Springer, Cham, pp 71–83

Khan ZH, Watson PJ, Ali HN, Chen ZJ (2018) Greater Jihad of society and self: religious and psychological implications in Pakistani Madrassa and University students. Int J Psychol Relig 28(4):271–280

Krishnaswami (n.d.) Islam and Pseudo-Secularists. Shradha Prakashan, Delhi

Lodhi Y, Bala N (2016) Caste system in India and role of education. Research Chronicler. Int Multidiscip Res J 4(5):100–104

Ludden D (ed) (1996) Contesting the nation: religion, community, and the politics of democracy in India. University of Pennsylvania Press, Philadelphia

McDonough J, McDonough S (2014) Research methods for English language teachers. Routledge

Mishra S (2020) Religious conversions: UP may bring ordinance. The Times of India. http://timesofindia.indiatimes.com/articleshow/78177777.cms. Accessed 11 Dec 2020

Mustafa F, Sohi JS (2017) Freedom of religion in India: current issues and supreme court acting as clergy. BYU Law Rev 4:915–955

Natarajan M (2016) Rapid assessment of "eve teasing" (sexual harassment) of young women during the commute to college In India. Crime Sci 5(6):1–11
NFHS-4: National Family Health Survey (2015–2016) International Institute for Population Sciences Deonar, Mumbai
Pandey N (2020) For VHP, Bollywood Khans' Hindu wives, New Year & birthday parties help spread 'Love Jihad'. The Print. Accessed 11 Dec 2020
Rajeshwar Y, Amore RC (2019) Coming home (Ghar Wapsi) and going away: politics and the mass conversion controversy in India. Religions 10(5):313
Richards JF (1995) The Mughal empire. Cambridge University Press, Cambridge
Rzucidło I (2020) Uzasadnienie orzeczenia sądowego. Ujęcie teoretyczne a poglądy orzecznictwa. Wolters Kluwer, Warszawa
Sethi M (2002) Avenging angels and nurturing mothers: women in Hindu nationalism. Econ Polit Weekly 37(16):1545–1552
Sharma N, Harikrishnan B, Nair P (2014) Neither love nor Jihad: the politics of hate-mongering. Mainstream Weekly 51(45):5–7
Stępień M (2019) Using case studies for research on judicial opinions: some preliminary insights. Law and Method
Strohl DJ (2018) Love Jihad in India's moral imaginaries: religion, kinship, and citizenship in late liberalism. Contemp South Asia 27(1):27–39
Stubbs JK (1993) Persuading thy neighbor to be as thyself: constitutional limits on evangelism in the United States and India. UCLA Pac Basin Law J 12(2):360–406
Subramanian N (2014) Nation and family: personal law, cultural pluralism, and gendered citizenship in India. Stanford University Press, Stanford
Tandon U, Luthra S (2016) Rape: violation of the chastity or dignity of woman? Feminist Critiq Indian Law 51:1–4
Tanishq Facebook (2020). https://www.facebook.com/Tanishq/photos/a.857519187610146/3930619476966753. Accessed 11 Dec 2020
Tanishq Twitter (2020). https://twitter.com/TanishqJewelry/status/1316033929791467520/photo/1. Accessed 11 Dec 2020
Tavares R (2008) Resolving the Kashmir conflict: Pakistan, India, Kashmiris and religious militants. Asian J Polit Sci 16(3):276–302
Tyagi A, Sen A (2020) Love-Jihad (Muslim Sexual Seduction) and ched-chad (sexual harassment): Hindu nationalist discourses and the Ideal/deviant urban citizen in India. Gender Place Cult 27 (1):104–125
Umber S, Ghauri MJ, Nawaz H (2018) Exploring the image of Muslims in India. South Asian Stud 33(2):475–490
USCIRF Special Report (2018) Limitations on minorities' religious freedom in South Asia. United States Commission on International Religious Freedom. https://www.uscirf.gov/sites/default/files/Limitations%20on%20Minorities%20Religious%20Freedom%20in%20South%20Asia.pdf. Accessed 11 Dec 2020
Way to Nikah (2020). https://www.waytonikah.com. Accessed 11 Dec 2020
Williams R (1998) The analysis of culture. In: Storey J (ed) Cultural theory and popular culture: a reader. The University of Georgia Press, Athens, pp 32–40
Zainal Z (2007) Case study as a research method. Jurnal Kemanusiaan 5(1)
Zia A (2019) Blinding Kashmiris. Interventions 21(6):773–786

Judicial Opinions and Case Files

AvS-fj: Verdict of the High Court of Kerala, Asokan K.M. v. The State of Kerala, from 25th of January 2016, WP(Crl.)/25/2016 — first judgement of the High Court of Kerala

AvS-sj: Verdicts of the High Court of Kerala, Asokan K.M. v. The Superintendent of Police, from 24th of May 2017, WP (Crl.).No. 297 of 2016 (S) – second judgement of the High Court of Kerala

SvA-cf: Shafin Jahan v. Asokan K.M. & Ors. – collection of case files of Hadiya case. https://drive.google.com/a/zgg.legal/uc?id=1FZuYbFBsBdDg9eMYCV-5wM0IlEavKw_Z&export=download, https://drive.google.com/a/zgg.legal/uc?id=1MA4aVVfNuhSbibzqTQd0bQfzRjKu6jI1&export=download. Accessed: 12 December 2020

SvA-sc: Verdicts of the Supreme Court of India, Shafin Jahan v. Asokan K.M. & Ors., from 9th of April 2018, Criminal appeal no. 366 of 2018 – Supreme Court judgement

SvS: Verdicts of the High Court of Kerala, Shahan Sha A vs State Of Kerala, from 9th of December 2009, Bail Appl. No. 5288 of 2009

Legal Acts

Constitution of India (1949). https://www.india.gov.in/my-government/constitution-india/constitution-india-full-text. Accessed 11 Dec 2020

Indian Penal Code, Act no. 45 of 1860 (1860). http://legislative.gov.in/sites/default/files/A1860-45.pdf. Accessed 11 Dec 2020

The Orissa Freedom of Religion Act, Act 2 of 1968 (1967). https://cjp.org.in/wp-content/uploads/2017/12/ORISSA-FREEDOM-OF-RELIGION-ACT-1967.pdf. Accessed 11 Dec 2020

Anna Juzaszek PhD candidate in sociology of law at the Interdisciplinary Programme Society of the Future in the Doctoral School in the Social Sciences at the Jagiellonian University; MA in law, MA in sociology, BA in cultural studies; author of several articles concerning law and culture, in particular personal law, Indian law and Muslims; Principal Investigator in the research project "The prohibition of entering into religious—only marriages from the perspective of human rights in Europe" funded by Preludium programme of the Polish National Science Centre; completed attorney apprenticeship; interested in the problems of religious freedom, Indian law, religious minorities, and the relations between law and culture.

Palestinian Culture Through a Legal Lens: A Case Study of Customary Legal Proceedings After a Homicide in Hebron

Ewa Górska

Abstract Arab customary law is strongly tied to Middle Eastern Arab culture and its traditions and, in Palestine, is still employed in parallel with state and religious laws. The most glaring, though becoming rarer, example of the application of customary law in the occupied Palestinian territories currently relates to criminal offenses such as homicide or bodily injury. This chapter is a case study of Palestinian customary law reconciliation procedures used in a legal conflict between two Hebronite clans: al—Haymounis and al—Jʿabaris, after murders in 2014 and 2016. Customary legal reaction to this crime aroused special interest in the community, and wide coverage by the local media because of its circumstances, the powerful clans involved, and certain unconventional decisions made during otherwise typical customary negotiations. The principal aim of this case study is, through the description and analysis of the above—mentioned case, to define the characteristics of customary law presently used in the country, and draw conclusions concerning contemporary Palestinian culture.

1 Introduction

At the beginning of March 2014, a serious criminal conflict between two clans broke out in Hebron (al—Khalil), West Bank, State of Palestine. On March 2nd, a few young men from the al—Jʿabari clan entered the estate of Abdul Ghani al—Haymouni (47 years old) to steal his son's bike. While trying to commit the theft, the perpetrators killed the man, and wounded his son and nephew. The case electrified the local society and aroused media interest. It became infamous in the area for several reasons, but probably the most important was that the al—Jʿabari clan was already (allegedly) guilty of four murders committed in the area over the preceding four years, but none of them was ever concluded with any reconciliation agreement. Therefore, when the al—Haymouni clan, smaller than the al—Jʿabaris,

E. Górska (✉)
Faculty of Law and Administration, Jagiellonian University, Cracow, Poland

M. Stępień, J. B. Klakla (eds.), *Law and Culture*, Law and Visual Jurisprudence 5,
https://doi.org/10.1007/978-3-030-81193-8_5

but influential and strong, promised to bring justice, the community in Hebron waited in anticipation.

The legal heritage of Palestine generally consists of the three parallel orders: state law, religious law and customary law. All three of these legal systems influence each other in formal and informal ways and are often used in parallel (Welchman 2009; Birzeit University 2006, p. 80, 94–97). Contemporary Arab customary law is rooted in the pre—Islamic, Arab and Bedouin legal traditions (Sergeant 1991; Terris and Inoue-Terris 2002, pp. 466–467). It is strongly tied to Arab culture and clan—segmented society and was always important in the Palestinian community. Often treated as an expression of independence and the cultural separateness of a people under foreign rule and occupations, it was further developed as a complementary or alternative legal system. Foreign rulers, in turn, frequently turned a blind eye, and even tacitly supported the local use of customary law because it served their purposes (Terris and Inoue-Terris 2002, pp. 468–470). Customary law still currently regulates everyday social conflicts and serious cases such as bodily injury, homicide or murder (Tsafrir 2006; Tarabeih et al. 2009).

The following chapter is an instrumental case study of Palestinian customary law following both the above—described murder, and a similar one in 2016. As such, it is a research strategy that focuses on selected fragments of a complicated whole in order to describe them, deepen understanding of them, and draw conclusions regarding the wider phenomena they represent in a specific place and period (see Verschuren 2003; Gerring 2007, pp. 19–20). The general aim of this case study is to, based on information regarding the above—mentioned legal conflict between two clans, define the characteristics of the customary law currently applied in the country, and draw conclusions about contemporary Palestinian culture.

In this research, the object under investigation is the legal conflict between the al—Haymouni and al—J'abari clans in Hebron. It was chosen as the focus for several reasons. First, Hebron is known for its commitment to tradition and clan loyalties, and Arab customary law is still highly active in the area. The proceedings in 2014 and 2016 are examples of the typical application of traditional informal legal procedures and, as such, allow for a thorough examination to be conducted. Second, even though most of the procedures followed in that case were regular, there was one atypical decision made by the clan to which the offenders belonged, which can shed light on possible changes in local culture. Third, the case is well documented as it was highly significant for the local community, widely discussed locally, and covered by the media.

The study is focused on the customary law practiced in criminal cases, particularly homicide, in Hebron. It should be noted that certain institutions and mechanisms described here are used only after the most serious crimes, and some may be local particularisms that differ from practices in other regions. Within the framework of this case study, the analysis is based on desk research in English and Arabic that includes literature and local newspaper articles, supplemented with in—depth unstructured interviews and field observations collected in Hebron over 6 weeks (March—April) in 2014 by the author. The interviews were conducted with local men who take part in local customary legal proceedings as conciliators, and the observations were conducted in Hebron during the proceedings following the 2014 murder.

Culture is a wide and flexible term with many meanings. This chapter uses Naomi Mezey's (2001, p. 42) working definition: sets of beliefs and practices shared by a given community or society. Within that conceptual background, customary law can be defined as sets of social practices pertaining to matters that are considered serious breaches of social norms and social order. However, certain issues arise in research that aims to study another culture through its customary law. First, law is often defined or understood in opposition to culture (Mezey 2001, p. 35), even though that only seems generally accurate in relation to positive Western legal systems in which the law ordered in codes is placed in opposition to flexible and ephemeral culture. On the other hand, informal legal procedures practiced by communities outside the Occident seem to be treated less as law and more as culture. Both those biases lead to the diminishing of non—occidental legal systems, and are based on a division between law and culture created over the seventeenth to nineteenth centuries. As Rosemary Coombe (1998, pp. 21–22) stated, concepts of law and culture were developed in European modernity, and were rooted in Eurocentrism, ideas of Western hegemony, and colonial goals. The concept of law was developed as the "antithesis of culture", while the Western understanding of ordered law was simultaneously essentialized as the basis of European civilization and proof of its superiority over the primitive, savage "others" (Coombe 1998, pp. 23–27; Fitzpatrick 1992, pp. 30–31).

What is known as "customary law" was a pejorative term given to all "other" normative systems as they were imagined by colonialists. However, if we stop employing this scission and follow the lead of those who perceive "law as culture, and culture as law" (Mezey 2001, p. 36) the belittling of so—called "customary law" may no longer stand. In this chapter I adopt the *a priori* assumption that such law should be treated equally to other legal systems. Based on this, I use the approach proposed by Mezey, treating law as "one of the signifying practices that constitute culture and vice versa", adapting a cultural interpretation of law to Palestinian customary law (2001, pp. 38, 61—62). This method, based on investigating and explaining the nature of discourses and practices, is applied here in one of the aspects that Mezey proposes: the interpretation of law at a site of its production (in this case: negotiating space between two clans). However, I understand the term "site of production" not spatially, but as a common space of meanings created by actors taking part in customary legal proceedings.

2 Customary Adjudication and Reconciliation Proceedings

Criminal offenses (even murder) are treated in Arab customary law as torts, and they are a source of liability between two clans (Tsafrir 2006). Violations of norms are sanctioned based on rules of reciprocity and compensatory justice. The aims are restoring peaceful relations, a sense of justice, and the honor of the family that may have been hindered when its member was victimized (Górska and Klakla 2017, p. 56). In Palestinian customary law, there are two means to achieve this: by paying the compensation decided by an informal judiciary system, or by exerting revenge (Thabit 2006; Tsafrir 2006; Hajjah 2011). Nevertheless, the matter is resolved according to what is subjectively considered as fair requital by the clans or community and, if both parties are Muslim, the Islamic system of *qiṣāṣ* (which denotes punishment by retributive justice according to the "eye for an eye" rule in which the perpetrator can be punished in the same manner as the crime he or she committed, or by payment of compensation (*diyya*), unless the family of the victim pardons him/her) is often invoked.

The first of the solutions to a conflict over a crime having been committed is a ritualized process of reconciliation called *ṣulḥ* or *ṣulḥa* (Irani and Funk 1998, p. 52; Gellman and Vuinovich 2008, p. 129). The custom of *ṣulḥ* dates to the pre—Islamic times (Pely 2011b) and has been preserved in all the religious denominations of the Arab community. To date, it is still practiced by Muslims, Christians, Druze, and representatives of other minorities in the Middle East (Lang 2002; Tsafrir 2006). It should be noted that the term itself is widely used in different legal contexts in the Islamic world, and not only in customary law. It is known in Islamic Law, and was incorporated into the state codifications of Muslim countries. For example, the Ottoman Mejelle defined *ṣulḥ* in Article 1531, and it is currently a term used in civil state courts and *sharīʿa* courts to denote processes of mediation—arbitration between disputants. In customary law, the process of negotiations is led and adjudicated by a reconciliation committee *(jāha)* consisting of respectable elders from other clans in the community (Pely 2009; Birzeit University 2006, pp. 77, 156–157; Hajjah 2011, pp. 188; 198–199). The reconciliation agreement is usually based on financial compensation—*diyya*. "Blood money" is generally expected and paid only in relation to serious conflicts such as murders, bodily injuries, car accidents, assaults on women and theft cases (Birzeit University 2006; Thabit 2006; Hajjah 2011, pp. 93–95). When the clans agree to finally reconcile, the settlement is sealed with a ritualized and public ceremony, also known as *ṣulḥ* or *ṣulḥa* (Abu-Nimer and Nasser 2013, p. 99; Górska and Klakla 2017), but sometimes called *'atwat at—tayyib* (Birzeit University 2006, p. 155). The negotiating process in serious cases such as homicide might extend for years before final reconciliation is achieved (Lang 2002; Tsafrir 2006; Pely 2009, 2010). Usually a temporary settlement for a year, called *'atwa*, is reached first. Later, it is renegotiated and renewed yearly, even for decades, until the parties are ready to finally reconcile (Hajjah 2011, pp. 162, 177–183; Birzeit University 2006, p. 152; Slemiah 2014).

There are no general or abstract norms that would bind the adjudication in such conciliatory procedures. There is only a framework of the process. The aim is to determine all the circumstances of the case and find a solution that could be considered fair not only to the parties of the conflict, but also to the society as a whole. To reach this goal, conciliators have flexibility in choosing a variety of measures according to the situation (Thabit 2006; Hajjah 2011). However, the reconciliation proceedings follow specific procedures and rituals established by centuries of tradition.

The family of the victim is approached and asked to agree to a truce (*hudna*) between the clans and to starting the settlement negotiations. Once three and one third days have elapsed after the crime, the representatives of the parties and the reconciliation committee (*jāha*) gather to negotiate the *'aṭwa,* which is considered a sign of the willingness to reconcile and a prelude to *ṣulḥa. 'Aṭwa* puts an end to any possible violence as, according to custom, the family of the victim may retaliate on the property of the culprit's direct relatives for several days before it is made (Birzeit University 2006, p. 156). That period is called the "raging of the blood" (*fawrat ad—damm)* and the perpetrators are usually not charged with any responsibility for such attacks.

Monetary compensation is usually negotiated, and the family of the victim may present other conditions. Often, the victim's family requests the relocation of the offender (sometimes alongside the offender's closest family) from his/her place of residence (*jalā'* or *jalwa* —"evacuation") after committing a serious crime (Pely 2009; Birzeit University 2006, p. 153). Currently, this custom is fading and often the evacuation is symbolic or limited to changing the place of residence within the boundaries of the same town. Sometimes, it is even sufficient for the family of the perpetrator to be prohibited from entering areas frequented by the victim's family (Lang 2002; Terris and Inoue-Terris 2002; Slemiah 2014). The relocation might be renegotiated by *jāha* during the renewal of the *'aṭwa,* and its conditions might change over the years (Hajjah 2011, pp. 177–183).

Monetary compensation paid as part of '*aṭwa* is counted as contributing to the final *diyya* payment (Birzeit University 2006, p. 152). These sums constitute a form of restitution; a life, bodily injury or other harm has an assigned financial value, which must be paid as compensation to the clan of the victim. The payment after a murder is considered an expression of goodwill in pursuit of reconciliation, preliminary reparation to the victim's family, and/or compensation for the costs of a victim's medical treatment, funeral and condolence ceremonies (Birzeit University 2006, pp. 76–78; Pely 2009; Hajjah 2011, p. 181). Some of the sums paid are traditionally fixed, and others are negotiated according to tradition and precedents, the specific circumstances in the area, rules concerning equality and the social positions of both parties, and other circumstances (Thabit 2006, pp. 157–160; Pely 2009; Hajjah 2011, pp. 94–95; Lang 2002; Slemiah 2014). In 2006, in Hebron, a clan agreement was signed stating that the *firāsh 'aṭwa* in a murder case has to be exactly 1000 Jordanian dinars (Hajjah 2011, p. 181), but 25 dinars are added to cover the expenses of the members of *jāha* such as for transportation, meals and the other expenses of hosting the *'aṭwa*. According to a report by Birzeit University (2006, pp. 79, 152), that sum is called *al—'aṭwa al—mushooka* or *morooq al—'aṭwa* and it is fixed in all Palestinian regions. This sum does not count when calculating the final *diyya*.

The *'aṭwa* signing ceremony should be attended by representatives of the official authorities such as the police or governorate. Such a representative of the state then co—signs the settlement document and keeps a copy of it. This represents an element of state control over the customary judiciary, as well as an additional measure of securing a temporary truce as the *'aṭwa* is also a guarantee of personal inviolability for the culprit's family as long as it is binding (Birzeit University 2006, pp. 70–80; Slemiah 2014). The perpetrator is excluded from the protection provided by *'aṭwa*.

As mentioned, *'aṭwa* agreements may be renegotiated and renewed for many years, and quite often a final *ṣulḥ* may not happen until the perpetrator dies, either as an outcome of a revenge killing, official authorities exercising capital punishment, or due to natural causes (Hajjah 2011, p. 162; Qafisheh 2014). Both parties then usually agree to reconcile according to local proverbs: "a grave faces a grave" and "blood meets blood".

3 Revenge Killing: *ath—thār*

As noted, a serious conflict involving bodily injury or homicide, if not resolved through clan negotiations, can be customarily settled through revenge according to the rule of "an eye for an eye". Such retaliation is also regulated by certain customary norms. Revenge should be taken on the perpetrator himself or, if that is not possible, closest male relatives up to the fifth degree of kinship (Lang 2002; Tsafrir 2006). The victim's party should take revenge only if the state authorities are not already executing punishment on the perpetrator (Hajjah 2011, pp. 163–165). Finally, the retaliation should take place within a few years after the original crime, though sometimes it is performed after decades (Thabit 2006, pp. 130–132; Hajjah 2011, p. 164; Slemiah 2014). A shorter term in which retaliation is permissible offers more stability to the community—if the revenge is taken, it should bring back peace and normal relations. However, a delay in taking vengeance is tolerated, presumably based on the assumption that, if such an act is executed after considerable time has passed since the original crime, the family seeking revenge must have justification. The most legitimate would be that the clan feels its honor (*sharaf*), crucial to their status and position in local society, has not been restored or must be enhanced in the perception of the community, and the past attack can be neither forgiven nor forgotten. Even if there is a strong will for retaliation, sometimes it is not taken directly after the first crime for pragmatic reasons such as the object being unavailable (i.e., the perpetrator was hiding, was abroad, or was being protected by his clan); personal and emotional factors (i.e., the closest family members of the victim tried to forgive but are inconsolable and they hope vengeance will restore their peace of mind); other honor—related events (i.e., the clan was victimized again by the same perpetrating clan); or other time—related reasons (i.e., the son of the victim was a child when his father was killed and takes revenge when he matures). As revenge killing – an eye—for—an—eye retaliation – usually settles the conflict, often *ṣulḥ* is made a short time after that (Thabit 2006, p. 165; Hajjah 2011, p. 192; Lang 2002).

It is argued (Lang 2002; Pely 2010) that contemporary manifestations of family feuds are becoming rare and most commonly the two feuding families agree to reconcile. However, in conservative areas like Hebron, many serious legal conflicts such as murder cases are followed by acts of revenge because clans deem it as a traditional and socially supported way to regain honor. Family solidarity demands taking action if one of its members is harmed. The honor of the family is not impaired only because its member became a victim of a crime; it is damaged if the family does not stand up to whomever violated the safety of its members, did not respect family's power of protection, and was not deterred by respect for the clan or fear of retaliation. If the clan cannot take care of its own members and solve the conflict according to the customary rules then it may lose its honor, and the influence that accompanies it. Not reacting to the murder of one's relative is perceived as a disgrace, a sign of weakness, and neglect of the family. In Hebron, some clans traditionally agree that the payment received during *'aṭwa* be deposited until they take revenge (Hebron Times 2014).

4 Al—Haymouni vs. al—J'abari: A Customary Reconciliation Procedure

The al—Haymouni vs. al—J'abari conflict broke out in Hebron in March 2014, after at least four young men from the powerful al—J'abari clan stabbed Abd al—Ghani al—Haymouni to death while breaking into his house to steal his son's bicycle (Al-Salaymeh 2014; Radio Siraj 2014; Raya News 2014). The culprits also wounded the victim's son and nephew. The case was deemed more reprehensible than a "regular" murder because the guilty men trespassed on private property and attacked the victims in their home (Hebron Times 2014). In local customs, homicide committed by an intruder during a theft is categorized as a separate type of aggravated murder, and the financial compensation for it may be four times higher than usual (Hajjah 2011, pp. 167–168).

The al—J'abari clan is one of the oldest in Hebron, and is considered powerful in terms of the number of its men and their social standing (The Palestinian Information Center 2019). The al—Haymounis are considerably smaller but could resist the al—J'abaris because they are well—respected, and because they received support from other Hebronites that made their position more significant. Moreover, both families are actually closely related – sheikh Hazim al—Haymouni, one of the representatives of the injured party at the *'aṭwa* negotiations, was exaggerating only slightly when he said that 99% of the al—Haymounis are in fact also members of the al—J'abari clan, and 99% of the al—J'abaris are members of the al—Haymounis (as cited in Hebron Times 2014). Nevertheless, in legal proceedings after the murder, the factional division separated both family groups.

The al—Haymounis opted for the reconciliation process, even though a more violent reaction also ensued directly after the murder when relatives of the victim reportedly attacked the house of the perpetrator and were only prevented from burning it down by the intervention of the Palestinian security forces (Radio Siraj 2014). In the first 3 days after the murder, fear of retaliation caused problems for hundreds of members of al—Jʿabari family, who were forced to not open their shops, not go work, and not send children to school (field observation). Eventually order was enforced by security forces and the heads of the clans, who started the negotiations to reconciliate both parties.

Three and one third days after the crime was committed, a meeting regarding the conditions of a one—year *'aṭwa* for a murder (the *'aṭwat ad—damm*) was held in a *dīwān* (traditional meeting place) of the al—Haymouni family, facilitated by a reconciliation committee of local elders (Hebron Times 2014; Radio Siraj 2014). The President of the Family Council, Abd as—Salam al—Haymouni, represented the al—Haymouni family, while the al—J'abari family chose Faiz al—Rajabi, a member of another prominent family from the city, to be their main representative (*lābis ath—thawb*) in the negotiations (Wattan News Agency 2014; Hebron Times 2014; Radio Bethlehem 2000 2016).

The meeting was open to the inhabitants of the city—*'aṭwa* and *ṣulḥa* signing ceremonies are organized in public spaces and witnessed by members of the community (Birzeit University 2006, p. 78). This allows a public display of repentance, forgiveness, and restoration of honor, and places social pressure on both parties to adhere to its commitments. Due to the seriousness of this conflict, the high profile of the actors taking part in it, and the involvement of other clans opposing the impunity of the al—Jʿabaris, the negotiations electrified the community. The final *'aṭwa* discussions and ceremonial speeches were broadcast by local radio for a whole day. In all the shops of the old city of Hebron, the radio was tuned to that frequency (field observation).

The family of the victim demanded at first 130,000 Jordanian dinars (JOD), approx. 183,500 USD, as compensation (Raya News 2014), a sum considered excessive under the customary law practiced in the area. According to Hajjah (2011, p. 94), such sums are between 60,000 and 80,000 Jordanian dinars. After long discussions, the representatives finally agreed on the immediate payment of 50,000 JOD (approx. 70,500 USD) of *'aṭwat ad—damm*, with an additional 1,000 JOD (approx. 1,410 USD) for the medical expenses of the injured son and nephew. Hamid Idris, head of the community organization facilitating the customary legal negotiations, National Committee for Civil Peace in Hebron, commented: "We agreed with the al—Haymouni family to resort to shariah, which stipulates the payment of *diyya* of 130,000 dinars, of which 50,000 were paid, and the remainder of the amount is pending until the demands and *ṣulḥ* between the two families [are fulfilled]" (Al-Salaymeh 2014; Wattan News Agency 2014).

There were also other conditions of the agreement. The al—Haymouni family demanded the expulsion of the perpetrators from the area of Hebron, and they called all the clans of Hebron to support them in that request (Raya News 2014). In this case, the negotiators managed to convince the relatives of the victim to agree to a ban on the offenders entering northern Hebron, with the exception of a neighborhood traditionally inhabited by al—Jʿabaris (Raya News 2014; Hebron Times 2014; Radio Bethlehem 2000 2016). As to removing them further from the area, the matter was left to the decision of the conciliatory committee. Al—Hajj Haj Abdul—Rahman Hajjah, the head of *jāha*, said: "We, as tribal elders, will study the issue of the four accused culprits and the issue of their deportation, and decide on this matter, with the participation of the al—Haymouni family, during the coming period" (Raya News 2014).

Thus, *'aṭwa* was signed for a year, and the truce between the clans was agreed to start on 6th of March 2014 (Raya News 2014; Wattan News Agency 2014; Hebron Times 2014). The temporary settlement was to be renegotiated and renewed each year to secure peace until the al—Haymounis were ready to accept a final reconciliation. The main perpetrator – directly responsible for stabbing the victim – was later arrested by state forces, and his trial was to take place in public court (ICHR 2016).

Until this point, the process and its outcomes are typical for customary legal proceedings in the Hebron area. However, this case was also unusual in some respects. During the *'aṭwa* ceremony, the al—J'abari family publicly announced a groundbreaking and unprecedented decision. They presented a "code of conduct" for their clan members in their relations with other families. It is a unique document, establishing a principle that, in the case of any criminal incident, the perpetrator will face the consequences of their actions alone. It states that the clan refuses to protect any member who commits a crime against another person or another person's property, and it refuses to be bound by any financial responsibilities resulting from such an act. The al—J'abari clan particularly denied its support to relatives who cause bodily injuries, commit financial fraud or commit homicide: "We declare that killing is the crime of the killer alone, and the family will not stand for his sake" (Al-Jʿabari Family Announcement 2014). The authors of the declaration made the exception for guilty of homicide in self—defense and while responding to attacks provoked by the victim. According to the document, the family should stay innocent as a whole and not respond collectively to the sins of individuals. Moreover, the clan should not help the perpetrator avoid punishment or protect them in any way from responsibility for their crimes. The document was reprinted, disseminated around Hebron, and other clans were called on to adopt it as well.

5 The Murder Case of 2016

The fragile settlement between the al—Haymounis and al—J'abaris was soon jeopardized when yet another murder threatened peace in the community, public order, and the safety of both clans' members. In January 2016, Mohammed Youssef Abdel—Khaleq al—Haymouni (25 years old) was shot dead by Haneen al—J'abari. The homicide was allegedly committed after al—Haymouni tried to stab al—J'abari, who was defending himself, but nevertheless it caused outrage in the area. An al—J'abari had again killed an al—Haymouni, and this time while the families had not yet been finally reconciled. Moreover, the 2016 case was also tied to the previous one, as the 2016 killer was said to be the father of the perpetrator from 2014 (ICHR 2016).

Members of the al—Haymouni clan responded with more violence ("raging of the blood") than in 2014. According to local records (ICHR 2016), they attacked the shops and private property of the Al—J'abaris, tried to set fire to two gas stations, burned two stores and shot at one, burned two cars and a bulldozer, attacked two restaurants, and threw stones at the Hebron University campus, wounding several security guards. They supposedly kidnapped a young member of the al—J'abari clan (releasing him shortly afterwards) and committed assault and battery on two other al—J'abaris. The outcome of the first days of the al—Haymounis' rage was detrimental to the community. Palestinian security forces were again called upon to secure order in the city. The revenge murder did not occur, but this was most probably a result of the perpetrator fleeing and hiding, and not of any restraint shown by the al—Haymounis.

Nevertheless, leaders of the al—Haymouni clan again decided to follow the reconciliation procedures. Interestingly, the document with the clan "code of conduct" from 2014 was not referred to in reports regarding the negotiations at all, and there is no proof that the statement of the al—J'abaris was accepted and put into further practice. The negotiations between both clans in 2016 went along traditional route, which suggests that al—J'abaris did not totally follow their own document 2 years later. It is possible that the arrest of the perpetrator by state forces in 2016 happened because his clan was not protecting him this time, but it might also be an outcome of regular police work. As to not taking collective, particularly financial, responsibility for the crimes committed by culprits belonging to the clan, the al—J'abaris did not comply and embarked on the customary negotiations. They might have retracted their statement, or the publication of the 2014 document may have been politically motivated and not intended to have much value in reality.

With order secured by state forces, both clans made an *'aṭwa* settlement three and one third days after the murder (Maan News 2016; Wattan News 2016). As in 2014, the signing of the *'aṭwa* took place in the *dīwān* of the al—Haymounis. It was attended by elders and large numbers of Hebron's inhabitants, and drew considerable attention in the city. The *'aṭwa* ceremonies from 2014 and 2016 were also recorded on the TV and clips can be found on YouTube (see i.e. Wattan News 2014; Maan Network 2016; Hebron HD 2016). In this case, the al—Haymouni family agreed to sign *'aṭwa* for a year, but refused any monetary compensation, considering the victim a martyr (Zaman Press 2016; Palestine24 2016; Raya News 2016). Such refusal is not atypical in customary law, as families sometimes decide to restore honor by showing generosity. However, the gesture might also imply that a revenge killing may occur.

The previous murder from 2014 was raised again during the negotiations, and the families ultimately agreed in the settlement conditions that expulsion from the area was necessary. The eviction should encompass the perpetrator responsible for the 2016 murders, three al—J'abaris who took part in the 2014 murder and who were not arrested, as well as their immediate families (Raya News 2016). Some of the members of the clan—the closest relatives of the 2016 culprit—were to be banned from entering areas of northern Hebron outside the al—J'abari neighborhood (Paltimes 2016; Palestine24 2016; Raya News 2016). The al—Haymounis pledged not to take revenge but to follow Islamic rules of retribution (Zaman Press 2016; Palestine24 2016). Both parties also agreed not to pursue any restitution, through either customary or formal state law, for properties damaged by the direct violent reaction of the al—Haymounis (Palestine24 2016; Raya News 2016). The family of the victim took this occasion to publicly address state authorities, officially demanding the highest penalty, death, to be performed by the state on the perpetrator, who had been detained by the security forces (Palestine24 2016; Raya News 2016).

6 Collectivism and the Clan—Based Culture of Hebron

Proceedings after the 2014 and 2016 cases of murder in Hebron are, in most part, typical examples of Palestinian customary law. As evident in both cases, reconciliation follows certain procedures and timelines. While details such as the amount of compensation, whether it will be received, and the conditions placed on the guilty party, may differ, the overall framework of the actions undertaken is the same.

Given the crime disrupts social order and peaceful relations, all members of the local community have an interest in solving it (Thabit 2006, p. 28). In Hebron, a separate organization—National Committee for Reform and Civil Peace in Hebron—facilitates proceedings, and even covers several parts of the compensatory sums. The reconciliation is intertwined with a whole network of relationships: local notables, politicians, neighbors, and the rest of the community, all of whom witness the final ceremony (Lang 2002). The state does not interfere with serving such justice, and although security services do intervene if violence is used against people or property after the crime, they do not disrupt the usage of customary law (Górska 2017). It is usual for state officials to attend ceremonies of *'aṭwa* and *ṣulḥa*. Their social standings and official positions raise the rank of the agreement and represent one of the guarantees securing it (breaking the agreement would be considered as acting against officials' respectability and honor). Compliance with the reconciliation committee's verdict, norms and provisions is subject to social control, however state authorities also supervise the results (Lang 2002; Terris and Inoue-Terris 2002; Birzeit University 2006, p. 132; Górska 2017). At the same time, the clans accept state law: the al—Haymounis in 2016 publicly asked the state to exercise capital punishment on the perpetrator, who was in custody. In this case, the customary and state legal systems coexist and mutually acknowledge their norms and adjudication procedures.

The interest of the society's members in solving the conflict is also related to power structures because the outcome of the feud between the two clans might change power relations in the community. In Palestinian customary law, the positions and strengths of the families play a crucial role. If the injured party is influential, it is often more difficult to negotiate a reconciliation because there is no pressure stemming from social positions, and financial considerations do not play a large role. In fact, the principal reason for reconciliation, in a case in which the perpetrator is from a weaker clan, is the desire to restore honor and raise the clan's position in the community by showing generosity. On the other hand, if the culprit is from a stronger family, reconciliation may have the opposite effect and result, not in the restoration of honor, but the loss of it (Lang 2002). In this case study, other Hebronite clans supported the al—Haymounis in their quest for justice. However, that support was probably motivated not only by an imperative to satisfy a sense of fairness in the community, but also by the fact the that outcome of such a legal case could weaken the al—J'abaris and their influence on the local social and political scenes.

The procedures and forms of Palestinian customary law's application also illustrate that the local social structure is based on clan divisions. Some of its most visible characteristics are the lack of the individualization of clan members, factionalization, and the dominance of clan solidarity over other forms. As in old tribal structures, a person belongs to a clan not only in their sense of affiliation, but also that of being a component of a collective led by the family's elders (*kibār al—'ā'īla*). Arab customary law does not confer the highest position in the legal system to the rights and obligations of individuals (Terris and Inoue-Terris 2002, p. 467), and an individual's life and physical integrity are not personal rights but goods of the group. Accordingly, while homicide is an unforgivable crime in Palestinian society, it is reprehensible not only because a life was taken, but also as an act harming the clan and community (Hajjah 2011, p. 16). Likewise, individuals involved in legal proceedings, both perpetrators and victims, are represented by relatives and do not act individually. It is the clan that chooses how to solve a conflict, what conditions are set, and whether they will seek revenge. At the same time, typical legal procedures focus on social solidarity and the duty of the entire family group to bear the burden of the violation of the law committed by one of its members. In such legal conflicts, it is not an individual perpetrator who faces legal charges, but their whole clan.

These traits are characteristic of so—called neopatriarchy. Neopatriarchal Arab societies, according to Hisham Sharabi (1988, pp. 6–8, 22–25), are somewhere in between traditional patriarchalism and modernity. They attempt to adapt their ways of life, organization of government, and civil society, to the model of modern Western societies, while internally cultivating familial patrimonialism and clientelism. In neopatriarchy, the institutions of a modern state and administration are superimposed on the client—patron relationship, while preserving clan rivalries and factionalism in which private interests are understood as the interests of the family. Social and political relations are based on *wāsṭa* ("cronyism", "connections", "clout"), a patronage system distributing privileges and protection (Sharabi 1988, pp. 45–46; Terris and Inoue-Terris 2002, p. 475). As Sharabi (1988, p. 28) wrote: "The essence of tribal practice is expressed in the individual's identification with the tribe, and this is reciprocated in the tribe's collective responsibility for the individual's actions, which in turn constantly renews and reinforces a person's kinship identification and loyalty".

Members of a clan are tied by loyalty and obligation to act in its best interest, which is particularly expressed in terms of guarding its honor. Therefore, the binding effect of the adjudication and settlement is founded on the values of honor and respect: the honor of families who cannot publicly break the assurances given, and the respect for the sometimes highly influential witnesses, who are the guardians of execution of the agreement. In the event of any legal proceedings, the problem of guilt and the penalty paid is less important than the reputation of the clan to which the accused belongs (Terris and Inoue-Terris 2002). As reciprocity governs the process in customary law, other goods must be evaluated and converted into common, usually financial, value. What becomes clear is that, in Arabic culture, the value of life (and the criminality of taking a life) is approached differently, depending on circumstances. The remuneration for taking a life or causing other types of harm to a person (or a group of relatives) is calculated based on the precedents and circumstances of the case. This does not mean that life is treated only as commodity, however. In such cases, money has a symbolic value and the financial punishment of the whole family for breaking societal norms should be a deterrent to crime.

Moreover, the value of a just requital in clan relations is so significant that it dictates how other key goods are calculated. The mechanisms available for the family to solve a dispute make it obvious that a "regular" murder is not criminalized and seen the same way in customary law as a revenge killing. Retaliation is one of exculpatory circumstances in customary law and taking a life in such situations is not considered a criminal offense (along with self—defense, defense of honor, and retaliation for an assault on honor such as indecent assault) (Hajjah 2011, pp. 163–165). Bloody revenge returns balance to relations between parties and demands no complicated and time—consuming reconciliation proceedings. It is considered to be justice served and an honorable, legal solution (though not a recommended one) to a conflict between two family groups. However, it can possibly lead to a vicious circle of conflict and violence in the community, and taking a life is always considered a grave act that cannot be considered lightly.

The sanctions and consequences in reconciliation procedures (financial compensation, expulsion) legally befall the perpetrator's next of kin (clan, closest family), and revenge may even be taken, if the perpetrator cannot be held personally accountable, on closest male relatives (Thabit 2006, p. 27). This collective responsibility is determined by blood ties only, not by any direct affiliation with the crime or by direct guilt for the act. This approach in customary law clearly exemplifies factionalization and the tribal solidarity of Arab neopatriarchalism. The contemporary importance of those traits is revealed by the fact that the "code of conduct" presented by the al—J'abaris in 2014 was widely discussed in Hebron because it stood in opposition to the clans' obligations to care for, control, and pay for the mistakes of its members.

Customary Palestinian law is also deeply patriarchal, which is not a unique feature –many customary legal systems, particularly in the Middle East or sub—Saharan Africa, generally share such traits (Chirayath et al. 2005). However, in Palestine, the customary legal procedures are significantly conservative in that regard, recreating and reinforcing conservative power structures dominated by one sex. The actors of the proceedings are men, and the families are represented by either a male head of the family or a chosen male representative. The case is investigated and adjudicated by the *jāha,* consisting of respectable male elders from the area. Although women have their roles in Palestinian customary law (Pely 2011a), in legal cases such as those studied here, representatives of only one gender officially participate in the proceedings.

7 Tracing Cultural Change Through Customary Law

While customary legal proceedings in Hebron follow traditional, centuries—old customs and rituals, the case study presented here also offers insight into the possible evolution of long—established cultural concepts. The central and most unique development during the application of customary negotiations in the above—described case was the announcement by the al—J'abari clan of the 'code of conduct' that would apply to its members. A legal and cultural precedent was created by the clan breaking solidarity by declaring that they would not protect any of their members who commit crimes. Nor would the clan participate in paying compensation according to customary reconciliations. These statements defy neo—tribal traditions, local social norms, and the culture of clan solidarity.

That departure from traditional attitudes could be caused by many factors. For example, attacks on private and public property by the enraged al—Haymounis, and fear of retaliation by the members of the al—Jʿabari clan, may have caused losses amounting to thousands of dinars of profits for the latter clan. The second reason relates to the honor and respect of the al—Jʿabari clan, which was already damaged by the other criminal actions of its members. There was also social pressure – the al—Haymounis were supported by other families in their efforts to reach customary justice. Nevertheless, those factors cannot fully explain the decision to abandon clan solidarity, as these considerations are often present in such conflicts.

A lack of subsequent references to this document, even in negotiations between the same clans in 2016, raises doubts concerning its meaning and importance. It might have been a well—calculated, politically motivated statement intended to calm the atmosphere in the town, or a genuine expression of grave condemnation by the clan elders regarding the violent crimes committed by the clan's members. The rejection of individuals belonging to the family when they face legal and social sanctions, and perhaps even threats to their lives, might be the most dire consequence in Arab neopatriarchal society.

Socially, introducing new "code of conduct" rules could lead to a diminishment of collective responsibility and punishment. However, it could also reduce the future efficiency of customary law as the family will be under less pressure to solve conflicts. Paying monetary compensation, freezing businesses due to the violent reactions of a victim's relatives, fear of revenge murders, possible forced relocation of a whole family—all are socio—legal tools of deterrence that strengthen a clan's control over its members to ensure they obey social norms.

From the perspective of a community such as the traditional society of Hebron, a clan breaking ancient legal customs by disowning members guilty of serious crimes might pose a problem. The still—existing system offers a means to reconcile parties and calm emotions through legal rituals and financial renumeration. However, the system is well—balanced and brings a sense of justice only as long as the whole community—all possible parties to such conflicts—take equal part in its practice. If a clan disowns a perpetrator belonging to it and refuses to pay the "blood money", it is highly unlikely that the perpetrator would be able to pay the whole amount individually. The outcome would be uncertain in such a situation: the victims' family may lower their expectations, the closest relatives of the perpetrator may take a loan (as the perpetrator would most probably be arrested or hiding), NGOs or other organizations may pay the settlement, or the victim's clan may feel forced to take revenge. In addition, how would the ritualized negotiations continue without the whole clan supporting and representing the offender. Perhaps a representative (*lābis ath—thawb*) would consult with the perpetrator individually and then singularly represent them before elders and other family. Possibly there would be political repercussions of one clan not undertaking any negotiations, as it would appear to the community that the clan is enabling the impunity of its members, and even making financial savings rather than amends.

It becomes apparent that accepting such a change in customs would pose more questions and problems for the community than following the traditional path. Nonetheless, the 'code of conduct' published by al—J'abaris might also signify a deeper change in local culture. It may represent not only a step toward recognizing the individuality of clan members, but also a repudiation of a clan solidarity so total that it forces a whole family group to take collective responsibility, allows attacks on property, and induces significant litigation and reconciliation costs. The adoption of this document by other clans would require a change in customary law to accommodate more space for individualism (if not an abandonment of customary law altogether), and would exemplify the evolution of Hebron's neopatriarchal culture.

8 Conclusions

The central assumption of this chapter was that the procedures implemented in customary legal proceedings may be revealing in relation to the culture of the community that employs them. This case study was an attempt to trace Palestinian customary legal proceedings in a murder case and, in doing so, define traits of contemporary Palestinian culture. In the wider perspective of the cultural analysis of law, this case exemplifies beliefs, traditions, behavior, social norms, and convictions concerning social order, justice, and fairness. The case also reveals what is considered valuable by the community, and how restitution is valued in different circumstances. The culture of Hebronite society is still honor—focused and organized around familial affiliations. It places significant value on continuing customs and traditions, considering them to be the main and most efficient tool to satisfy a sense of justice. That justice appears flexible and relative, dependent on circumstance and subjective feelings of personal suffering and humiliation, and closely connected to collective perceptions of honor.

Analyzing mechanisms of customary law in Hebron allows the identification of traits that can and should be categorized as cultural, even if they are most visible during the application of law. Those attributes could be divided into three general groups. The first is traditional clan collectivism exemplified by features such as clan solidarity, a limited recognition of the individuality of clan members (in the face of law and other clans), a feeling of responsibility, factionalism during conflict and reconciliation, and patriarchalism visible in the power relations within families and society.

The second group could be described as the values characteristic of traditional clan collectivism that are, in this case, particularly visible in notions of honor and reciprocity. Honor is a broad term with different meanings and understandings. It can be described as an immaterial commodity that can be lost and regained and, while it is perceived subjectively, it has objective ramifications. On a subjective level, honor exists as an imaginative family asset that is experienced emotionally. It is an obligation, a sense of pride, a fear of humiliation, and a source of self—confidence and security. Those feelings are a response to perceptions of reality by the group and its members. However, these psychological phenomena have material, and more objective, dimensions. The external perceptions of a family group's honor by those outside the group determines that family's social and political position. It also leads to a feeling of it being necessary to exert control over members of the clan (thus leading to a lack of individualism). Finally, the clan acts toward outsiders (i.e. retaliates) based on those internal perceptions. Reciprocity, closely connected to a communal sense of justice, is another such value. It simplifies relations between clans and constitutes the basis for establishing unwritten rules (e.g., concerning the financial value of norm transgressions), while also being flexible and adaptable to the circumstances and emotions of various parties.

The third group of cultural traits, more marginalized in this case study due to its focus solely on customary law, are tensions between the traditional justice and state justice systems. The reconciliation proceedings described reveal that their users accept state law and appeal to it (when useful). Moreover, representatives of state authority contribute to customary proceedings in their official capacities. However, Hebronites employing customary law articulate distrust toward the state judiciary, notably in disbelieving that it can calm emotions or deliver justice in accordance with the values of traditional collectivism. This conventional sense of justice seems flexible and relative, dependent on circumstances and subjective feelings of personal suffering and humiliation that are intricately connected to collective perceptions of honor. On cursory inspection, the modern state justice system seems to be built on different foundations. However, its ability to respond to those traditional sentiments requires further research.

The characteristics of contemporary customary law defined above cannot be segregated from culture as they are, in fact, illustrations of it. This case study of Palestinian customary law particularly highlights the traditional elements of local culture. Examining it through the lens of the neopatriachalism concept, customary law exemplifies the patriarchal, tribal, factional aspects of contemporary Palestinian society. Nevertheless, customary law procedures are implemented alongside state and religious laws, and it remains to be seen what position that legal system will hold in the future, and whether—as is suggested in this analysis—certain cultural attributes (e.g., collective responsibility) that define the scope and mechanisms of this law might be subject to change.

References

Abu-Nimer M, Nasser I (2013) Forgiveness in the Arab and Islamic contexts: between theology and practice. J Relig Ethics 41:474–494

Al-Jʿabari Family Announcement (2014) Copy in the archive of the author

Al-Salaymeh H (2014) Bil—video... tafaṣīl al—ʿaṭwa bayn ʿāʾilatīn al—Jʿabarī wal—Haymūnī fī al—Khalīl. In: Wattan News. https://www.wattan.net/ar/news/87822.html Accessed 15 May 2014

Birzeit University (2006) Informal justice, rule of law and dispute resolution in Palestine: National Report on field research results. http://www.ldf.ps/documentsShow.aspx?ATT_ID=2035. Accessed 04 May 2020

Chirayath L, Sage C, Woolcock M (2005) Customary law and policy reform: engaging with the plurality of justice systems. backround paper for the World Development Report 2006: Equity and Development. http://citeseerx.ist.psu.edu/viewdoc/summary?doi=10.1.1.574.6598. Accessed 13 May 2020

Coombe RJ (1998) Contingent articulations: a critical cultural studies of law. In: Sarat A, Kearns T (eds) Law in the domains of culture. University of Michigan Press, Ann Arbor, pp 21–64

Fitzpatrick P (1992) The mythology of modern law. Routledge, London

Gellman M, Vuinovich M (2008) From Sulha to Salaam: connecting local knowledge with international negotiations for lasting peace in Palestine/Israel. Confl Resolut Q 26(2):127–148

Gerring J (2007) Case study research. Principles and practices. Cambridge University Press, Cambridge

Górska E (2017) Arab customary law in contemporary palestine: remnant of the past or a part of a modern Arab Society? In: Ożarowski R, Gardocki S (eds) Religion, Society and Economic Issues in the Islamic World. Rambler Press, Warsaw, pp 107–128

Górska E, Klakla JB (2017) Arab customary law and the modern Western idea of restorative justice. Pol J Arts Cult New Series 5:31–50

Hajjah AM (2011) Al—Urf al—sha'ri fi—l—islah, Hebron

Hebron Times (2014) ʾAhl Al—Khalīl yaḥqinūn al—dimāʾ wa ʿāʾilat al—Haymūnī yuʿtūn ʿaṭwa li—muddat sana. Hebron Times 84:108–109

ICHR (2016) Al—hiʾiah al—mustaqilla li—ḥuquq al—ʾinsān tadīn ḥāla al—fuḍī wal—faltān al—Āmanī al—laḏī ḥaṣala fī madīnah al—Ḫalīl wa—tadʿaū īlā tʿazīz saīādah al—qānūn wal—salam al—āhlī. Independent Commission for Human Rights. https://ichr.ps/ar/1/26/1320/الهيئة—المستقلة—لحقوق—الإنسان—تدين—حالة—الفوضى—والفلتان—الأمني—الذي—حصل—في—مدينة—الخليل—وتدعو—إلى—تعزيز—سيادة—القانون—والسلم—الأهلي. Accessed 2 Aug 2020

Irani GE, Funk NC (1998) Rituals of reconciliation: Arab—Islamic perspectives. ASQ 20(4):53–73

Lang S (2002) Sulha peacemaking and the politics of persuasion. J Palestine Stud 31(3/2002):52–66

Maan News (2016) tarḥīl qatla ʾībnāʾ al—Haīmūnī wa—ʿaṭwa li—muddat ʿām mʿa ʿāīlat al—Jʿabarī. Maan News. https://www.maannews.net/news/820517.html. Accessed 10 Aug 2020

Mezey N (2001) Law as culture. Yale J Law Human 13:35–67

Palestine24 (2016) ʿAṭwa bayn al—Jʿabarī wal—Haymūnī. Palestine 24. https://www.pal24.net/news/74825.html. Accessed 10 Aug 2020

Paltimes (2016) Al—ʿaṭwa bayn ʿāʾilatīn al—Haymūnī wal—Jʿabarī fī al—Khalīl. https://paltimesps.ps/post/117880/انتهاء—العطوة—بين—عائلتي—الهيموني—والجعبري—في—الخليل. Accessed 02 Aug 2020

Pely D (2009) Resolving clan—based disputes using the Sulha, the traditional dispute resolution process of the middle east. Dispute Resol J 64(4):80–88

Pely D (2010) Honor: the Sulha's Main Dispute Resolution Tool. Confl Resol Q 28(1/2010):67–81

Pely D (2011a) Women in Sulha – excluded yet influential. Int J Confl Manag 22(1):89–104

Pely D (2011b) Where East not always meets West: comparing the Sulha process to Western—style mediation and arbitration. Confl Resol Q 28(4):427–440

Radio Bethlehem 2000 (2016) ʿAqada hudna mud—hā ʿām bayn ʿāīlatīn al—Haīmūnī wal—Jʿabarī bʿad difʿa al—ākhīr al—diyya. https://www.rb2000.ps/news/267890.html. Accessed 10 Aug 2020

Radio Siraj (2014) Maqtalu mūāṭṭani wa—ṣābat īṯnaīn min āqāribīn fī shajār ʿāīlī bil—Khalīl. Radio Siraj. https://sirajfm.com/مقتل—مواطن—واصابة—اثنين—من—اقاربة—في—شج. Accessed 4 Apr 2020

Raya News (2014) ʿAqada ṣulḥ ʿashāīrī li—muddat ʿām bayn ʿāʾilatīn al—Haymūnī wal—Jʿabarī bil— Khalīl. Raya News. https://www.raya.fm/news/853299.html. Accessed 4 Apr 2020

Raya News (2016) Natāīj al—ʿaṭwa al—ʿashāīri bayn ʿāīlatī al—Haīmūnī wal—Jʿabarī bil—Khalīl. https://www.raya.ps/news/930856.html. Accessed 2 Aug 2020

Sergeant RB (1991) Customary and Shari'ah Law in Arabian Society. Ashgate Publishing, Aldershot

Sharabi H (1988) Neopatriarchy: a theory of distorted change in Arab society. Oxford University Press, Oxford

Tarabeih H, Shmueli D, Khamaisi R (2009) Towards the implementation of Sulha as a cultural peacemaking method for managing and resolving environmental conflicts among Arab Palestinians in Israel. J Peacebuilding Dev 5(1):50–64

Terris R, Inoue-Terris V (2002) A case study of Third World Jurisprudence – Palestine: conflict resolution and customary law in neopatrimonial society. Berkeley J Int Law 20:462–495

Thabit MS (2006) Al—Qada al—'asha'iri 'and qaba'il Bir al—Saba. Filastin, Gaza

The Palestinian Information Center (2019) Farīd Al—Jʿabarī "mukhtār al—Khalīl" allaḏī hājamuhu al—wazīr Al—Aʿaraj. https://www.palinfo.com/news/2019/1/20/%d9%81%d8%b1%d9%8a%d8%af—%d8%a7%d9%84%d8%ac%d8%b9%d8%a8%d8%b1%d9%8a—%d9%85%d8%ae%d8%aa%d8%a7%d8%b1—%d8%a7%d9%84%d8%ae%d9%84%d9%8a%d9%84—%d8%a7%d9%84%d8%b0%d9%8a—%d9%87%d8%a7%d8%ac%d9%85%d9%87—%d8%a7%d9%84%d9%88%d8%b2%d9%8a%d8%b1—%d8%a7%d9%84%d8%a7%d8%b9%d8%b1%d8%ac. Accessed 2 Aug 2020

Tsafrir N (2006) Arab customary law in Israel: Sulha agreements and Israeli Courts. Islam Law Soc 13(1):76–98

Verschuren P (2003) Case study as a research strategy: some ambiguities and opportunities. Int J Soc Res Methodol 6(2):121–139

Wattan News (2014) 50 Ālf dīnār wa—hudna bayn ʿāīlatīn al—Jʿabarī wal—Haīmūnī fī al—Khalīl. https://www.wattan.net/ar/news/87638.html. Accessed 10 Aug 2020

Wattan News (2016) Bil—video... ʿAṭwat damm bayn ʿāʾilatīn al—Jʿabarī wal—Haymūnī li—muddat ʿām. https://www.wattan.net/ar/news/160153.html. Accessed 2 Aug 2020

Welchman L (2009) The Bedouin Judge, the Mufti, and the Chief Islamic Justice: completing legal regimes in the occupied palestinian territories. JPS 38(2):6–23

Zaman Press (2016) Bunud 'aṭwat al—Jʿabarī wal—Haymūnī fī al—Khalīl. http://zamnpress.com/news/90718. Accessed 2 Aug 2020

Videos

Hebron HD (2016) Mulakhaṣ ʻaṭwa al—Jʻabarī mʻal—Haymūnī. You Tube. https://www.youtube.com/watch?v=wBWVzNmwmec. Accessed 10 Aug 2020

Maan Network (2016) Qarīr dʻā' īaḥia al—Khalīl tarḥīl quṭlat 'ībnā' la—Haymūnī wa—ʻaṭwa li—muddat ʻām m'a ʻāīla al—Jʻabarī 10—1 —2016. You Tube. https://www.youtube.com/watch?v=Jdlh76uJddc. Accessed 10 Aug 2020

Wattan News Agency (2014) Tafaṣīl al—ʻaṭwa bayn ʻā'ilatīn al—Jʻabarī wal—Haymūnī fī al—Khalīl. You Tube. https://www.youtube.com/watch?v=D7n—gItuPNA. Accessed 10 Aug 2020

Personal Interviews

Qafisheh, Muneer, personal communication, Hebron, 12.03.2014

Slemiah, Khalil, personal communication, Idhna, 04.03.2014 & 31.03.2014

Ewa Górska Doctor of Law; earned MA in Law, and MA in Middle Eastern Cultural Studies from the Jagiellonian University (Poland). Author of the book "Contemporary Dynamics of Islamic Law regarding bioethical problems", and multiple articles with a focus on law in the Middle East. Awardee of the Polish Ministry of Science and Higher Education programme "Diamond Grant", and the Ryoichi Sasakawa Young Leaders Fellowship Fund (SYLFF) scholarship. Has extensive experience working with CSOs and NGOs in Poland and the Middle East. Her research interests include formal and informal legal systems in the Arab world, normative pluralism, legal Orientalism, Islam and new technologies, and medical anthropology studies focused on the Arab World.

“In This Case, Can There Be No Talk About Such a Justification Through Circumstances”? A Case Study of the Invocation of Cultural Defense Outside the Common Law

Joanna Ptak-Chmiel

Abstract Cultural defense as a court strategy was developed in the countries of common law, which are characterized by contradictions of criminal proceedings and a wide scope of a party’s impact on the course of a trial. However, its appearance is not limited to any particular legal system. The subject of this chapter is a case study of a court case in which arguments based on cultural defense were raised in particular conditions—within the Polish legal system, in a country that is relatively homogeneous and in which the main process initiative is within the judges’ competence. In accordance with the characteristics of an intensive case study, the research consisted of examination of court files, which included testimony of an expert in culture, critical analysis of the text of judicial opinions and analysis of relevant media publications. Application of such multi—method approach enabled detailed consideration of the issue of admissibility of invocation of cultural defense in particular institutional and formal settings. It also depicted necessity of adaptation of the framework of the case study in reference to court case as a particular subject of research.

1 Introduction

The first part of this chapter’s title is a quotation from a judicial opinion formulated by the Court of Appeal in Warsaw, Poland. The case it refers to was unique because over its course, the attorneys attempted to invoke cultural defense within the frames of the Polish legal system, in a country characterized at the time by relative homogeneity in the context of ethnic differentiation (which does not mean that Poland is completely homogeneous [see Bek 2018, pp. 138–142], however, the percentage of ethnic differentiation is lower in comparison to such countries, as the

J. Ptak-Chmiel (✉)
Department of Sociology of Law, Faculty of Law and Administration, Jagiellonian University, Kraków, Poland
e-mail: joanna.ptak@alumni.uj.edu.pl

M. Stępień, J. B. Klakla (eds.), *Law and Culture*, Law and Visual Jurisprudence 5,
https://doi.org/10.1007/978-3-030-81193-8_6

United States or the United Kingdom, which in this case were the base for reference). The necessity of comprehensive analysis of the case and its context indicates its potential suitability for a case study as a specific research framework that embraces a multiplicity of methods and techniques and is focused on details of the analyzed material.

Noteworthily, court cases and judicial opinions as subjects of research are characterized by various peculiarities and unique features. In reference to the completed court case, the list of available sources is limited and includes mainly various written documents collected during the trial. The evaluation of the usability of a case study as a framework for analysis of such material constitutes the added value of the research presented herein.

The remainder of this chapter includes a brief presentation of the phenomenon of cultural defense and a discussion of the details of the analyzed case. The main focus is given to judicial opinions issued by the District Court (District Court in Warsaw, VIII Criminal Division, verdict from the 21st of February 2013, VIII K 265/12; Verdict of the District Court in Warsaw, VIII Criminal Division 2013); and the Court of Appeal (Court of Appeal in Warsaw, II Criminal Division, verdict from the 21st of June 2013, II AKa 183/13; Verdict of the Court of Appeal in Warsaw 2013). The analysis is preceded by a presentation of the methodology and research questions in the following section.

2 Methodology and Research Questions

The case study as a research approach is complex. Its application to the context of law and judicial opinions increases the challenge. In general, a case study may be defined as "an in—depth exploration from multiple perspectives of the complexity and uniqueness of a particular project, policy, institution, programme or system in a 'real life' context" (Simons 2009, p. 21). As it was already shown in the chapters "Indian "Love Jihad" Goes to Court" and "Palestinian Culture Through a Legal Lens: A Case Study of Customary Legal Proceedings After a Homicide in Hebron" of this book by Drwal and Górska, it is possible to distinguish numerous types and variations of this approach. Although it is beyond the scope of this chapter to discuss this matter in detail, it is important to indicate that the case study presented in this chapter fits into the classical, intensive type. From a researcher's perspective, this means that it was focused on in—depth and thorough analysis of a narrow research area. However, because of the specificity of the research subject, particular adaptations were necessary.

Such an approach justified the choice of analyzed court case, which fits the category of "typical" cases of cultural defense. Despite the fact that the scope of this framework is not limited to any specific areas of law, the most well—known examples of this phenomena occurred in the context of criminal law (see the most classical examples are the case of Fumiko Kimura, Helen Wu or Dong Lu Chen; Kim 1997, pp. 101—102). Noteworthily, the case is also unique because the perpetrator of the crime in question was of Turkish origin, whereas in the Polish context cultural defense is usually considered in reference to Roma people (Bek 2018).

The aforementioned in—depth perspective requires a multi—method approach. The choice of particular methods and techniques to be used in a given context should depend on the case itself. In reference to this aspect, particularities of the court case and judicial opinions as the subjects of research justified the use of the detailed analysis of court files, and the interpretation of the text of judicial opinions, inspired by critical discourse analysis (CDA; see Wodak 2007; Ven Leeuwen 2008; Shuy 2015; Van Dijk 2015). In reference to CDA, matters such as the following were taken into consideration (Wodak 2007, p. 194): (1) what characteristics, qualities, and features were attributed to the actors of the case; (2) which arguments were used in this context; and (3) from what perspective were they expressed. Furthermore, the issue of inclusion/exclusion and creation of dichotomy between various groups, as well as the distance of power and its manifestations, were discussed. Last but not least, the material was completed through the examination of various media coverage of the case in question. However, during the research only two publications of local media related directly to this case were revealed.[1] Both were very brief and limited to basic facts of the case, such as the age of the perpetrator or his citizenship. Therefore, they could not be subjected to an extensive analysis. The initial research plan also consisted of interviewing involved parties and judicial bodies; however, attempted efforts to reach these actors were not successful.

In further sections of this chapter, I take into consideration characteristics of the judicial opinions as a specific genre of text. Furthermore, I focus on textual and contextual dimensions of the analyzed material, especially in reference to means of construction and conceptualization of culture and cultural differences, manifested in the creation of a division between "Us" and "Them" or "We/They" groups (Van Dijk 1984, p. 138). Notwithstanding, all of the analyzed data were originally formulated in Polish and translated for the purposes of this research. As such, particular characteristics and specificities of the text may have been lost in translation.

Taking the abovementioned into account, the research question I attempt to answer in the chapter is as follows: On the base of the analyzed case, what are the frames of admissibility of invocation of cultural defense in the context of the Polish legal system? Additional research questions are connected with such matters: What was meant by the term "culture" in the particular case and how was its indicated meaning constructed? What did the invocation of cultural defense in this particular case consist of? How did the judges refer to the cultural arguments raised by the defense? How was the relationship between culture and criminal law in the context of the Polish legal system constructed and conceptualized by judges in the analyzed judicial opinions? Which circumstances of the case, referring to the cultural background of the perpetrator, were taken into consideration in the decision—making process, as declared in the judicial opinion? Before these questions can be answered,

[1] *Dlaczego zabił konkubinę?,* http://warszawa.tvp.pl/5780802/dlaczego—zabil—konkubine> (accessed: 11.02.2020), *Zabójstwo w stolicy* https://video.wp.pl/i,zabojstwo—w—stolicy—paragraf,mid,927061,cid,4051,klip.html?ticaid=11be1f (accessed: 11.02.2020).

a brief presentation of the issue of cultural defense and its main assumptions should be presented.

3 What Is Cultural Defence?

The debate over cultural defense started in the USA in the 1980s (Grzyb 2016, p. 307). On the one hand, it was rooted in the system of common law, which in comparison to continental law is characterized by adversarial criminal procedure and a wider scope of defense initiatives. On the other hand, it was influenced by the specific approach towards the multiplicity of cultures and ethnicities that coexisted in the territory of one country. Cultural pluralism had opened frames for consideration of whether particular cultural backgrounds of litigants should be taken into account by judicial bodies in the decision—making process, for example, as a mitigating factor. Because the matter of cultural defense has been widely discussed, from various perspectives and in a multiplicity of contexts (see for example Foblets and Renteln 2009; Van Broeck 2001), its comprehensive presentation would require the capacity of a separate monograph. Due to space limitations, in following part of this chapter, I focus on the main assumptions about cultural defense.

Although the most well—known cases in which cultural defense was invoked were fatal, this strategy was also considered in the context of less violent breaches of law, such as "victimless crimes" (Dudek 2011). Within this theme, E. M. Held and R. G. Fontaine, who generally criticized the concept, allowed "cultural arguments" to be taken into consideration in case of "relatively harmless acts that they [perpetrators] never dreamed would be the kind of behavior that might be regulated criminally" (2009: 251). In reference to the aspects of "defense" itself, used arguments may vary from justification to an excuse, from acquisition to mitigation of a punishment. In case of killing, an invocation of cultural defense could result in reducing charges from murder to manslaughter due its recognition as a "lesser wrong" (Woodman 2009, p. 9).

One of the most classical works that refers to the concept of cultural defense is a book by Alison Dundes Renteln (2004). The author described the aim of her research as being "to examine the nature of the debate surrounding the admissibility of cultural evidence in the courtroom" (Renteln 2004, p. 5). Her main arguments in favor of the discussed concept were based on the notion that "enculturing shapes individuals' perceptions and influences their action" (Renteln 2009, p. 62). In such a perspective, acting in accordance with patterns of culture, even if contrary to binding law, was regarded through analogy to other social attributes that might have an impact on sentencing in the context of a particular case due to individualized justice, such as gender, age, or mental state. However, cultural defense is not limited to the sphere of issuing the verdict and determining severity of punishment. Its scope embraces almost every stage of a procedure, as it may—for example—be manifested in an introduction of expert testimony to evaluate the validity of a party's claims based on references to their culture. Such a conceptualization widens the spectrum of potential applications of this court strategy to cases outside of criminal law. The implementation of cultural defense may encompass such aspects as the termination of parental rights or the evaluation of the size of damages or validity of requests for asylum (Renteln 2009, pp. 61–63).

The application of cultural defense has been widely criticized (Bek 2018, pp. 109–114; Grzyb 2016, pp. 313–337; Sikora 2001, pp. 1708–1714). Whilst it is beyond the scope of this chapter to discuss this issue in detail, it should be noted that in general, according to Damian W. Sikora, arguments against cultural defense usually refer to such matters: "cultural defenses may promote stereotypes; immigrant women and children's rights are undermined by the defense; it would be impossible to draft legislation that defines when, where, and how the defense can be used; and the defense would cause a balkanization of the criminal justice system" (2001: 1708). Furthermore, various concerns refer to the danger of misusing or overusing this strategy (Held and Fontaine 2009; Renteln 2009).

In spite of all of the critique, it must be acknowledged that various arguments related to the cultural background of the perpetrator are raised over court trials in practice as a defense strategy. As the analysis of the chosen case indicates, their appearance is not limited to a particular legal system. The details of the case are presented in further sections of this chapter.

4 Background: Analysis of Case Files

The analyzed court case concerned the murder of a young woman of Polish descent, which was committed in November 2011. Analyzed material included documents gathered by various institutions, such as police forces and prosecution, from the moment of gaining the first information about the commission of crime until the execution of judgement. It also consisted of various protocols and documents depicting the course of the trials in both the District Court and the Court of Appeal.

4.1 The First Stages of Proceedings

According to the case files, the perpetrator, who was a Turkish citizen, was the partner of the victim.[2] He had arrived in Poland 4 years prior to the crime in question. The couple lived together with their young daughter and an older daughter of the victim from her previous marriage. Notwithstanding, on the birth certificate of the younger child, the fatherhood was indicated as "unknown". They were not married. On the day of the murder the couple had an argument, one of many that had

[2]Unless explicitly indicated otherwise, all of information and citations presented in the next sections of this chapter was collected on the base of analysis of the court files.

happened before, and both drank alcohol. Their relationship was stormy, with a history of his infidelity and jealousy. However, this time the consequences were tragic. The victim was stabbed with a knife and strangled, and died on the spot due to the wounds. Afterwards, the perpetrator attempted to commit suicide by jumping into a river, but he came out of the water on his own. The police report stated that during the arrest, the man behaved normally and confessed to committing the crime. At the initial stages of proceedings, his declared motive was that the victim "had misbehaved and abused alcohol". The perpetrator himself indicated that he had killed his partner due to anger.

The perpetrator was examined by experts in psychology and psychiatry, who evaluated his mental state at the moment of the act. In their opinion, the gathered data did not justify a statement that the crime was a consequence of rapid sheering of strong emotions, which as a consequence would have enabled its classification as a crime of passion. No arguments relating to either ethnicity or culture of the accused were raised at that point.

The perpetrator was accused of murder (article 148 § 1 of Polish Penal Code). During the court trial, on the basis of alleged difficulties with communication with the translator, the perpetrator revoked part of his preceding explanations. However, the issue of his guilt remained undoubted. As such, further proceedings focused on the analysis of the case in the search for eventual extenuating or aggravating circumstances.

Although in that part of the trial the aspect of eventual cultural differences was not highlighted by the perpetrator himself, some of the witnesses mentioned the issue of culture in the context of the case. The most comprehensive statement was given by the employer of the perpetrator, also of Turkish descent, who described Turkey as country that was diverse in terms of culture and morality. He focused on differences between Polish and Turkish society, especially in the context of a family. Notwithstanding, until that moment the cultural background of the perpetrator had not played an important role in the court trial.

4.2 Cultural Expert Testimony

In the defense's assessment, data gathered by that point of the proceedings was not comprehensive. It was the very first moment the attempt to apply the strategy of cultural defense could be observed. They requested an introduction of an opinion of an expert in Turkish culture. The attorney observed that particular circumstances, which could be related to the culture of the perpetrator, were not examined by the expert in psychology, who in the defense's perception had analyzed the behavior of the accused from the perspective of "our" [Polish] principles and "our" system. According to their standing, such aspects were significant from the point of view of estimation of both a motive and the intentions. At that point, the court accepted the arguments of the defense that referred to the necessity of cultural expertise to fully assess the circumstances of the case and introduced the expert testimony.

The evidence was presented as an oral statement of the expert. The expert was a Polish researcher specialized in Turkish culture, holding an academic degree. The opinion referred to such issues as the characteristics of Turkey, differences between Poland (or other European countries) and Turkey, the Turkish model of a family, and *namus* ("honor" in Turkish). The expert mentioned the fact of the cultural and social heterogeneity of Turkey and noted that this factor led to difficulties in making general statements about the whole society; particular matters might have differed dependent on the social stratum of an individual.

In reference to the model of a family, on the basis of the testimony of the accused, the expert assumed that he was from a middle—class family of rather poor financial status, which was not overly conservative, but rather traditional. She observed that usually such families were characterized by men playing the main role as the heads of a household. Apart from gender inequalities, conservative families were characterized by an emphasis on a collective and the importance of public opinion, especially in reference to *namus.*

The expert conceptualized *namus* as an equivalent of honor. Nevertheless, while discussing the sense of this term, she highlighted difficulties in a direct translation and referred to it partially through the phrase "a good name". The expert presented *namus* in a collective dimension, as a property of a family as a whole, regulating the entirety of the life of an individual. In the presented opinion, *namus* was regarded as "a particular collection of principles and rules, which maintain leads to a positive reception of a family by others". Furthermore, the expert referred to this concept in relation to decency and respect. In the expert's opinion, it differentiated the situation of men and women in such a sense that its rules were stricter in the context of females, for example, within the scope of social allowance towards premarital sexual intercourse.

In reference to differences (or similarities) between Poland and Turkey, the expert discussed such issues as the consequences of infidelity and perception of quarrels, especially in the context of female behavior in the public sphere, or attitude towards suicides and the frequency at which they are committed. The expert stated that Turkish men were more impulsive than inhabitants of "these geographical areas". She connected this impulsiveness with an assumption that the infringement of a good name required immediate reaction and acting without consideration of consequences. However, in the expert's opinion, these reactions were mostly merely verbalized and did not cross the boundary into physical aggression.

Last but not least, the expert highlighted that to the best of her knowledge, the percentage of homicide in Turkey was higher compared with European countries. She justified it through lenses of cultural and religious perceptions, according to which "the odium towards a killer is much lesser than in case of a thief". The expert stated that she was informed that it was caused by the fact that stealing was always premeditated, while killings were usually murders of passion. In her opinion, all of these convictions were connected with *namus.*

4.3 Further Formulation of a Defense Line

On the basis of the presented expert's opinion, the attorneys continued the strategy of cultural defense, arguing that the cultural background of the perpetrator potentially had an impact on his mental state and impulsiveness of his reaction to the victim's behavior at the moment of the crime. After the cultural evidence was presented, the main focus returned to the testimony of experts in psychiatry and psychology, who examined the accused. The question was whether the culture of the perpetrator should have been taken into consideration in the assessment of his mental state.

In the additional opinions, the expert in psychology acknowledged the fact that the surroundings in which the perpetrator was brought up and stayed for a long period before arriving in Poland must have had an impact on his current personality. However, the expert stated that the cultural evidence did not have an influence on her examination of the emotional state of the accused.

The defense in the question session attempted to undermine this standing. For example, they asked whether the expert in psychology was familiar with particular scientific publications referring to issues of aggression and culture. Furthermore, the attorneys employed many rhetorical operations that constituted a particular image of the perpetrator and his culture. The most evident example of such efforts was a question that referred to a potential infringement of the results of the expert's examination due to gender and cultural differences. The attorneys asked whether the expert took into consideration that the perpetrator, who "as we all know was raised in a patriarchal family", could have experienced discomfort while being examined by a woman. The expert's answer was negative.

The defense then attempted to undermine the expert's testimony at a variety of levels. The majority were related to the omission of cultural imperatives as the factor that could have had an impact on the evaluation of the perpetrator's mental state. The attorneys argued that the psychological opinion was not comprehensive and additional examination, conducted by an expert of the same cultural background as the perpetrator, was required. Furthermore, they made an effort to introduce evidence from a private opinion of a psychologist, which supported their claims. However, on the basis of an evaluation of the gathered material being valid and comprehensive, the court rejected this claim.

4.4 Court Verdict and Appeal

The debate over the psychological testimony was one of the concluding stages of the trial. The court sentenced the accused to 12 years of imprisonment. The exact content of judicial opinions is the subject of a further part of this chapter. At this point, it is worth mentioning that both parties challenged this verdict in the Court of Appeal. The prosecution argued that taking into consideration the social noxiousness of the act, such punishment was grossly disproportionate and it infringed conditions of general prevention in both of the aspects—negative and positive. In reference to potential perpetrators, including those living in Poland, but originating from “other cultural circles, characterized by a different than European approach towards women”, it was assumed that such a verdict—due to its leniency—would not have had an impact on their emotional sphere. Moreover, the prosecution argued that the assumed disproportionality of the sentence was harmful in the context of enhancing the sense of validity of legal norms and the hierarchy of social values.

The defense’s standing was based on arguments referring to cultural defense, such as not taking into consideration all circumstances of the case, especially those related to the culture of the perpetrator and the methodological incorrectness of the psychological examination, as well as the lack of its adjustment to the context of cultural differences. Furthermore, the attorney claimed the expert’s lack of basic knowledge of such terms as enculturation and culture of honor. In reference to this matter, the defense mentioned the work of R. Nisbett and D. Cohen, which was described as classical in the field of social psychology (1996). In the concluding remarks, the attorney argued that the proper examination of the perpetrator’s emotions and mental state at the moment of the crime was decisive to its categorization, as the results of a reliable trial could have led to classifying it as a crime of passion (Article 148 § 4 of Polish Penal Code), which would have resulted in the sentence being lowered.

5 Analysis of Judicial Opinions

In this section, I indicate how the issues of culture and its relations with law were manifested in the analyzed judicial opinions. However, such considerations should be preceded by an outline of the context of the analyzed material and indication of the speech event (Shuy 2015, p. 824). To do so, it is worth mentioning that judicial opinions as a genre are characterized by a multiplicity of particularities. First of all, their basic goal is to indicate the factors that had an impact on the sentence and decision—making processes of judges. Furthermore, as one of the elements of procedural justice that was discussed in details by Różyczka further in this book (chapter “The Procedural Justice in South Korean Popular Culture. An Analysis of Court Hearings Using the Example of the K—Drama *Your Honor*”), through a variety of available rhetorical devices, they may influence the parties’ convictions about the equity of the verdict. However, it is important to note that the scope of their addressees is wider than just the participants of a particular case, because after the anonymization of their content they are widely accessible to the public and may serve as a source of information about binding law and the content of legal norms. In consequence, judicial opinions fulfill various functions, such as those presented by Drwal in chapter “Indian “Love Jihad” Goes to Court”. Furthermore, especially in the case of the occurrence of rare circumstances, arguments presented in the judicial opinions may have an impact on the further lines of interpretation of law, presented in the following court cases. The process of sentencing is depersonalized, as the verdict is given by the court as an organ that acts on the behalf of the Republic of Poland. It is reflected in the wording used by the authors of the text. Linguistic structures are not formulated in a first—person narrative.

Moreover, from the point of view of discourse analysis, it is crucial to note that authors of the judicial opinions use specific legal language, which is primarily formal. At the same time, one of the aims of judicial opinions is to convince the parties and relevant actors and institutions about the propriety of the ruling. Consequently, as is shown in the following sections, particular rhetorical operations, also referring to the emotional sphere, are used in this context. Another specificity of the wording of judicial opinions is connected with the fact that those documents are directed simultaneously to professional and unprofessional users of legal language.

In addition, the frames of research are impacted by the fact that the judicial opinion of the Court of Appeal constitutes a constant reference to the sentence and statements of reason, formulated by the District Court. Taking listed matters into consideration, in further parts of this chapter I compare how the mentioned issues were constructed and manifested in both of the documents. The starting point is the judicial opinion of the District Court.

5.1 Background: Judicial Opinion of the District Court

In the mentioned judicial opinion, the matter of culture played a rather minor role. The main focus was given to the evidence and circumstances of the case revealed during the trial, which referred to events preceding the commission of crime, such as repeating disagreements and sustaining disputes between the victim and the perpetrator. In general, the image that arises from the statements depicts a situation of a long—lasting conflict between partners, the consequences of which were tragic. However, this does not mean that the issues that may be connected with the strategy of cultural defense were completely omitted. Quite the opposite, the issue of the ethnic background of the perpetrator was also included, but in a very particular context—one of analysis of perpetrators' mental state at the moment of a crime.

In coherence with the part of the defense's arguments, the exact problem that was taken into consideration was whether the culture of the perpetrator had an impact on his behavior and violent reaction. The court stated that opinions formulated by the expert in psychology were "reliable, professional, and the conclusions included in them fully indicate the state, in which the perpetrator was at the critical moment (. . .)". As I mentioned, one of the aims of the judicial opinions is to justify the equity of the verdict. In the sphere of rhetorical operations, this goal was reflected in the fact that the court referred to the external source and used wording that highlighted the perceived veracity of the expertise.

In reference to the culture itself, the court presented its own standing and assumed that the 4—year period of stay in Poland prior to the events in question was sufficient to become familiarized with Polish culture and norms, and consequently to evaluate the process of the perpetrator's [cultural] adaptation as "accomplished". Apart from the time period, no other arguments referring to this aspect were mentioned. Ethnic differences were constructed in reference to issues such as consuming alcohol, cohabiting, not participating in the financial maintenance of the family, taking care of honor, controlling the partner, being excessively jealous, and rationalizing one's own aggression towards the victim. The majority of the arguments referred to the sphere of gender equality. Consequently, the court outlined a particular vision of differences between Polish and Turkish culture. As can be concluded from the statements cited above, the created image of Polish culture (notably, native to judges) consisted of such aspects as consuming alcohol and living in cohabitation. Components of the perpetrator's behavior, assumed to be derived from Polish culture, were created on the basis of their contradiction of Turkish norms and notions about the lack of allowance towards such behavior in Turkey. Similar to what was observed in reference to the perpetrator's mental state, in this context the source of the court's information about the norms of Turkish culture was the opinion of the cultural expert discussed above.

On the contrary, Turkish culture was presented as being composed of aspects such as taking care of honor, in addition to controlling one's partner, being excessively jealous, and rationalizing the aggression. On the basis of the abovementioned statements, the court evaluated that "the perpetrator was intentionally choosing favorable elements of both Polish and Turkish culture". In reference to linguistic structures, the contradiction between particular norms of culture was constructed with the use of specific phrases that explicitly created an impression of opposition (On the one hand... On the other...).

To sum up at this point, the court created a specific image of culture and its diversity. Its construction was based on the assumed differences between norms of accepted behavior in both countries. The assumption was overly simplistic and could be reduced to one statement—if some aspects of the perpetrator's behavior, observed by the Court, were not mentioned in the cultural expert's testimony, they were derived from Polish culture. The majority of these issues referred to the sphere of gender relations. In this context, Turkish culture was depicted as characterized by gender inequalities, manifested in excessive jealousy and aggression towards the partner. Taking this into consideration, the analyzed judicial opinion was based on the stereotypical, generalizing, and simplified assumptions about both Polish and Turkish culture and established contradictions between them. Noteworthily, such a creation of the notion of "national" culture as a fixed idea was criticized rightly by Klakla in chapter "Customary Law is Like an Onion: A Multilayered Approach to Customary Law and Its Status in the Contemporary World" in this book. All of the mentioned statements were presented as justified by the expert's opinion, which created an impression of objectivity of relevant judgements. Due to subject limitations, it is impossible to unambiguously indicate whether particular judges' beliefs about Turkish culture, especially in the context of gender inequalities, preceded the expert opinion or were the result of it. Nevertheless, the fact the expert mentioned the heterogeneity of Turkish society and impropriety of generalizations in this context was not taken into consideration in the analyzed material.

However, at the same time, such a reasoning indicates that particular aspects of cultural defense were taken into consideration by the court. The strategy of the defense resulted in the analysis of the potential impact of the native culture of the perpetrator on his behavior. Even though in this case such an influence was excluded, its negligence was not based on the general rejection of 'culture' as a factor that could be potentially relevant to the legal assessment of one's actions. Quite contrarily, the perpetrator's behavior was in fact evaluated in terms of various characteristics that were distinguished by the court as derived from either Polish or Turkish culture, and the potential impact of his cultural background on his actions was considered. As such, in this context the defense's strategy was successful. However, due to the fact that the process of the perpetrator's cultural adaptation was evaluated by the court as accomplished, in this case cultural defense seemingly had no impact on the sentence. At least, such an influence was not expressed in the judicial opinion. As Drwal observed in her chapter in reference to discovering judges' personal beliefs from judicial opinions (chapter "Indian "Love Jihad" Goes to Court"), taking into consideration the characteristics of such documents, a reader cannot be entirely sure that absolutely all of the factors that impacted the sentencing were fully presented in the written opinion. Nevertheless, due to the lack of first—hand sources of information, any further analysis would be suppositious.

5.2 Judicial Opinion of the Court of Appeal

As I mentioned previously, both parties appealed the discussed verdict. Judicial opinion, formulated by the Court of Appeal, constitutes a direct reference to the judicial opinion of the District Court. Analyses of both documents led to the conclusion that the arguments and language devices used by both institutions were similar, but not identical. In general, it was ruled that the arguments of both parties were not justified and the Court sustained the sentence.

In reference to the aspect of culture, the Court rejected the arguments of the defense that related to the eventual impact of cultural imperatives on the mental state of the perpetrator and his behavior at the moment of crime, as well as the improprieties of the examination conducted by the expert in psychology. This negligence in the strategy of cultural defense was based on the assumption that the accused did not expose his background and nationality in the course of the trial and did not invoke "unquestionable cultural differences, including *namus*" in the description of his life with the victim. However, at the same time, the admissibility of cultural defense was partially highlighted as the Court stated that "without a doubt, the perpetrator—like everyone—is not capable of the complete elimination of some patterns of behavior, characteristic to one's own cultural circle".

As I have mentioned, part of the strategy of the defense was directed against the propriety of the opinion of the expert in psychology. In this context, the Court was highly categorical and used firm statements. For example, it was argued that "the choice of the method used during the formulation of an opinion is in the expert's competence, not party's". The Court ruled that the decision of the District Court regarding the rejection of additional cultural evidence, requested by the defense, was justified, since the expert's opinion was comprehensive and based on multiple sources of information, such as direct contact with the accused, consultation with the psychologist, and other data gathered during the case.

Arguments raised in the defense's appellation, especially those related to the gender of the expert in psychology, were partially ridiculed. To be exact, the Court observed that "her [expert's] opinion cannot be questioned by the fact that she is a woman (similarly to the experts in psychiatry and one of the accused's defenders, which does not disallow actions and actions taken by them)". Furthermore, the Court highlighted that the defense's expert who formulated the private opinion, presented by the defense as a part of the strategy, did not have contact with the accused and had based his evaluation on the disputed expertise. The Court assumed that since circumstances that were regarded by the party's expert as indicating abnormal personality development were taken from "nothing else than" the opinion of the expert in psychology, this meant that those data were not excluded; quite contrarily, it provided that she "evaluated them and included in the opinion".

Furthermore, the Court of Appeal confirmed the presupposition of the District Court that the period of 4 years was sufficient to "get to know moral norms of the country of residence (...)". Similar to the opinion of the District Court, the Court of Appeal assumed that aspects indicating what could be described as acculturation (although the Court did not use such a phrase) consisted of not legalizing the relationship, as well as leading a lifestyle that "did not depart from the Polish model, including drinking alcohol and recognizing the equal position of both of the partners". All of these circumstances were regarded as justifying the observation that the accused accepted Polish norms, did not focus on "transplanting the customs, in which he was brought up to the current stage of life", and adapted to new surroundings. As such, the admissibility of cultural defense was once again finally rejected on the basis of the assumption that the process of cultural adaptation of the perpetrator was accomplished.

Taking this into consideration, arguments referring to the matter of cultural defense and the culture of the perpetrator, raised by both the District Court and Court of Appeal, were based on similar observations and led to comparable conclusions. However, the Court of Appeal denied part of the statements of the Court of lower instance, and to a certain extent overcame the image of differences between Polish and Turkish societies that was created by the District Court.

First of all, it was assumed that circumstances, which by the District Court were evaluated as based in the culture of honor, such as jealousy, "happen independently of the nationality" and that the importance of *namus* was not confirmed in the testimony of the accused. Issues referring to this sphere were regarded as "characteristic to a description of a conflict between two people, but not because of the lack of mutual adjustment of partners descending from the regions of different morals or culturally diverse (...)". Furthermore, the Court of Appeal rejected the opinion that the perpetrator had chosen those elements of both cultures that were suitable to him.

Noteworthily, the exclusive matter, in which the Court acknowledged the potential impact of the perpetrator's culture on his behavior, was the alleged defensive and introverted attitude of the accused during his psychological examination. The Court observed that it could have been enhanced by cultural motives and declared a reluctance to talk about the problems, since it was the only aspect in which the accused referred to cultural differences. In a result, the Court stated that taking into consideration all mentioned circumstances, the opinion of the expert in psychology could not have been effectively undermined.

In reference to the eventual qualification of the act in question as a crime of passion, which was the main aim of the invocation of cultural defense, the Court used categorical and strict wording. It stated the following:

> The Article [148 § 4 of Polish Penal Code] requires that the commotion – in case of its occurrence – was justified by the circumstances, which should be evaluated with the use of the objective criteria and it is the court's obligation. In this case there can be no talk about such justification by the circumstances – in Polish conditions and Polish legal system, even if the strong commotion, accompanying the acts of the perpetrator, was acknowledged, so—called culture of honour, which was invoked by the defence, and not by the perpetrator himself, cannot constitute such circumstance.

Noteworthily, arguments referring to described matters were more extensive and detailed than in the case of the judicial opinion of the District Court, also in terms of the sphere of their measurable length and quantity. As can be seen from this quotation, the Court of Appeal categorically rejected the possibility of taking the aspects of the "culture of honor" into account, which were raised by the defense and not by the perpetrator himself, as potentially impacting the sphere of sentencing and coherent with the category of "objective criteria". As such, in this particular case, the Court dismissed the possibility of acknowledging cultural imperatives as justifying the eventual state of commotion in the context of the Polish legal system.

However, one may argue whether the Court generally rejected the admissibility of cultural defense in the Polish legal system or the specific circumstances of the case prevailed. The Court explicitly highlighted that the issue of cultural differences and their potential impact on the behavior was raised by the defense and not by the perpetrator himself. However, it was not clearly stated if, had the perpetrator behaved differently during the trial, the admissibility of cultural defense would have been accepted (and what the eventual outcome would have been). Consequently, on the basis of the judicial opinion, it may be discussed whether the argument referring to the perpetrator's avoidance of the issue of inevitable cultural differences was raised to strengthen the general rejection of acceptability of cultural defense, or whether it was in fact the deciding factor. Independently, making such a differentiation between the words of the perpetrator and the arguments of his defense is disputable, as it is the defense's role to represent the accused.

Noteworthily, the Court did not define the term "culture of honor". Instead, it used a reference to the defense and its previous arguments. This aspect is particularly worth highlighting because the analysis of the available court files led to the conclusion that the first of the actors involved in the case to use this exact term was the expert in culture, not the defense. Consequently, on the basis of the research material, without access to other sources of information, it is challenging to clearly settle what the Court of Appeal's exact approach to the general admissibility of cultural defense in the Polish legal system was. In this context, the constraints of judicial opinions as the research material are particularly evident.

Components of the construction of culture can also be found in fragments that refer to the arguments raised by the prosecution, especially in the sphere of assumed infringement of the requirements of general prevention by the leniency of the sentence. The Court argued that,

> there is a lack of data, which would prove that the perpetrator through his lifestyle in Poland and the way of functioning in the context of the family had pursued to adopting by the victim rules of behaviour differing from those accepted in Europe, that he was imposing on her rules foreign to European culture, that he dominated her; what is more, that cultural differences were leading his behaviour and determining his actions, although undoubtedly he did not completely break away from his own culture.

The Court framed general prevention and cultural differences in the context of gender equality. It was assumed that its principle was the deterrence of other people who descend from "distinct cultural circles", characterized by a "different than European" approach to women. Furthermore, the Court explicitly argued that the general prevention shaped the legal awareness of those who were from different cultural circles through "making them aware through adjudicating on the penalty of the effects of forcing habits or solutions unacceptable in the light of Polish law". However, the Court ruled that in the given case, those matters were not dominant.

When it comes to the multiplicity of potential uses of the term "culture", the text of the judicial opinion consists of such variations: [own] culture, other cultures, Turkish culture, culture of honor, European culture, [other] cultural circles or [own] cultural circle, [unquestionable] cultural differences, cultural barrier, distinct cultural area, Turkish cultural patterns, components of culture, and cultural motives. By contrast, in the judicial opinion of the District Court, only four versions are to be found: culture, Turkish culture, Polish culture, and elements of culture [of the accused]. Furthermore, the number of references to culture is higher. This disproportion, also in the context of the quantity of arguments referring to various aspects of culture, is justified by the fact that matters connected with this sphere were the bases for both of the appellations.

All of these phrases and structures create an impression of differentiation between the "cultures", namely that of the accused and Polish/European culture. Taking this into account, both of the judiciary bodies framed these matters into a dichotomy of "Us" (Poles/Europeans) and "Them" (Turks). When it comes to a foundation of such division, in both of the judicial opinions, this issue can be reduced to the sphere of morals, especially in the context of an approach to gender equality. This aspect was particularly evident in the judicial opinion of the Court of Appeal. The rhetorical operations, used by judges, were persuasive and based on contrast and generalization (van Dijk 1984, pp. 139–141).

Consequently, Polish and Turkish culture were presented as in fact contradictory. On the one hand, the creation of such a dichotomy opened the frames for the analysis of whether cultural background should have been considered an important factor in the comprehensive assessment of the circumstances of the case. However, on the other hand, one may argue that the goal of creating such a dichotomy was in fact the opposite; it was not to focus on differences but rather to turn the attention in the direction of similarities. Comparisons of the lifestyle of the perpetrator with perceived characteristics of Turkish culture actually enhanced the impression that the process of his cultural adaptation was accomplished.

In the Courts' perspective, the mentioned dichotomy was broken through specific circumstances, such as the length of stay of the accused in the territory of Poland, as well as the fact that he drank alcohol and had not married. Aspects related to gender equality through the assumption that the accused recognized the equal position of both partners were also listed by the Court of Appeal. This "breaking" of the dichotomy served as an additional justification of the standing of the court that there was nothing "particular" in the committed crime in terms of cultural differences between the perpetrator and victim. It additionally strengthened the motives of the ruling, especially in the sphere of rejection of the necessity of focusing on the cultural background of the perpetrator during the assessment of his mental state at the moment of the act. Noteworthily, despite the fact the District Court described the testimony of the cultural expert in detail, in the statement of reason of the Court of Appeal it was merely mentioned, and the main concern was given to other aspects of the case.

The rhetorical operations adopted indicated that the Court formulated its standpoint from the point of a higher position. This was especially evident in reference to various devices that were used to ridicule arguments formulated by the parties. At the same time, the Court tended to highlight the idea of objectivity as the priority of its performance. Such an impression was also enhanced indirectly, such as in the context of constantly referring to the provisions of the Penal Code or experts' opinions. It is worth considering whether such operations could have served as a safe "veil" for the real convictions of the judges. Without a doubt, they had an impact on the increased impression that in the process of their formulation, judicial opinions were separated from the authors and their personal standpoint.

6 Conclusions

In conclusion, when it comes to the framework of cultural defense, the analyzed case fulfils various prerequisites for it to be included in this category. First of all, the defense requested an introduction of the testimony of the expert in culture to assess the potential impact of cultural imperatives on the perpetrator's behavior and mental state. Furthermore, acting in accordance with relevant behavioral norms, derived from one's culture, was presented by the defense as justifying the classification of the act of the perpetrator as a crime of passion, which, if successful, would have resulted in the sentence being lowered. Consequently, the analyzed case shares common features with most 'classical' examples of cultural defense that were discussed in the relevant literature.

On the contrary, the prosecution argued that the perpetrator's cultural background should have been considered in the context of requiring general prevention to be enhanced as well as a clear signal passed to members of cultures other than Polish about the lack of acceptance for particular unlawful behavior. The parties used arguments based on the particular relation between law and culture to support their standings. Nevertheless, all of them referred to different aspects connected with sentencing and none were used as justification for a complete acquittal.

Furthermore, a particular conceptualization of the relation between criminal law and culture was present in both judicial opinions. However, it is worth considering whether both institutions, despite their declared standpoints, actually rejected the possibility of acknowledging cultural imperatives on the basis of their relevance over the course of a court trial and judicial decision making. In fact, the party's request to introduce evidence from the testimony of the cultural expert was accepted. This sole fact leads to the conclusion that, at least at that point, the judges evaluated its introduction as necessary to fully evaluate all circumstances of the case. Furthermore, the District Court assessed this opinion as informative in reference to the state of the perpetrator at the moment of the commission of the crime. This further leads to the conclusion that despite the potential rejection of admissibility of cultural defense in the context of the Polish legal system, at least in this particular case, specific frames exist that enable consideration of those aspects over the course of a court trial. First and foremost, they include the possibility of introducing an expert's testimony. Other means, connected with the postulate of individualized justice, may also be applied. For example, they may consist of the necessity for adapting the methods used to assess the mental state of the accused or the circumstances of a case. Nevertheless, they depend on the individual perspective of the involved actors, especially judges.

Noteworthily, the choice of an expert lies within the court's competence. In this context, the crucial question is who was regarded an expert. In the analyzed case, the assessment of the level of expertise was the most probably based simply on one's academic degree and affiliation. The collected material did not include any reference to additional circumstances that could have an impact on the choice of the particular expert. Because it is impossible to examine this issue comprehensively due to source limitations, one may only consider potential factors that could have an influence on this choice, such as accessibility. In this context, the lack of full clarity should be evaluated negatively because the research results have shown that the matter of choice of a personal source of information is particularly important. The expert's testimony had a direct impact on further proceedings and was quoted in the judicial opinions as the justification for particular standings.

In reference to culture itself, in both judicial opinions, no explicit definition of this concept was included. It suggests that in spite of all of the difficulties with the exact meaning of "culture" that were presented by Stępień (chapter "Exploring New Avenues for Studying the Legal Culture: Drawing on Homi Bhabha's Theorization of "Culture"") or Wojdala (chapter "Does Visual Culture Pose a Threat to Law?") in this book, discussed term was understood by judges as fixed and self-explanatory. However, a particular conceptualization of cultural differences and components of both the cultures, namely Polish and Turkish, can be derived from the content of the analyzed documents. First and foremost, the term culture was considered through the terms of varying nationalities in a sense of belonging to a specific ethnic group (see Wodak 1996). In this context, Polish culture was included in a wider category of European culture. It was assumed that the major differentiating factor was the approach to gender equality. The culture itself consisted of components referring to the sphere of morals and particular patterns of accepted behavior, which were presented in detail in previous sections.

What is particularly crucial is that the issue of cultural differences, based on approaches to gender relations, was mentioned by many of the involved actors, starting from the employer of the perpetrator. This issue was also the central point of the testimony of the expert in culture, who created a general impression of patriarchalism and the subordinate position of women in Turkey. Its influence on the judicial opinion was particularly evident in the case of the District Court. However, the fact that the expert explicitly mentioned that the culture of Turkey was heterogenous and any generalizations would have been improper was not taken into account by the Court. Nevertheless, the Court of Appeal rejected such categorical differentiation and observed that aspects such as jealousy were not ascribed exclusively to one nationality.

In addition, contradiction and differentiation between "Us" and "Them" were created through the use of various linguistic structures. Noteworthily, the distance of power between the Court and both involved parties was especially evident in the rhetorical devices used by the Court of Appeal. I assume that it was particularly visible in the fragments based on the ridicule of the parties' arguments included in the appellations. Such operations could also be regarded as enhancing the validity of the Court's claims, similar to referring to such 'objective' sources of information as the expert's opinion.

Despite sharing a particular vision of Turkish culture, based on stereotypes and generalization, both Courts formulated the standing that the perpetrator was adopted into Polish culture. Various aspects of his behavior were evaluated as overcoming the differentiation between Poles and Turks. Notwithstanding, some were also generalized and based on auto—stereotypes related to the judges' native culture. Nevertheless, it could be observed that despite the fact the circumstances of the case that were connected to the descent of the perpetrator were taken into consideration in both judicial opinions, it seems, at least at first glance, that they did not result in either lowering or harshening the sentence. Noteworthily, the possibility of determining a universal period that would enable whether the process of cultural adaptation has been accomplished to be assessed, assumed by both of the Courts, and presented in the testimony of the expert in psychology, should be evaluated negatively.

Despite the extensive discussion of various aspects connected with the nationality of the perpetrator, the case was evaluated as a "typical" situation of conflict between two partners, the consequences of which were fatal. A similar perspective was presented in the analyzed media coverage of this case. The fact the perpetrator was

Turkish was mentioned only briefly as a basic fact of the case. No articles referred to the issue of cultural differences between Poland and Turkey.

Last but not least, regarding the application of a case study as the research framework, it can be concluded that the adoption of such a perspective was useful for a comprehensive analysis of the chosen case and its context. Such a detailed approach enables the researcher to observe and consider the whole spectrum of the court case and judicial opinions. Due to the uniqueness of this case, this matter was particularly critical. However, the peculiarities of this research material—connected especially to a reliance on documents that are both constructed and constructive, and also to the limited availability of first—hand sources—require particular adaptations of applied methods and techniques. Consequently, not all of the research questions could be answered through using the case study perspective. Nevertheless, if awareness of these restrictions is maintained, the case study is an inquiring and prompting framework for further research on the matter of court cases and judicial opinions.

References

Bek D (2018) Obrona przez kulturę. Analiza na gruncie polskiego prawa karnego. C.H. Beck, Warsaw

Dudek M (2011) Czy każda kultura zasługuje na obronę? Kilka wątpliwości dotyczących cultural defence i prawa karnego w dobie multikulturalizmu. Archiwum Filozofii Prawa i Filozofii Społecznej 2:47–60

Foblets M-C, Renteln AD (2009) Multicultural Jurisprudence. Comparative perspectives on the cultural defense. Hart, Oxford

Grzyb M (2016) Przestępstwa motywowane kulturowo. Aspekty kryminologiczne i prawnokarne. Wolters Kluwer, Warsaw

Held EM, Fontaine RG (2009) On the boundaries of culture as an affirmative defense. Ariz Law Rev 51(1):237–251

Kim SN (1997) The cultural defense and the problem of cultural preemption: a framework for analysis. N M L Rev 27(1):101–139

Nisbett RE, Cohen D (1996) Culture of honour. The psychology of violence in the south. Westview Press, Boulder

Renteln AD (2004) The cultural defense. Oxford University Press, New York

Renteln AD (2009) The use and abuse of the cultural defense. In: Foblets M-C, Renteln AD (eds) Multicultural jurisprudence. Comparative perspectives on the cultural defense. Hart, Oxford, pp 61–82

Shuy R (2015) Discourse analysis in the legal context. In: Tannen D, Hamilton HE, Schiffrin D (eds) The handbook of discourse analysis. Wiley Blackwell, Chichester, pp 822–840

Sikora DW (2001) Differing cultures, differing culpabilities?: A sensible alternative: using cultural circumstances as a mitigating factor in sentencing. Ohio St Law J 62(5):1695–1728

Simons H (2009) Case study research in practice. Sage, London

Van Broeck J (2001) Cultural defence and culturally motivated crimes (cultural offences). Eur J Crime Crim Law Crim Just 9(1):1–32

Van Dijk TA (1984) Prejudice in discourse. An analysis of ethnic prejudice in cognition and conversation. John Benjamins Publishing Company, Amsterdam

Van Dijk TA (2015) Critical discourse analysis. In: Tannen D, Hamilton HE, Schiffrin D (eds) The handbook of discourse analysis. Wiley Blackwell, Chichester, pp 466–485

Ven Leeuwen T (2008) Discourse and practice. New tools for critical discourse analysis. Oxford University Press, New York

Wodak R (1996) The genesis of racist discourse in Austria since 1989. In: Caldas-Coulthard CR, Coulthard M (eds) Texts and practices: readings in critical discourse analysis. Routledge, New York, pp 107–128

Wodak R (2007) Critical Discourse Analysis. In: Seale C, Gobo G, Gubrium JF, Silverman D (eds) Qualitative Research Practice. Sage Publications, London, Thousand Oaks, New Delhi, pp. 185–201

Woodman GR (2009) The culture defence in English common law: the potential for development. In: Foblets M-C, Renteln AD (eds) Multicultural jurisprudence. Comparative perspectives on the cultural defense. Hart, Oxford, pp 7–34

Judicial Opinions

Verdict of the Court of Appeal in Warsaw, II Criminal Division, from 21st of June 2013, II AKa 183/13

Verdict of the District Court in Warsaw, VIII Criminal Division, from 21st of February 2013, VIII K 265/12.

Internet Sources

Dlaczego zabił konkubinę?. http://warszawa.tvp.pl/5780802/dlaczego—zabil—konkubine. Accessed 11 Feb 2020

Zabójstwo w stolicy. https://video.wp.pl/i,zabojstwo—w—stolicy—paragraf,mid,927061, cid,4051,klip.html?ticaid=11be1f. Accessed 11 Feb 2020

Joanna Ptak-Chmiel A sociologist of law and lawyer, holding a PhD in Law, granted in 2019 at the Faculty of Law and Administration of Jagiellonian University. Her main research interests focus on the various aspects of law and the diversity of cultures, especially in the context of migration. In her PhD dissertation that was titled “Strategies of combatting honour—related violence” she focused on the state’s approach towards tackling the issue of honour—related violence in three European countries: the United Kingdom, Germany and the Netherlands. Awardee of the Polish Ministry of Science and Higher Education programme “Diamond Grant”.

Part III
Law and Cultural Production

Copyright and Culture: The Case of Poland

Ewa Radomska

Abstract This chapter is aimed at exploring the relationship between continental copyright law and culture regulated by this law on the example of Poland. The theoretical objective consists of searching for the most important areas of intersection between copyright and culture, including cultural production and participation. The empirical objective is to reconstruct understandings of the interrelations between copyright law and culture functioning within the Polish public discourse on copyright in order to investigate the most visible interdependencies of discourses on copyright and culture. The inferences from the empirical material show that the way in which culture is defined is the most important factor determining the perception of the relationship between copyright and culture. Moreover, it can be concluded that Polish non-governmental organisations play a crucial role in describing and explaining the "copyright–culture" relationship. Finally, on the basis of both empirical and theoretical data, a typology is proposed of four essential areas in which this relationship is the most intense. Because a balance between copyright fixity and cultural variability is needed (as the more general conclusion from the data indicates), the proposed typology is also an indication of the spheres where maintaining equilibrium has the greatest importance.

This chapter is a result of the research project "Social conflict over intellectual property rights on the example of Polish discourses on copyright" (No. 2015/19/N/HS6/00783) financed by the National Science Centre and carried out at the Institute of Sociology of the Jagiellonian University.

E. Radomska (✉)
Jagiellonian University, Department of Sociology of Law, Cracow, Poland
e-mail: ewa.radomska@doctoral.uj.edu.pl

M. Stępień, J. B. Klakla (eds.), *Law and Culture*, Law and Visual Jurisprudence 5,
https://doi.org/10.1007/978-3-030-81193-8_7

1 Introduction

The problematic character of the relationship between copyright and culture makes this relationship one of the most common themes appearing in the public discourse on copyright. In the case of Polish copyright discourse, the complexity of the "copyright–culture" relation seems to be especially visible, since its understanding requires taking into consideration many economic, social, and historical factors. Until recently, Poles have perceived culture as a quite important source of national identity, as it was culture that helped the Polish people to survive as a nation during the times when Poland was not an independent country. However, nowadays, in the era of cultural commodification and globalization, the main role of culture, not only in the Polish society, is—apart from providing content that can be monetized—to enable people to take part in extended social relations that cross national borders. Similar revolutionary changes can be observed in the ways in which copyright norms regulate cultural production and consumption. In the beginning, copyright laws concerned mainly the professional creators and intermediaries. Whereas today, most online activities fall within the scope of copyright protection. Keeping all this in mind and assuming that copyright law, as any other law, has an impact on culture, as well as assuming that changes in culture influence the rules of the copyright (for more detailed considerations on relations between law and culture, see Chapter 'Exploring New Avenues for Studying the Legal Culture: Drawing on Homi Bhabha's Theorization of "Culture"' and Chapter 'Customary Law Is Like an Onion: A Multilayered Approach to Customary Law and Its Status in the Contemporary World' of this book), it is evident that defining both nature and scope of interdependencies between copyright and culture requires complex and in-depth analysis.

The main goal of this chapter is to explore the relationship between continental copyright law and culture regulated by this law on the basis of the Polish discourse on copyright. To achieve this goal, both theoretical and empirical objectives have been established. The theoretical objective consists of exploring the intersections of copyright and the dominant culture (mostly European and Anglo-Saxon culture). Such an exploration is focused on interdependent relations between law and culture characterized by consecutive cycles of definition, slippage, and redefinition (Mezey 2001), within which copyright law and culture evolve together. To be more precise, the most important areas of intersections between copyright and culture are examined, including between copyright and cultural production, and participation. The empirical objective of the chapter is to reconstruct understandings of the relationship between the copyright law in force in Poland (i.e., international copyright law, European copyright law, and Polish copyright law) and the culture (produced and consumed by Poles) that function within the Polish copyright discourse. An in-depth analysis of the narratives that create such understandings will help investigate "moments of collision between the dependent discourses of law and culture" (Mezey 2001, p. 38).

The chapter consists of two main parts corresponding to the theoretical and empirical objectives. In the first part (see Subsection 'Theoretical Framework for Relations Between Law and Culture'), three groups of conceptions are described, in which indications can be found of how the relations between copyright and culture are or could be arranged: (a) classical copyright justifications, (b) theories on relations between copyright and creativity, and (c) two conceptions focused on the necessity of introducing proper limitations to copyright law due to the need to support cultural development—the right to culture and the conception of free culture. Additionally, copyright policy as an element of cultural policy is presented. These conceptions are mainly of a theoretical-normative character. Only the free culture concept, which takes as a starting point the difficulties encountered in the course of cultural practices, has some empirical basis. However, this conception is mostly interested in Anglo-Saxon culture and the system of common law that regulates it (Lessig 2004); thus, it has a limited application to Polish society. With this kept in mind, in the second part of the chapter (see Subsection 'Polish Discourse on Copyright'), theoretical considerations of the relations between copyright and culture are enriched with empirical data from an analysis of the Polish press discourse on copyright. Due to the special role of Polish non-governmental organizations in copyright debates, the scope of discourse was narrowed to the discourse led by these organizations. Additionally, to deepen the conclusions obtained from the discourse analysis, the results from expert interviews with representatives of these organizations have been presented. Furthermore, to consider perspectives that are different from that of non-governmental organizations, results have been provided from expert interviews with Polish lawyers who specialize in copyright and with selected Polish publishers and music producers.

The exploration of the copyright–culture interrelation requires prior preparation of conceptual foundation that includes, among others, making general assumptions about the type and scope of both phenomena. As mentioned, copyright law, for the purposes of this chapter, is understood as continental copyright law. It is also treated as a social system aimed at introducing "fixity, clarity, and predictability" to social relations and practices; it is a system that is not separated from other social systems (Cohen 2007, p. 194). However, it is much more difficult to propose a definition of culture as a phenomenon regulated by copyright (for other types of definition of culture, see Chapter 'Does Visual Culture Pose a Threat to Law?' of this book), as culture is one of the concepts that is "extremely difficult to absorb and define by law" (Młynarska-Sobaczewska 2018, p. 35). Trying to propose such a definition is even harder if one takes into account that copyright does not often directly refer to culture (at least that is the case with Polish copyright). Nevertheless, copyright law is above all a complex system that tries to resolve the conflict between the public interests of society and the individual interests of the creators of copyrightable work. These works are quite often the products of culture, which are also called cultural property or cultural goods. Cultural property is a concept in the field of international law that includes, except works of art, "objects of artistic, archaeological, ethnological or historical interest" (Merryman 1986, p. 831). However, "cultural goods" is a term most often used in the context of market exchange of the cultural products. Although this chapter is mainly about works of art and products of popular culture, including those that are outside market circulation, all of these notions are used here interchangeably.

Despite the focus of copyright on works that are fixed in a tangible form, the relationship between copyright and culture cannot be reduced to the interdependences between copyright regulations and "documentary culture", which is understood as "the body of intellectual and imaginative work" (Williams 1965, p. 57). First, the fact that modern copyright laws do not give sufficient scope for the protection of every form of cultural expression opens a space for reflection about cultural sensitivities or the "cultural life" of copyright (Bowrey 2001). Second, since art "is a kind of human activity whose characteristics assume their final form only during the contact between the work and the audience" (Młynarska-Sobaczewska 2018, p. 88), attention should also be paid to the non-material dimension of cultural property that consists of the "reflection" that is comprised of, above all, the emotional states of both creators and "users" (Pałecki 2007). The issue of the cultural limits of copyright law has been thoroughly explored in past studies on the relations between intellectual property and indigenous folklore (see, e.g., Coombe 1998). Because this issue is not a problem widely discussed in Polish copyright discourse, it is not a subject of this chapter. However, other elements of so-called "social culture", understood as "a particular way of life", which expresses certain meanings and values (Williams 1965, p. 57), are included. The social dimension of culture is an important factor in determining the scope of both the moral rights of the author as well as the right to culture. The latter, as shown below, plays a substantial role in setting the boundaries of copyright protection.

While preparing the conceptual basis for considering the copyright–culture interrelation, one should adopt other conceptual categories for describing culture that are relevant from the point of view of the copyright protection of cultural property. As many legal definitions of culture take the shape of aggregate definitions (Zeidler 2016), in particular the different typologies of culture should be taken into account. Among the typologies that are important in the sphere of copyright protection are the following distinctions of culture: dominating/ethnic culture, universal (cosmopolitan)/national culture, elite (high)/egalitarian (low or popular culture), and professional/amateur culture (for limitations of this type of typologies see Chapter 'Customary Law Is Like an Onion: A Multilayered Approach to Customary Law and Its Status in the Contemporary World' and Chapter 'Does Visual Culture Pose a Threat to Law?' of this book).

At first, copyright laws applied mostly to the works of dominant, elite, and national cultures. Similarly, in the initial period of protection of cultural goods (e.g., the protection of participation in cultural life and the protection of heritage), the prevailing approach was to treat them as cultural resources important for the state community (Młynarska-Sobaczewska 2018). The dominant culture, in this context, means, in reference to P. Bourdieu (1984), the culture that imposes the discourse, cultural themes, and constituents of community identity. However, elite and national cultures are simply cultures that can be assigned to particular classes of society or to particular nations and states, but all these categories of culture can overlap.

Moreover, starting in the middle of the twentieth century, the role of opposite types of culture (i.e., ethnic culture, the universal culture, and popular culture) began to be noticed. It was then when cultural research was increasingly emphasizing that each culture exhibits both universal and emic characteristics. As a result, the way of interpreting the concept of cultural life by creators and enforcers of international regulations has evolved following appreciation of the need to preserve cultural diversity (O'Keefe 1998). In addition, a system of international cooperation to protect of world heritage were established. At the same time, because access to cultural goods has changed in a revolutionary way, the distinction between elite and egalitarian culture has started to lose significance (Młynarska-Sobaczewska 2018) and as a consequence, popular culture has been placed at the center (for more detailed considerations on popular culture see also Chapter 'The Procedural Justice in South Korean Popular Culture. An Analysis of Court Hearings Using the Example of the K-drama *Your Honor*' of this book), becoming the dominant culture (van den Haag 1957). Similar process has been recently observed in case of the distinction between professional and amateur culture. The main reason for this is that nowadays both the constant development of communicative technologies as well as new types of public copyright licenses, such as Creative Commons licenses, are opening up new possibilities for creating, sharing, and supervising the creative output of amateur artists. These creators are quite often a part of so-called remix culture (Lessig 2008), which is closely related to the concept of free culture. The latter is the subject of more in-depth consideration in the further body of the chapter. All these mentioned definitions and divisions of culture consist the frame of reference for the analyses described in the following parts of the chapter.

2 Theoretical Framework for Relations Between Law and Culture

2.1 Culture and Copyright Justification

Although modern Western copyright law developed without much recourse to theoretical justification, an understanding of its philosophical foundations can help to indicate the sources of widespread disagreement over the nature and legitimacy of intellectual property rights institutions. Such disagreement can be widely observed in contemporary public debates on copyright regulations. Culture plays an essential role in the arguments raised both by authors of traditional (but still "after-the-fact") copyright justifications and participants of current copyright debates.

Traditional copyright justifications can be categorized as either based on their belonging to one of the grand theories (Hughes 1988) or based on their main philosophical-ethical assumptions. On the basis of the latter, deontological and consequentialist justifications can be distinguished. According to deontological rationales, "rights are enforced with respect to persons who are entitled to intellectual property as a matter of natural rights or as a matter of classical liberal or human rights or as a matter of duty" (Dutfield and Suthersanen 2008, pp. 51–52). Copyright law is justified with arguments parallel to "those commonly found in the law of obligations" (e.g., the "unjust enrichment" argument known also as the principle against reaping without sowing) or to "those used to underpin the institution of property" (e.g., the argument from desert, argument from personhood, or argument from personal autonomy) (Spence 2002). Contrary to this, consequentialist theories of copyright contend that copyright protection is necessary because of the valuable consequences it brings about in a society such as providing incentives for knowledge and cultural production. The most commonly used consequentialist justifications are utilitarian justifications and justifications on the basis of public policy (Stokes 2001). Some authors also include in this group the capabilities approach (Cohen 2007). In pursuance of the utilitarian justifications, "the grant of exclusive rights to the author is an incentive for the author to create. It is also a very significant incentive to entrepreneurs such as publishers who rely on the copyright protection afforded to authors". However, public policy arguments state that "authors should be encouraged to publish their works to ensure as wide a dissemination of knowledge and culture as possible" (Stokes 2001, pp. 10–12).

Regardless of the deontology–consequentialism divide, there are also two grand theories of intellectual property and copyright: labor theory (based mainly on Locke's theory of property) and personality/personhood theory (derived from the theoretical concepts of philosophers such as G. W. F. Hegel and M. Radin). The Lockean justification enables normative and instrumental interpretations of the assumption that labor should be rewarded (Hughes 1988) and hence can be jointly used with both deontological and consequentialist justifications. At the same time, the second main philosophical justification for copyright is based mainly on moral rights and personality claims. This justification emphasizes that granting authors full control over the copyrighted works they create is necessary for their personal self-actualization, as these works "materialize" their personal traits (Hughes 1988).

Culture understood as a "cultural property" created by artists is not only visible in all of the copyright justifications, it is also a common denominator of these justifications. Namely, all mentioned theories of copyright directly or indirectly demonstrate the importance of culture for society. On the grounds of consequentialism and labor theory, it is presumed that to ensure cultural production and the wide availability of cultural goods, rights that restrict the current availability and use of cultural property should be established (Hettinger 1989). This is stated with the reservation that if copyright is unregulated (e.g., by not introducing exceptions to copyright protection on the basis of "fair use" or "fair dealing"), it may act "as a fetter on those who need to copy the works for desirable purposes" (Stokes 2001, p. 12), such as artistic creation or inspiration. Much less obvious are relations between the protection of moral rights and the social role of culture. However, there are at least a few assumptions made by rights theorists that indicate the general need to protect or support culture. For example, R. Kwall has observed that protection for creators' personal rights, such as the right to the integrity of their work, "enables society to preserve the integrity of its cultural heritage", as well as "to enjoy the fruits of a creator's labors in original form and to learn cultural heritage from such creations"

(1985, p. 69). Moreover, in this context, it is also worth mentioning that Hegel's personality theory provides affirmative justifications for the complete alienation of copies of the cultural property (as opposed to complete alienation of intellectual property, which is "morally analogous to slavery or suicide because it is the surrender of a 'universal' aspect of the self") due to concern for the economic well-being of authors (Hughes 1988, pp. 348–349). According to Hegel, creators sell copies of their works to obtain resources which they can invest in things that increase their self-actualization (Hughes 1988). The latter will help to gradually multiply the "capital" in the form of cultural property accumulated by the whole society.

2.2 *How Does Copyright Affect the Process of Culture Creation?*

Most copyright scholars, regardless of which copyright justification they adopt, agree that, to assure the availability and dissemination of cultural production, a copyright system should seek to promote creativity. Rights theorists describe creativity in terms of an individual liberty, while economic theorists try to divine the optimal rules for promoting creativity (Cohen 2007). The latter are proponents of the economic rationale for copyright—that is, the most common utilitarian justification—which states that the copyright law "provides an incentive to create by enabling authors and publishers to recoup their outlays on the time and effort of creating the work on the part of the author and the cost to the publisher of making the master copy" (Towse 2001, pp. 10–11). These theorists assume that "people are more likely to create when they can monetize their creation" (Simon 2011, p. 313). The best known, often regarded as definitive, economic analysis of copyright law is the analysis conducted by Landes and Posner (1989). They believe that to maximize creative output, copyright must strike a balance between protection of the author and the search costs for novel means of expression (e.g., the costs of obtaining permission to use the copyrighted works of others). Hence, the exclusive right of authorization should be limited in copyright statutes, and exceptions for certain types of "fair use"—the use of copyrighted works without the author's consent and without remuneration—should be provided (Towse 2001).

Although it is universally agreed that copyright should account for the creative process when rights are granted, copyright scholarship and policymaking, as J. Cohen properly observed, have proceeded to a great extent on the basis of assumptions about what creativity actually is (2007). Moreover, in the case of the economic model, it is the creative process where the shortcomings lie (Simon 2011). As R. Towse puts it, "for all the sophisticated analysis by economists, economic historians, law-and-economists and lawyers, (...) we still cannot say with any conviction that intellectual property law in general, and copyright law in particular, stimulates creativity" (2001, p. 21). According to others scholars, there are at least two reasons for this failure. The first one is connected with the economic model's inability to account for nonmonetary motivations to create (Simon 2011). Namely, artists are motivated not only by economic means (or extrinsic motivation, in reference to the distinction introduced by B. Frey (1999)) but also by intrinsic motivation. In the context of culture production, the former is a response to pecuniary rewards and the latter is an artistic drive to create. However, what is more important is that monetary payment is not only inappropriate for intrinsic motivation, but it also could act as a disincentive to create.

The second reason why copyright scholars are unable to answer the question of whether and how does copyright affect cultural creation is that they are not treating creativity as a process (Simon 2011). For example, as O. Arewa (2007) rightly observes, copyright scholars fail to account for the copying necessary in the creative process. As a result, despite that much of the creative process entails borrowing from many different ideas and expressions, copyright law focuses on the complete copyrighted products that spring full-blown from the minds of creators. For similar causes, the classical copyright conception of creativity cannot be reconciled with the so-called "internet-inspired creativity" (Simon 2011). The latter is a new category of nonmonetary, collaborative creativity that has opened up as the freedom provided by the internet has enabled people to engage with culture much more freely than before. The idea of autonomy is what is underlying this type of creativity (Benkler 2006).

Among the concepts that have challenged copyright's understanding of creativity, the Cohen's concept that is based on cultural theory (Cohen 2007) stands out. According to Simon, Cohen's account of creativity "re-conceptualizes the creative process to reflect the realities of the creator as an individual submerged in a sea of culture" (2011, p. 326). Cohen has sketched a model that treats creative processes as "complex, decentered, and emergent" (2007, p. 1153). Within this model, it is neither creators nor social patterns that produce artistic culture, but it is the dynamic interactions between them. The process of "working through culture" is tied both to the semantic links within content and to the spatial distribution and material forms of cultural goods. However, the spatially distributed set of cultural resources, which Cohen (2007) has characterized as the "cultural landscape", does not map onto the category of public domain. Nevertheless, constraints on creativity do not flow just from a time and place, but also from the "situatedness", as the culture with which individuals engage contains evolving and contested meanings. This is mainly caused by the fact that social institutions, groups, and human behavior also constrain and shape creativity, for example, by promoting and validating certain kinds of creativity at different times (Simon 2011). As a result, "the play of culture" is the "to-and-fro" in flows of cultural goods and in cultural practices. Play in this sense is an essential condition of cultural progress, as it "supplies the unexpected inputs to creative processes, fuels serendipitous consumption by situated users, and inclines audiences toward the new" (Cohen 2007, p. 1192).

The model of creativity proposed by Cohen challenges the widespread assumption about the nature and direction of copyright's influence on creativity. First, this model suggests a more modest conception of copyright's role in stimulating creativity. Specifically, Cohen indicates that even though "creativity is not especially amenable to social engineering" and as a result "copyright is not the most important factor in stimulating creativity" (2007, p. 1193), the system of copyright still may be the paramount factor that is within control. This observation is more important when one remembers that copyright law also serves other social goals, such as the organization of cultural production and the distribution of artistic goods. Namely, control of copying and derivation enables the organization of economic activity in ways that produce a variety of desirable goods. The second contribution of Cohen's model of creativity is that it provides the foundation for arguments about the systemic harms of the copyright regime (2007, p. 1193). Namely, as critics of copyright maximalism have indicated, overly rigid control of access to and manipulation of cultural goods can stifle cultural innovation. The possibility of the latter is the main reason why, according to Cohen, a copyright regime must be assessed based on its effects on creativity, with special attention to "the extent to which it renders elements of the cultural landscape more or less accessible" (2007, p. 1194).

2.3 Copyright and Access to Culture

Because copyright law has some impact—regardless of its level and direction—on the process of creation, it determines not only the amount of cultural goods created by artists, as utilitarian justifications assume, but also the quality of cultural goods. Hence, there is an inevitable interrelation between a system of copyright and access to culture, in particular to one that is high or dominant. There are a great deal of conceptions indicating opportunities and threats for the culture that may occur depending on the extent to which an ongoing copyright system takes into account the needs of the members of society to participate in cultural life (see, e.g., Bollier 2008; Boyle 2008; McLeod 2005). Many of these conceptions have a great impact on social attitudes towards copyright (see, e.g., Benkler 2006; Lessig 2004). Two of them are especially important from the point of view of this chapter—the right to culture and free culture, as they are directly referred to by the participants of Polish copyright discourse. As indicated below, both conceptions are closely related to each other.

According to Młynarska-Sobaczewska, two understandings of the right to culture can be distinguished. The first one is "the right to common culture, concerning universal artistic culture, or (...) the dominating one" (Młynarska-Sobaczewska 2018, pp. 51–52). The second meaning concerns the right to one's own culture, such as an ethnic culture. From the point of view of the relations between copyright and access to culture, the first understanding is of a much greater importance. Such an understanding was also adopted while the Universal Declaration of Human Rights and the International Covenant on Economic, Social and Cultural Rights

(ICESCR) were written, when the right to culture was defined as a human right that assured every member of the public the enjoyment of so-called high culture.[1]

The right to participate in the dominant culture, despite being included in canonical documents regulating human rights protection, has not become a necessary element of the catalogue of rights in international or national systems. Instead, it has remained "one of the most mysterious and undervalued corners of the galaxy of rights and freedoms" (Młynarska-Sobaczewska 2018, p. 9). The reason for this is, on the one hand, the complex character of culture and, on the other hand, the reluctance of public authorities to enter into new obligations towards their own citizens. As a consequence, the right to culture became the right of transversal nature that consists of elements of many other spheres of entitlements (Donders 2007), as it is not a second-generation law nor is it the mere correlation of the public duties of authorities with the rights of individuals. The conceptualization of this right requires an analysis of cultural freedoms, as well as the presentation of legislative, political and administrative instruments providing access to artistic culture. What is more, such a synthesis should be made in the context of the doctrine of human rights and the constitutional acquis of contemporary states (Młynarska-Sobaczewska 2018). An excellent example of the first is general comments of the Committee on Economic, Social, and Cultural Rights (CESCR). One of these Commentaries (General Commentary no. 21) differentiates three components of the right to participate or take part in cultural life protected by Article 15 of ICESCR: "participation in", "access to", and "contribution to" cultural life (CESCR 2009, p. 3). Participation covers the right to choose cultural identity and engage in cultural practices, access means the right to become familiar with one's own culture or gain access to cultural heritage of other communities, and contribution refers to the right to be involved in creating "the spiritual, material, intellectual and emotional expressions of the community" (CESCR 2009, p. 3).

However, the right to culture under Article 15 of the Covenant does not mean exclusively the right to satisfy certain claims to participate in cultural life, as it is closely linked to other freedoms and rights, which determine borders of the right to access cultural life. Participation in cultural life is above all closely related to the rights of creators to benefit from their creation (Article 15.1.c of the ICESCR). It is also delimited by copyright protection, since the intersection between right to culture and copyright has become crucial due to the widespread access to cultural goods. Nevertheless, it is justified to distinguish the category of the right to culture as the individual right to participate in artistic culture that entails specific obligations of states. According to General Commentary Number 21, there are three types of such

[1]According to article 27 of the Universal Declaration of Human Rights "Everyone has the right freely to participate in the cultural life of the community, to enjoy the arts and to share in scientific advancement and its benefits. Article 15 of the International Covenant on Economic, Social and Cultural Rights states that "The States Parties (. . .) recognize the right of everyone: (a) To take part in cultural life; (b) To enjoy the benefits of scientific progress and its applications; (c) To benefit from the protection of the moral and material interests resulting from any scientific, literary or artistic production of which he is the author."

obligations: “the obligation to respect”, “the obligation to protect”, and “the obligation to fulfil” (CESCR 2009, p. 9). The obligation associated with the sphere of respect is aimed at protecting the sphere of freedom of artistic creation and free access to cultural assets. The obligation to protect is mainly designed to guarantee the right to culture in the sphere of horizontal relations and to protect cultural heritage. Finally, the state’s obligation to fulfil is primarily linked to the need for formation of effective mechanisms for participation in cultural life (also for people with reduced participation opportunities), as well as to the creation of policies for the protection of cultural heritage (CESCR 2009, pp. 9–11).

In line with the human rights regulations and doctrine, the Polish constitutional acquis, which devotes a great deal of attention to cultural heritage and its role in the life of the national community, include the right to culture within catalogues of political principles and economic, social, and cultural freedoms and rights. In Article 6 of the Polish Constitution, the programme norm was introduced, which states, “The Republic of Poland shall provide conditions for the people’s equal access to the products of culture which are the source of the Nation’s identity, continuity and development”. A specification of this principle can be found in a latter passage of the Constitution, which states ”the freedom of artistic creation and scientific research as well as dissemination of the fruits thereof, the freedom to teach and to enjoy the products of culture, shall be ensured to everyone” (Article 73).

As Młynarska-Sobaczewska (2018) has acutely observed, the fundamental issue in the sphere of interrelations between the right to culture and copyright protection is to determine the share of a copyright regime—developed regardless of the human rights order—in exercising the right to culture. This issue includes also answering the question of whether there is an inherent conflict between the order of copyright and the cultural rights. Setting this dilemma is relevant for the practical definition of mutual relations and borders between these rights; it also has a significant impact on the scope and content of the right to culture.

Although at the time of the Universal Declaration’s signing there was an atmosphere in which wide access to the goods of artistic culture was favored (Shaver 2010), new forms of communication and an unpredictable increase in the exposition of cultural goods in a digitalized environment have caused the barriers to access to culture to become particularly visible (Młynarska-Sobaczewska 2018). The main reason is that the revolutionary changes in access to cultural goods enabled by digitalization have made the tension between copyright holders and the right to culture much more evident, within both the framework of repressive and preventive protection (Shaver and Sganga 2010). Moreover, the inevitable side effect of the contemporary development of the sphere of intellectual property protection is the conflict between copyright and freedom of expression, including artistic expression; this conflict is especially characteristic of Anglo-Saxon countries. The digital revolution has also changed the model of creating and presenting works of art, as market forces have started to enter the relationship between the audience and the author with much more energy, resulting in the latter transferring copyrights to commercial entities (Młynarska-Sobaczewska 2018).

Despite all the aforementioned changes, the copyright system has provided surprisingly little response to the requirements of the market of digitalized cultural goods. To date, only a few legal compromises between unrestricted access to digitalized content and the protection of the rights of copyright holders have been made (e.g., the regulation imposing a levy on blank media and devices) (Młynarska-Sobaczewska 2018). Similarly, far-reaching proposals to increase the limits on the freedom of artistic creation at the expense of protecting copyrights—going beyond creating new fields of permitted use or liberalizing access to unavailable or orphan works—do not bring satisfying results. On the contrary, defenders of ongoing copyright focus only on a dissemination activity that violates copyright regulation, ignoring the need for becoming acquainted with art and culture. As a result, two orders become increasingly separated—on the one hand, the demands and declarations concerning access to culture in the order of human rights and actions aimed at guaranteeing this access and, on the other hand, a rigid system of protecting copyright holders, open to new phenomena only if they can be described using the existing legal categories (Młynarska-Sobaczewska 2018).

Although, it seems to be forgotten that the users' activities, "consisting in the exchange of files, the processing of cultural content online and the use thereof (...) broaden access to culture to an extent previously unknown" (Młynarska-Sobaczewska 2018, p. 158), a great development of social movements focused on reducing the primacy of copyright can be observed. The crusade began in 1998 in the United States, when American law professor L. Lessig failed to tackle the Sonny Bono Copyright Term Extension Act extending the length of copyright protection (see Eldred v. Ashcroft, 537 U.S. 186, 2003). Shortly afterwards, Lessig founded Creative Commons, offering a new formula of copyright protection. He also introduced the conception of free culture, a concept which was later developed in his book of the same name.

Lessig's main goal with the concept of free culture was to accentuate the necessity of taking into account the social need of culture by those who pass copyright laws. His idea gave birth to the free-culture movement, which operates mainly in the United States and is aimed at promoting the freedom of distribution and processing of cultural content by using the possibilities offered by modern media, in particular the internet.

The main thesis of Lessig's book *Free Culture* is that the emergence of the internet led to important, albeit unrecognized, changes in the process of culture creation. Namely, radical change in the effective scope of the law not only produced concentration of power among creative industry corporations, but also it altered the way in which culture is made and consumed. Lessig believes that transformations of the actual scope of copyright law arise from the fact that in distributed, digital networks every use of a copyrighted material produces a copy and hence is subject to copyright. As a result, uses that before were presumptively unregulated are now "presumptively regulated". No longer is there a set of fair uses that define a freedom associated with copyrighted works. Aware of these limitations, the representatives of the content industry were, and still are, trying "to use the law to directly regulate the technology of the Internet so that it better protects their content" (Lessig 2004, p. 193).

All changes described by Lessig in areas such as technology, the creative industry, and the law are the causes of the excessive protection of copyrights that threatens a free culture, as it makes it difficult (and sometimes impossible) for a wide range of creativity to exist legally (Lessig 2008). A free culture, according to Lessig, supports and protects creators. It does this directly (by granting intellectual property rights) and indirectly "by limiting the reach of those rights, to guarantee that follow-on creators and innovators remain as free as possible from the control of the past" (Lessig 2004, p. XIV). Free in this context is understood as "free" in "free speech", "free trade", and "free enterprise". Hence, the idea of free culture is based on a balance between anarchy and control, just as a free market is filled with property rights and contracts protected by the state. The opposite of a free culture is a "permission culture", in which "creators get to create only with the permission of the powerful, or of creators from the past" (Lessig 2004, p. XIV).

Lessig pointed out that "the norm of free culture" has been, until recently and except within totalitarian regimes, quite universal and broadly exploited. Unfortunately, nowadays, in response to a real, if not yet quantified, threat that the internet presents to the twentieth-century business models for producing and distributing culture, the law and technology are being transformed in a way that can undermine the tradition of free culture. Because "the purpose of copyright is to enable the commercial market that spreads culture" (Lessig 2004, p. 227), the restrictive system of copyright regulation poses a threat mostly for non-commercial culture and so-called "read/write" culture (Lessig 2008). Non-commercial culture, including the second (non-commercial) "life" of commercial culture not only makes up most of human creativity, but also is extremely important for the spread and stability of a whole culture. Therefore, it is necessary to enable non-market forces, inter alia, by limiting the excessive influence of market forces, at least to archive non-commercial culture. Free culture, like free markets, depends on vibrant competition, which when suppressed produces an "overregulated culture" (Lessig 2004). A manifestation of the latter is when copyright blocks social activities within the read/write culture (e.g., remix culture), which, unlike the "read/only" culture, encourages active participation in cultural life as well as promotes a more democratic culture (Lessig 2008).

To prevent further restriction of creativity, copyright, according to Lessig, "should regulate culture only where that regulation does good" (2004, p. 305). Copyright law is, after all, a regulation of speech "justified if it produces incentives to create speech that otherwise wouldn't be created" (Lessig 2008, p. 96). With this in mind, it is hard to agree with the situation in which one can talk about free culture only when its "commercial life" has ended and when it has no longer been subject to copyright regulations, which representatives of the creative industry take advantage of. In such a situation, copyright does not serve any purpose related to the dissemination of culture or knowledge about culture. On the contrary, it acts as a curb to the freedoms necessary for cultural production (Lessig 2008).

2.4 Copyright as a Tool of Cultural Policy

Development of positive obligations of the state in terms of the right to culture takes place mainly within the framework of cultural policy (Młynarska-Sobaczewska 2018). Cultural policy, in this context, can be understood as the sum of a government's activities focused on art, cultural heritage and humanities in the sphere of support, promotion, and dissemination of cultural goods (Mulcahy 2006). Strategies applied under such policy include not only legal regulations and the activities of administrative bodies and government agencies in terms of creating and maintaining traditional cultural institutions, but also instruments for supporting artistic creators and facilitating access to culture (Młynarska-Sobaczewska 2018).

The concept of cultural policy stems from the tradition of the patronage of artists, in which it was the sponsor who determined taste and artistic value. In the language of modern politics, the traditional model of patronage can be described as political, in the sense that both funding and the scope of creative freedom depend on the will and intentions of persons and entities holding power (Młynarska-Sobaczewska 2018). Nowadays, basically the same challenges are faced by cultural policy, which has adopted different attitudes towards artistic life. The typology proposed by Chartrand and McCaughey (1989) is one of the most well-known and distinguishes four types of policies, that are differentiated by the application of the criterion that concerns the political influence on a culture and in particular the way of supporting creativity through public funds. These policies are classified by the roles adopted by the state: engineer, patron, facilitator, and architect (Chartrand and McCaughey 1989). Except for the engineer state which is attractive to totalitarian regimes, all models of cultural policy are conducted with declared respect for artistic freedom and the assumption of influence on the content of the culture through the use of aesthetic criteria (Młynarska-Sobaczewska 2018).

The main role of the patron state is to support artistic activity only on the basis of the evaluation of quality and according to the "arm's length principle", which is the principle of allocating funds for artistic activity by expert bodies. The United Kingdom is the best-known example of a patron state. The facilitator state is characteristic of the United States and originates in the principle of state neutrality. It is a system of "cultural Darwinism" that is aimed at diversifying cultural activities only by facilitating their operations and sponsorship by non-govermental actors, mainly through tax exemptions (Młynarska-Sobaczewska 2018). Finally, the architect state supports cultural life "as part of its social welfare objectives" (Chartrand and McCaughey 1989). It also tends to shape the policy of financial support for artistic creation, based on the needs of the community rather than standards of artistic excellence. The latter is the reason why the policy dynamic of the architect tends to be revolutionary (Chartrand and McCaughey 1989).

According to Młynarska-Sobaczewska (2018), the Polish model of financing cultural life is based on the architect system, with the reservation that it is uncertain if such a status can be assigned to it at all, since in Poland it is difficult to identify a cultural policy which is clearly defined and coherent (see, e.g., Głowacki et al. 2009;

Wąsowska-Pawlik 2013). There are two main reasons for this state of affairs. First, the basic structure of Polish cultural activities is constituted by cultural institutions—run by state or local governments—that are not financially independent, which results in their administrative dependence and practical incapacitation. The second factor is the lack of a transparent system for evaluation of the functioning of cultural institutions correlated with their financing. Namely, there are many cases when participation of advisory and expert bodies is rather of a facade character, as it creats only the appearance of a substantive mode of making decisions on cultural issues (Młynarska-Sobaczewska 2018).

Institutional solutions adopted by particular models (as briefly outlined above) reveal fundamental problems that accompany contemporary cultural policy. These problems, above all, concern answering questions as to who is to decide on support for specific artistic actions and whose cultural needs the artists receiving public funding should satisfy (Młynarska-Sobaczewska 2018). The answer to the second question is inextricably related to a fundamental paradox of cultural policy, which according to Młynarska-Sobaczewska (2018) manifests itself as a necessity to subsidize those genres and types of culture that do not perform well in market conditions—those that are not in high demand. What is more, the new model of participation in cultural life—individual, easily accessible and relatively cheap—has made this paradox glaringly visible. Namely, since culture reaches people through the new media, rather than through government subsidies, it is legitimate to say that nowadays the latter supports culture addressed to a small percentage of recipients. As a result, subsidized high culture is that part of culture that people do not want to pay for (Młynarska-Sobaczewska 2018). This paradox is also important from the perspective of those elements of cultural policy which are aimed at improving accessibility to cultural life. Among them are instruments concerning access to cultural infrastructure and protection of cultural assets and cultural heritage, as well as market-accessibility instruments, such as measures eliminating economic barriers to the availability of cultural works (Młynarska-Sobaczewska 2018).

Since, as mentioned earlier, the right to participate in culture remains in a certain conflict with intellectual property law, copyright policy should be treated as a part of cultural policy. As Towse puts it, "copyright, like subsidy, is an instrument of cultural policy" (2001, p. 22). Therefore, "copyright policy should (. . .) be integrated into cultural policy for the sake of the health of the creative industries" (Towse 2001, p. 22). Nevertheless, the extent to which copyright policy can be freely pursued by the state is limited. In case of Polish copyright, the scope of legislative freedom is delimited by both international and European law. The acts of international law set universal standards and define the minimum scope of copyright protection. At the same time, harmonization of copyright rules regarding the scope of rights, their content, and permitted use is carried out at the EU level, mainly through the issuance of directives. However, regardless of the international and European legal framework, the state still can take a great deal of legislative action in the field of copyright policy. Excellent examples of legal regulations in the sphere of copyright which can be treated as manifestations of state cultural policy are regulations imposing levies on blank media and recording or reprographic devices intended as compensation for copying works within permitted personal use, as well as regulations imposing rules on opening public resources.

The Polish Copyright Act provides the so-called "private copying levy" in Article 20. In accordance with this article, producers and importers of blank media (e.g., DVDs and CDs) and devices that enable making copies of copyrighted works (e.g., DVD recorders, photocopiers, scanners) are required to pay fees to collective societies in the amount of no more than 3% of the sale value of such media and devices.[2] Unfortunately, the ongoing ordinance of the Minister of Culture and National Heritage (from 2003), defining particular categories of media and devices for which the fee should be charged, is striking for its anachronism. While a list of carriers and devices attached to the ordinance comprises cassette tapes and VCRs, devices which are nowadays the most popular tools used to access content protected by copyright—such as smartphones, tablets, and laptops—are not included. However, when it comes to opening public resources, a bill on open resources prepared by the Ministry of Administration and Digitization in 2012 is of a special importance. The prepared act was aimed at, inter alia, guaranteeing access to public resources created by employees of public cultural institutions or financed from public funds. Unfortunately, due to the huge opposition from artists and collective societies, it has never been enacted.

In the first part of this chapter, three groups of conceptions were described, in which indications can be found of how the relations between copyright and culture are or could be arranged. Traditional copyright justifications treat culture as a kind of common good that can be multiplied by introducing legal regulations that either motivate artists to create or guarantee that their artistic creation will be protected from distortion. In these approaches, statutory exceptions to copyright protection are also important, as they can ensure members of the public an adequate level of access to culture. The possibility of stimulating processes of cultural production by means of legal regulations is still explained by theories of the relations between copyright and creativity. The necessity of introducing proper limitations to copyright law, due to the need to support cultural development, has been comprehensively presented in the dogma of the right to culture. It was also widely elaborated by Lessig (2004) in his concept of free culture. Finally, cultural policies implemented by particular countries determine the way in which the right to culture—understood as the right to choose cultural identity, to engage in cultural practices, and to become familiar with one's own culture—is guaranteed by the state. All of these theories confirm Cohen's observation that "copyright theory and jurisprudence are powerfully structured by a set of interlinked anxieties about the appropriate tools for understanding

[2] According to Article 20 of Act of 4 February 1994 on Copyright and Related Rights, "Producers and importers of: 1) magnetic tape recorders and players, video recorders and players, and other similar devices, 2) photocopiers, scanners and other similar reprographic devices that enable copying of the whole or part of a copy of a published work; 3) blank media for fixation, for private use, of works or the subject matter of related rights, using the devices listed in subparagraph 1 and 2 — shall be obliged to pay to collecting societies (. . .) fees not exceeding 3 per cent of the amount due on account of sale of those devices and media".

the interactions between copyright and culture. Those anxieties (...) concern the justification for assigning rights, the nature of the progress that copyright is meant to promote, and the mechanics of creative processes" (2007, p. 1154). According to Cohen, each of these anxieties spring from first-order commitments associated with liberal political theory that define "the boundaries of copyright's epistemological universe" (2007, p. 1154). Despite being aware that such a universe excludes many other approaches to investigating and theorizing the copyright–culture relation, Western liberal political philosophy and its vision of copyright is the main frame of reference for the following discourse analysis.

3 Polish Discourse on Copyright

3.1 The Place of Culture in the Polish Public Debate on Copyright

The public discourse on copyright is an excellent example of the social space in which the interdependencies between copyright and culture can be freely observed. In case of Poland, such discourse takes the form of both an institutional discourse (which includes, inter alia, the discourse conducted by social organizations) and a media discourse co-created by journalists. The Polish copyright discourse is also only to a small extent a "discourse of politics", as understood by Czyżewski et al. (1997) as part of the public discourse, including speeches of persons belonging to the power elites, which speeches are related to political roles and functions of these persons. The main reason for this is the high level of complexity and abstraction of copyright law. Namely, notwithstanding the fact that copyright can be a political issue, it still remains a topic that representatives of the Polish establishment tend to ignore. The most important exceptions were the Polish debates on Anti-Counterfeiting Trade Agreement (ACTA) and Directive 2019/790 (called in Poland "ACTA2") when social reaction forced politicians to take a position on copyright regulations. As a result, the Polish copyright discourse is a fragmented discourse with diverse groups of participants. It has also incidental character, in the sense that copyright issues are publicly discussed mainly when there is a debate on a specific legal act or when there is a copyright dispute in which a well-known person is involved.

In the Polish discourse on copyright, it is the representatives of non-governmental organizations that mostly speak about the copyright–culture relation. Therefore, the analysis of copyright discourse described in this chapter, that is aimed at reconstructing the understandings of the relationship between copyright law and culture has been narrowed to the analysis of the press discourse of these organizations.

Within Polish organizations that officially include copyright policy (and copyright education) in the scope of their work, two main groups can be distinguished:

organizations representing the interests of the creative industry (e.g., creators and intermediaries) and organizations representing citizens in general (in particular users of culture). The first group consists mainly of copyright-collecting societies, the Legal Culture Foundation (LC), and Creative Poland (CP), whereas the second group includes above of all the Modern Poland Foundation (MPF), the Digital Centre Foundation (DC), and the Panopticon Foundation.

The largest, most recognizable, and at the same time the most active Polish collecting society is the Polish Society of Authors (known by the Polish acronym ZAiKS). It was founded in 1918 by outstanding Polish artists and its current statutory objectives are, among others and apart from collective rights management, "developing and disseminating Polish artistic creations and culture" and "improving copyright" (ZAiKS 2019, pp. 1–2). In addition, the Polish Society of the Phonographic Industry (known by its Polish acronym ZPAV), mainly due to its anti-piracy campaigns and incidental lobbying in the area of copyright, should be mentioned. It was founded in the early 1990s by representatives of the Polish music industry. On the list of its goals are (apart from "the protection and collective management of the rights of producers of phonograms and music videos") the production and promotion of music of high artistic value, as well as intellectual property education (ZPAV 1991). The LC was established to teach citizens that the way in which cultural goods are used is essential for the condition of culture. According to the foundation's statute, the LC aims act for the common good in terms of "culture, art, protection of cultural goods and national heritage", as well as "limiting the illegal distribution of cultural products and their use with the violation of rights and interests of producers of cultural goods" (Legal Culture 2011). Finally, CP is a typical example of an umbrella organization, as it represents many creative and innovative organizations, including the ZAiKS, ZPAV, and LC. The most important goals of CP are "acting for the development and protection of Polish culture, science, creativity and innovation" and "inspiring and participating in all activities related to the law-making process and decision-making that affects the situation and possibilities of the actions of creators and scientists, as well as the shape of the Polish creative and innovative industry" (Creative Poland 2014).

The MPF was the first Polish non-governmental organization caring about the interests of users of culture that has become interested in copyright. In 2007, J. Lipszyc, who had already taken part in the public debate on copyright, became the president of the foundation. The MPF has adopted as its main goal "promotion and protection of the freedom to use cultural goods" (Modern Poland Foundation 2019), and its flagship projects are "Wolne Lektury", "Prawo Kultury", and the "CopyCamp".[3] Soon after the MPF launched its first project, the DC begun its

[3] "Wolne Lektury" is a free online library that archives books (including school readings) that have already fallen in the public domain; Prawokultury.pl is an educational website that teaches about matters related with the subject of copyright; "CopyCamp" is "an event on law", during which people share their experiences in international and interdisciplinary group of artists, experts, scientists, and social activists and show how law related to copyright is important to everyone.

activity in the field of copyright.[4] For many years the president of the DC was a A. Tarkowski, who, like Lipszyc, is a long-time activist in the area of copyright policy. One of the strategic objectives of the foundation is "adjusting regulations and using legal tools to support the needs and rights of users, as they participate in open circulations of resources online".[5] The foundation is also part of the creative commons movement that supports free culture, works for copyright reform, and promotes universal access to research and education. The last of the listed organizations representing citizens, the Panoptykon, is an organization in which members, despite the foundation not mentioning either copyright or culture on the list of its priorities (as the priorities of the Panopticon Foundation include above of all protecting freedom and human rights in the surveillance society; https://en.panoptykon.org/), have actively participated in Polish public debates concerning ACTA and the "ACTA2".

The analysis of the press discourse on copyright of all the mentioned organizations was based on a corpus comprised of 296 journalistic texts from dailies[6] and weeklies[7] with nationwide coverage from the period of 2000–2019. Within this scope, only texts about copyright that presents the position of at least one of the organizations characterized above were included.[8] In the final corpus of texts, prevail journalistic articles (139), information articles (89), and interviews (30) and articles from external sources (22). There were also a few press releases (8), reports (6), and letters to the editors (2). Because the subject of the analysis was the press discourse of specific organizations, the content analysis covered only those parts of the texts which contains "communiqués" from the organizations' representatives. Among these communiqués were mainly original statements, statements paraphrased by journalists, and information about undertaken activities and initiatives. There were also a few interviews with organization representatives, as well as independent articles written by them. The ZAiKS was the organization that issued (alone or jointly with another organizations) the largest number of communiqués (127) during the analyzed period. Subsequently, the most active participants of the copyright discourse were the ZPAV (73), DC (67), and MPF (50). The LC (25), Panopticon (15), and CP (6) were the organizations that least frequently made public statements on copyright issues in the press. As a consequence, the public narratives concerning the social aspects of copyright law were mostly produced by

---

[4] Although the DC foundation in its present form was founded in 2015, it is a continuation of the "Centrum Cyfrowe Projekt: Polska"—the research institute established five years earlier. The later was one of the first institutions in Poland conducting research on the social aspects of copyright.

[5] Description of the DC mission is available via: https://centrumcyfrowe.pl/en/co-robimy/ [Accessed 7 Oct 2021].

[6] Gazeta Wyborcza (GW), Rzeczpospolita and Dziennik Gazeta Prawa (DGP)—earlier Gazeta Prawna (GP).

[7] Polityka, Wprost, Newsweek and Tygodnik Powszechny (TP).

[8] Some texts presenting statements of Lipszyc and Tarkowski published before they have become the formal leaders of the MPF and DC were also included. These statements are consistent with the later narratives of the MPF and DC.

organizations representing the interests of authors (the ZAiKS) or intermediaries (the ZPAV). Only second to these were the narratives generated by organizations caring for the interests of the users of culture.

The quantitative analysis of all the communiqués shows that the notion of culture appears in the content of 117 (43%)[9] of the communiqués. Every fifth communiqué (59) pertained to culture by using argumentative narratives referring to the general need for supporting culture, including supporting its creators. Nine communiqués presented activities undertaken by organizations focused on creating tools to facilitate the use of culture, six communiqués highlighted the overall positive impact of the organization's initiatives on culture, and four communiqués presented accusations that other organizations acted against culture. Furthermore, 70 communiqués (over 1/4) contain statements whose authors—often unintentionally—raised the issue of the relations between copyright and culture. The attempts to define this relationship were often made with reference to research results (mainly findings from the research carried out by the DC) or while discussing undertaken initiatives. However, much more important, some participants of the discourse characterized the nature of the copyright–culture relation directly by referring to the theoretical concepts outlined in the first part of the chapter. Namely, ten communiqués mentioned the right to culture, nine communiqués described various types of copyright restrictions on culture, and eight communiqués evoked the idea of free culture.

Within the discourse of social organizations operating in the field of copyright, the concept of culture was mostly defined in a broad way, departing from a narrow understanding of culture typical of legal approaches. Examples of the broad understanding of culture were found mainly in the statements of representatives of the MPF: "We legalize any non-commercial use of culture, whether it is uploading a profile photo on Nasza-klasa[10] or a song on Facebook" (GW 2009).[11] Such examples were also found in statements of the DC:

> This is a serious step towards culture 2.0 (. . .). [I]t's not just that culture uses modern technologies. It is more about that, thanks to them, participation in culture is expanded. The focus is shifting from professionals to the so-called amateurs (GW 2010).

Nevertheless, this was not the main distinguishing feature of the definitions of culture used by the discourse participants. It was the fact that these definitions took into account the legal status of practices that make up the culture. Namely, while the founder of the LC understood culture "as reciprocity, the art of giving and taking on mutually agreed terms" (GW 2012), the leaders of the DC and MPF thought that practices considered as unethical, and sometimes even as illegal, also deserve to be included. For example, the DC stated the following: "Some of these practices are definitely illegal (. . .) We are not talking about pirates and thieves, because we do

[9]Proper nouns containing the word "culture", such as the Legal Culture or the Ministry of Culture and National Heritage were excluded.

[10]Nasza-klasa is a Polish school-based social networking service founded in 2006.

[11]Fragments of journalistic texts are described by acronym or the full name of the newspapers and the date of the release.

not want to stigmatize anyone, but to show how Poles use cultural goods" (Rzeczpospolita 2012). Similar statement appeared in MPF's communiqué one year later: "[Piracy] is a negative expression that suggests that someone has robbed. It condemns people who simply want to actively participate in the cultural circuit" (DGP 2013). What is more, according to the co-founder of the DC, the illegal nature of activities undertaken by both creators and users may have a positive impact on the culture: "Illegality encourages culture; artists like actions [that are] on the edge of the law. But they rarely think that the vitality of culture depends on sharing" (Rzeczpospolita 2010). As another represented of DC observed: "The respondents [from research conducted by the DC] de facto violate copyright, but they cannot be treated directly as criminals (. . .) because they are helping to spread the culture. They should be compared to non-profit institutions that realize a public mission" (DGP 2013).

Building arguments on the basis of the general need for supporting culture (i.e., the most common way of referring to culture in the analyzed discourse) was typical of the narrative of the DC, MPF, and LC. Arguments invoking the need to support culture were found only in a few communiqués from the ZAiKS and ZPAV. There was also one such argument in CP's statements, and there were no such arguments in the statements of the Panopticon. The CP referred to the market more often than to culture. The Panopticon focused mainly on the need to protect freedom of speech and the right to privacy in the online sphere.

The arguments referring to the general need for supporting culture used by representatives of particular organizations took different forms. Some of them consisted in simply reminding one about the role and importance of culture. For example the ZAiKS made the following statement: "in times when there is no understanding of the culture, we must strive for it more" (Polityka 2019), whereas the DC argued that "by focusing on the protection of intellectual property, we lose sight of such important values as creativity and vivid, unhampered culture" (GW 2008). Moreover, arguments invoking the need to support culture appeared in the course of debates concerning the assumptions or changes in the copyright system. Within these debates, such arguments took the form of a diagnosis, a description of the desired state, a proposition of general or specific solutions to the perceived problems, and an indication of potential risks; all in the relations between law and culture. There were also cases of referring to the need to protect or support culture during discussions of specific legal regulations.

The general diagnosis for the ongoing copyright system in the context of its impact on culture, presenting the desired state in this regard, as well as accentuating risks posed by excessive copyright regulation were discursive activities typical of the MPF and DC. Excellent examples of arguments in the form of the diagnosis are the following statements of the DC: "Copyright in its current, restrictive shape is not always conducive to the use of cultural goods" (GW 2008) and, "The ongoing [copyright] system was created as a regulation of analog technologies (. . .). Digital technologies have opened the gateway to culture and now there are many new ways of communication" (Rzeczpospolita 2010). The desired state was presented inter alia in the following argumentation of the MPF: "Maintaining the public domain, the sphere of non-commercial exchange of cultural goods, is in the vital interest of society" (GW 2005). Finally, accentuation of the risks posed by excessive copyright regulation can be found in the following statement of the DC: "Increased control will cause that network culture which is rich today to soon resemble the relatively monotonous programmes of television stations" (GW 2008). Similar focus on potential risks caused by copyright regime was observed in many communiqués of MPF: "The policy of tightening copyright law does not work for the benefit of society and creators: the more restrictions, the smaller the space for participants in cultural life" (GW 2011). Both the MPF and DC used all mentioned arguments to underline the excessively restrictive nature of the current copyright regime, as well as to present possible scenarios for further development of the situation.

When it comes to general and specific proposals to help solve the problems regarding the tense relation between copyright and culture, they were put forward by the LC, MFP and DC. Propositions of general changes in the copyright system concerned such issues as restoring balance ("The balance between the rights of different users of culture should be restored" [GW 2006]), changing the practices of the users of culture ("Legal sources will arise only when the recipients of culture will use them. By using legal sources, you support culture!" [GW 2013]), or de-penalizing activities related to the creation and distribution of cultural goods ("In our opinion (. . .) it is important to consider, whether the law does not artificially restrict some forms of creation or distribution that could be legalized without harm, and even for general profit" [Rzeczpospolita 2013]). However, the most frequently mentioned examples of specific solutions were creating an alternative to the existing copyright system and shortening the duration of copyrights. Presenting the alternatives was typical of the DC:

> Creative commons is a model of open licensing (. . .) This type of license creates an alternative model within the copyright system (. . .) The copyright system regulated by the act, in many cases, does not serve either creators or recipients well, as it excessively limits further artistic creation and the use of cultural goods (DGP 2007).

The MPF most often propose shortening copyrights: "The duration of the copyright monopoly, which is currently 70 years after the author's death, should be changed (. . .). It is an absurdity that has no economic justification and has negative consequences for culture" (DGP 2013).

Regardless of the form adopted, some of the narratives referring to the important role of culture fall within the scope of broader debates on specific legal acts. The largest number of such narratives appeared in the course of the debate on a bill on open resources that took place during the period of 2013–2014. The main participants and, at the same time, opponents in this debate—the DC and ZAiKS—were referring to the imperative of protecting and supporting culture in different ways. The DC perceive the open public resources act as an opportunity to increase access to culture:

> Why should we do this? First, in order to equalize the chances of access to culture (. . .) There is still a shortage of legally available and high-quality content in Poland. This gap may be filled by open public resources (DGP 2013).

At the same time, the director of the ZAiKS was afraid of the opposite:

> Until 1989, contract templates were required in all areas of creative activity. For example, cinematographic activity was regulated by 44 executive acts issued by ministers, the Cinematography Committee, and the Council of Ministers. Returning to the idea of regulating contracts and making culture available through acts of the Council of Ministers, contract templates (...) sends chills down your spine (GW 2013).

Moreover, the impact of copyright regulations on the condition or availability of Polish culture was indicated by representatives of the MPF and DC in the discussion about the amendment to the Polish Copyright Act adopted in 2015 that implemented the provisions of the EU directives.[12] As part of this discussion a representative of the MPF made the following statement:

> Let's try to talk openly not about copyright but about the public financing of cultural production; an important effect of the amendment may be the transfer of some part of the budget that has so far paid for making culture available to the authors selected by officials (...) and to people organized in the institutional system of collective management organizations (Rzeczpospolita 2014).

Later, during the same debate the DC stated: "We do not understand why institutions such as museums or libraries (...) will not be allowed to use fair use. We are not using the potential provided by the EU directive" (DGP 2015).

At the same time, authorities from the ZAiKS referred to the important role of culture in the course of a long-lasting dispute concerning the private copying levy:[13] "According to the Polish Copyright Law, importers and producers of electronic devices should pay up to 3% of their value for culture" (Polityka 2015). Whereas the ZPAV's representatives were focusing on the need to protect culture during the discussion on Directive 2019/790:

> The decision that will be made (...) in the European Parliament will be crucial for the development and future of Poland and Europe, because the future of the next creative generations will depend on it. Our culture is our identity, our uniqueness, but for it to develop and survive, it must be supported, and creators must be fairly remunerated in the online sphere (DGP 2018).

---

[12] Amendment Act of 11 September 2015 amending Act on Copyright and Related Rights and Gambling Act (Dz.U. 2015 item 1639). The aim of this amendment was to, inter alia, implement the Directive 2006/115/EC (the Directive on rental right and lending right) and the Directive 2012/28/EU (the Directive on certain permitted uses of orphan works).

[13] A long-standing dispute between the ZAiKS and ZIPSEE (Association of Importers and Producers of Electrical and Electronic Equipment—ZIPSEE "Digital Poland") about the ordinance of the Minister of Culture and National Heritage defining particular categories of blank media and devices that enable making copies of copy-righted works for which the fee should be charged from producers and importers of these media and devices. The ZAiKS has demanded amendment of the ordinance and believed that the ZIPSSE is responsible for the fact that amendment has not been enacted until today. At the same time, the ZIPSSEE was argued that the costs of new levies will be borne primarily by ordinary users, as well as it was pointing to the lack of competence of the ZAiKS.

Finally, among the narratives referring to the general need of supporting culture that are worth mentioning, there is also the "The Law of Culture" campaign launched in 2012 by the MPF:

> The campaign called "The Law of Culture" was organized by the Modern Poland Foundation (...) The Foundation (...) informs [people] that it is allowed to download movies from the internet, copy books or share music. In Warsaw's underground, speech bubbles like those from comic books were stuck to the windows, and in them you can read "I have the right to download films", "I have the right to copy books" and "I have the right to share music". Under each slogan, a reference to the website www.prawokultury.pl. Those who visit this page will find the legal basis for these slogans (GW 2012).

Especially, the reaction of the director of the ZPAV to this campaign, described in Gazeta Wyborcza's article, needs special attention:

> It's like showing people how to steal in supermarkets (...) It is acting to the detriment of artists and, more generally, to the detriment of culture. In a legal sense everything is fine, but it is undoubtedly robbing from artists and—I repeat—acting to the detriment of culture (GW 2012).

The quoted excerpts show another key difference in the definitions of culture by organizations representing users and organizations representing creators, which is that the latter quite often identified culture with its creators. The obvious reason of using such an understanding of culture was to emphasize the importance of creators' interests.

In the copyright discourse of non-governmental organizations, the assumption of the special importance of culture can be observed not only in the arguments that were used. Namely, representatives of particular organizations—especially representatives of the ZAiKS—had a habit of bragging about their own contributions to culture. For example, one of the ZAiKS' representatives stated: "I am not prone to bombast, but I believe that Polish culture would be much worse without ZAiKS" (TP 2016), while according to the other: "If not for ZAIKS's money, society would be deprived of a significant part of the Polish culture" (GW 2016). The ZAiKS was also pointing out how other organizations act to the detriment of culture:

> For many years, ZIPSEE has preferred to do everything so that the next Minister of Culture issues an appropriate ordinance as late as possible, because as long as it is not issued (...), the enemies of Polish culture think that they do not have to pay any fees (Polityka 2015).

In the case of the ZAiKS, the following was a typical way of expressing dissatisfaction with the actions undertaken by other organizations: "ZAiKS has one answer to everything: broadcasters avoid paying royalties – the national culture suffers and the creative milieus are getting poorer" (Wprost 2000). This was especially visible in the ZAiKS's comment on the report on Polish copyright collecting societies and their financial data, published by the DC in 2015 (Strycharz et al. 2015):

> The report proves the incompetence of authors in the matter of collective management in Poland and around the world. (...) What is the purpose of such action? Perhaps nothing more than weakening of the position of the creators. This report works against the national culture (GW 2015).

Moreover, in line with what has already been mentioned, in the narratives created by Polish non-governmental organisations, one could find direct references to two theoretical conceptions described in the first part of the chapter, that is, to the right to culture and free culture. The right to culture, understood as a "right to access culture", was even one of the flagship postulates proclaimed by the initiators of the social movement called by one journalist "the spring of internet users":

> Defense of freedom on the internet, the right to privacy and the right to access to culture, entertainment, science and information on the internet: these are the slogans of the strongest global social movement since the times of the hippie contestation (DGP 2013).

In particular by Lipszyc stated that: "The authors' right to remuneration and the recipients' right to access to culture are at stake" (GW 2005). Interestingly, the MFP's president, having recalled the right to culture, not only indicated its legal sources: "Index 73 is named after the number of an article in the Polish constitution (. . .) The freedom to use cultural goods is also a human right enshrined in the Universal Declaration"[14] (GW 2008). He also distinguished two of its most important components. The first is the right to access culture: "Adding restrictions will be ineffective at best. At worst, it will cause enormous losses to culture (. . .) and make the constitutional right of access to cultural goods a literary fiction" (GW 2006). The second is the right to participate in culture: "The right to participate in culture, modify it and make it available to other people. Besides, the 'freedom to use cultural goods' is enshrined in the constitution" (GW 2007). The latter was understood by Lipszyc in a quite broad way, taking into account the freedom to process and share cultural property, hence without including copyright reservations. It is also worth pointing out that the MPF was most often referring to the right to culture in the context of its actual or potential non-compliance. Single references to the right of access to culture appeared in the statements of the DC.

References to the idea of free culture appeared in the communiqués of almost all organizations and had quite different characteristics. In the cases of the MPF and DC, such references took the form of either simply recalling pivotal work of the concept's initiator or showing specific examples of its implementation. The following statements exemplify the latter: "We cooperate with cultural, scientific and educational institutions. The most important ones are implementing free culture" (Rzeczpospolita 2010) and, "We are just launching the 'Free textbooks' project in Poland (. . .) Teachers are jointly creating textbooks that are then available to anyone, anywhere, at any time" (GW 2007). At the same time, the representatives of collecting societies—mainly the ZPAV—treated free culture as a symbol of the assumptions and values shared by organizations striving to liberalize copyright, to which collective societies have a negative attitude:

---

[14] "Index 73" is a nationwide initiative that aims to defend the freedom of artistic creation and scientific research, and the free access to cultural goods guaranteed in the Article 73 of the Polish Constitution. Official website of the initiative is available via: http://indeks73.blogspot.com/ [Accessed 7 Oct 2021].

> For the money they earn, concerns promote new artists and new media. Thus, I do not agree that, in the name of free culture, anyone should be deprived of the possibility of deciding what in his or her work is his or her property and what is not (GW 2008).

Additionally, statements of the ZAiKS and LC's representatives regarding the issue of "free access to culture" may be treated as examples of references to the idea of free culture. The ZAiKS' representative argued the following: "Free access to culture—please, as widely as possible. But not at the expense of those who made it. Let's use a 6,000-year-old directive. The seventh directive: do not steal" (Newsweek 2012). While according to the LC "Freedom regained 25 years ago also includes free access to culture, which to a large extent has previously functioned in the 'second circulation'" (GW 2014). Although both organizations were trying to negate the concept of free culture, only the LC did it by proposing an alternative understanding by referring to the historical context. Furthermore, it is also worth mentioning that some participants of the Polish copyright discourse equated free culture with the so-called "openism",[15] which was manifested in interchangeable use of terms such as "open culture" and "free culture" or "freedomists" (Polish term "wolnościowcy") and "openists". Such tendency can be observed in the following statement of one of the Polish lawyers: "Freedomists, with the publicist Jarosław Lipszyc at the helm, refer to the argument of the open culture of the internet and call for the legalization of downloading" (Polityka 2006).[16]

Finally, it should be noted that in the Polish copyright discourse, the complex character of the copyright–culture relation found its best reflection in narratives about piracy. Piracy, which is not a legal term, is understood by the authors of these narratives as either making profits from the illegal distribution of someone else's work or using someone else's work without the consent of the author (or producer or publisher), which also includes not paying the remuneration. In the case of using the first definition, the legal status of piracy was quite clear, and its stigmatization did not raise many objections among the discourse participants. The situation was completely different when, within the piracy concept, the sharing of cultural works by internet users was also included. What is more, according to Lipszyc, such a broad approach to the phenomenon of piracy may have a negative impact on culture:

> Piracy has (...) two dimensions. The first is the obvious one, when someone creates a business model on the basis of the deliberative violation of the law (...). [T]he second—

[15] In Poland the term "openists" ("otwartyści") was used to name the supporters of the bill on open resources from 2012. The concept of "openism" ("otwartyzm") can also be associated with such movements and initiatives as: open source movement, open access, open data movement or open innovation. The DC, one of the greatest proponents of open resources in Poland, treats "openness" as a value and understands it as "openness to the recipient and people with specific needs; as a technological and legal openness of products and resources that enables the free sharing of knowledge; as openness to changes and readiness to adapt to new circumstances, as well as promoting free and open software" (https://centrumcyfrowe.pl/obszary_dzialan/otwarta-kultura/, Accessed 7 Oct 2021).

[16] This is a fragment of the press article "Więzienie za ściąganie" by Ł. Ptak, which was not included in the corpus of journalistic texts.

> when mass violations of the existing law arise not from the desire for profit, but from the normal activities in the field of culture (GW 2006).

> Fair use (. . .) is quite narrow in the era of internet. When it comes to simple communication with others, e.g. uploading a photo of a kitten on a blog, the [copyright] system should be more flexible. The basic problem is that two phenomena are not properly separated – infringement of exclusive rights in order to obtain a profit, that must be punished with severity, and infringements by ordinary users who simply share cultural goods (Rzeczpospolita 2014).

The importance of the problem highlighted by the president of the MPF can be seen with full clarity in the public debate surrounding the report "The Circulations of Culture: On the Social Distribution of Content" prepared by the DC (Filiciak et al. 2012). Its publication took place, according to M. Kuźmiński, "just in time: on January 25 [2012], when demonstrations against ACTA were taking place in Polish cities. The research concerns access to cultural goods, one of the most important slogans on protesters' banners" (TP 2012).[17] What is more, this report for the opponents of ACTA became "a kind of manifesto, because it undermined the opinion that downloading illegal content from the internet is harmful to the culture" (GW 2012).[18] The premise of this "undermining" was one of the main theses of the report, according to which people who take part in the so-called "informal circuits of culture" are its most active participants. The thesis was mentioned in many press articles, some of them written by the authors of the report:

> Our report shows that participation in the informal circulation does not entirely exclude buying cultural goods. On the contrary, (. . .) one in three buyers of books and films, and one in two customers of the music industry are people who download free content (. . .) such people are culturally very active, especially when compared to the rest of Poles (GW 2012).

> The old order cannot be fitted into the internet. For people who feel robbed, I would recommend reading the report "The Circulations of Culture" (. . .) The report shows that consumers who go to concerts, buy T-shirts, etc., are mostly those who download music from the internet (GW 2012).

However, it is not the scope of the media reception of the report that is most interesting, but the numerous attempts to discredit its results. An excellent example of such attempts can be observed in the following press statement: "Unfortunately, I do not share Filiciak and Tarkowski's optimistic faith in human truthfulness, so I treat the conclusions of this report with great skepticism" (GW 2012).[19] The quoted excerpt clearly shows how difficult it is to make any attempts to determine the impact of copyright on culture. Moreover, the difficulties result not only from different visions of culture and associated values, but, as will be shown later in the article, also from the conflicting interests of participants in the exchange of cultural goods.

---

[17] This is a fragment of the press article "Szybcy i wolni" by M. Kuźmiński, which was not included in the corpus of journalistic texts.

[18] This is a fragment of the press article, "Ściągamy, ale niekoniecznie kupujemy" by E. Błaszczak, which was not included in the corpus of journalistic texts.

[19] This is a fragment of the press article "Ściągamy, ale niekoniecznie kupujemy" by W. Orliński, which was not included in the corpus of journalistic texts.

3.2 *The Relation Between Copyright and Culture in the Opinion of Practitioners*

The statements of people who come into contact with copyright law on a daily basis can also contribute to the efforts of understanding the interrelation between copyright and culture. Therefore, the results of the qualitative analysis of 27 individual, in-depth interviews are presented here. The interviews were conducted with Polish lawyers specializing in copyright, intermediaries (Polish book publishers and Polish music producers), and representatives of non-governmental organizations characterized earlier (except for the Panopticon Foundation, whose representatives refused to participate in the interview). All interviews were conducted in the period of 2019–2020 in three large Polish cities (Warsaw, Cracow, and Łódź). In this chapter, only the interview results concerning the relations between copyright and culture have been taken into consideration.

Although lawyers themselves have doubts if copyright is a tool of cultural policy—as one lawyer stated: "If (. . .) copyright is to be a tool for cultural policy, then somewhere on the margins" (L1),[20]—the representatives of social organizations think that copyright plays an even more important role, as it is "a key cultural institution – as important as libraries or museums" (Rzeczpospolita 2010). According to a representative of the MPF, one of the reasons why the rules for creating and sharing cultural goods should be the subject of Polish public policy is the need to protect Polish culture from market forces and from the domination of foreign cultures:

> If we leave the culture-forming sphere exclusively to the market, it will have an impact on the shape of culture (. . .). [I]f we have strong public patronage, (. . .) we will have an influence on the culture area (. . .) Public patronage is currently one of the few tools of society that somehow defends the culture area (. . .) in the situation in which (. . .) we are dealing with a very strong phenomenon of cultural imperialism (MPF).

However, as the interviews with intermediaries have shown, this and others postulates put forward not only by the MPF but also by other organizations seeking to liberalize copyright are not positively assessed by intermediaries. The main reason is the lack of funds:

> This is ultimately a financial problem, when we publish a book, this money must bring profit (. . .) There are some branding projects where they could be in a public domain, in public access, but such activity of a commercial publisher is purely charitable (. . .) I don't know who would finance it (BP1).

Both book publishers and music producers believe that, without adequate financial resources, there will be no culture, at least not one that professional intermediaries can provide:

[20] Statements of particular lawyers were marked as L1, L2,. . . L11; statements of book publishers as BP1, ..., BP6; and statements of music producers as MP1,. . ., MP6.

> The publisher (. . .) feels a great responsibility to provide the reader with the highest quality and sees the same in other people—demands from them and pays them proportionally to how they work for him, what content they generate. This is why paying for culture is so important (BP3).

> Going in the direction of open domains, releasing without rights, without publishing houses, will end up in being flooded with crap literature (. . .) I would be against (. . .) opening licenses and open texts in general, because in a moment no one will control it (BP4).

Of course, this does not mean that publishers and producers completely reject the idea of making cultural goods widely available, as supported by "freedomists". They usually disagree only with promoting those forms of use of copyrighted works that are free of charge:

> They say that art should be widely available and everything should be widely available on the internet, because it is important for human development. I believe that it should be widely available, but this does not mean that it should be free of charge (MP1).

> Cultural products are not property that can be used without renumeration, those are such difficult questions and actually a difficult discussion, because (. . .) one would like this culture to be as accessible as possible and that as many people as possible could use it (BP2).

Much greater difficulties in reacting to the postulates put forward by adherents of free culture or by "openists" are encountered by organizations representing the interests of artists and organizations representing entities that monetize artists' work. Some of their statements even indicate their inability to reconcile conflicting interests:

> There is an ethical dissonance that, on the one hand, we treat the culture and clearly the artists' creations as extremely important, identity-related (. . .) [and on the other hand] how not to create regulations that constitute a barrier against such greedy appropriation of rights, striving to be entitled. An artist has created something and I will be entitled to manage his work (ZAiKS).[21]

> It feels stupid to forbid a man to use cultural goods (. . .). On the other hand (. . .) our state as well as any other state does not secure culture or the creators in such a way that it could become the common good of all of us (. . .). In my opinion, it will never work (LC).

The only exception was the ZPAV representative, who thinks that copyright is a sufficient guarantee of the freedom and independence needed in the creative process:

> It used to be "lord's grace", namely generally some patron of the arts was taking and paying. Generally speaking, I think that a much better form is that their rights are protected, and they get money for it (. . .). The creator needs to be independent and free (. . .) regardless of the creator's views (. . .). It matters whether he makes good or bad art, and copyright ensures that (ZPAV).

As shown in the latter part of the chapter, such a vision of copyright policy and related cultural policy is also shared by some lawyers.

---

[21] In case of ZAiKS, this reaction is especially significant if we take into account the arguments referring to culture that were used by representatives of this organization in the press discourse.

The reasons for the lack of a common denominator between intermediaries (and organizations representing them) and organizations caring for the interests of users of culture can be found in the definition of culture. Namely, according to representatives of organizations such as the MPF or DC, every manifestation of interpersonal interactions can be treated as culture: "I believe that [culture] is a continuum. I believe that high culture is some kind of extension of completely basic communication (...), an extension of the sum of all conversations we have" (MPF). At the same time, many producers and publishers, when asked about the need to support culture by creating appropriate copyright regulations, quite often point out that it is important to ensure adequate access only to the high culture:

> They say that (...) everything on the internet should be widely available, because it is important for human development (...). I say (...) tell me what impact on human development has a hit had like "bum-bum, fa-la-la" that sells well ? There is none, because it is stupid as a shoe. It is good to bow to such music (MP1).

> [Book publishing] becomes an ordinary trade and nowadays there are no good ideas on how to do it commercially, to support publishers in publishing, in investing in higher literature, more culture-forming, one that has a deeper contribution to culture, to the social fabric (BP1).

Thus, cases of perceiving culture as more "democratic" are only occasionally found among intermediaries:

> [Copyright] serves [us] primarily because we have a culture (...) because we become authors, we become creators, we become performers in various situations. When we are not necessarily doing it professionally (...) the digital world enables us (...) to become editors of our portals, have (...) fan pages, of which there are millions at the moment (...), and this law will enable us to stop others from copying (MP2).

Defining culture in a narrow way, when considering cultural goods that should be made available to society (e.g., by providing exceptions within the copyright system), is also typical for copyright lawyers:

> We have to ask ourselves a question (...) about this "culture-genic", culture-forming role, which we are talking about. Whether we are talking [about] turning on the TV, watching something means that someone is using culture or not? When someone goes to the museum, he or she is probably using it [culture]; it is more associated [with culture] (L2).

Interestingly, these lawyers have adopted a narrow definition of culture also in the scope of works that should be protected by copyright law: "Copyright should be an instrument that protects new cultural values, so if an object has no cultural value, it shouldn't be protected by copyright" (L5).

The second reason why intermediaries and organizations representing citizens have a different view on the optimal relation between copyright and culture is that they have a different vision of how the development of culture should be supported. Most intermediaries, especially publishers, are aware of the negative impact of market mechanisms on the works that they publish: "Such capitalist-consumerist commodification makes it very difficult to think of a book not as a consumable commodity, a good that we trade" (BP1); "The market is not some god who decides what is good and what is bad; indeed, many of our books – it is a pity to say, very good ones – have been underestimated by the market" (BP3). Nevertheless, they still want to publish and disseminate works that are or may be of great importance for the culture. Namely, some of intermediaries allocate a certain part of their profits to the publication of works that are less popular but are valued by art experts or by the intermediaries themselves:

> Occasionally, we publish books for "the honor of the house" (...), I think that we should stick to this disproportion, because (...) this is a company, this is a corporation that must survive (...). I would only condemn such publishing houses that, despite the money they earn, do not publish things for "the honor of the house", i.e. books that we know will bring us losses, but we have a sense of mission (BP4).

At the same time, others are making sure that the content they produce is of high quality: "We just have to take care of qualitative content, which gives our nations an identity that we value" (MP2). In both cases, the basis of the strategy adopted by intermediaries is the assumption that more attention should be paid to quality than to the quantity of copyrighted works. This assumption is different from the general premise underlying the postulates of "freedomists" and "openists", according to which the quantity and variety of goods in the circulation of culture is the most important. Such premise can be found in the following press statements of the MPF and DC: "The creative commons movement with which I am associated is looking for solutions that would enable creators to make money and share their works as widely as possible – films, music files" (GW 2008); "Ultimately, a teacher should have a huge amount of commercial-free and free-of-charge educational content to choose from" (Wprost 2014).

With reference to various approaches to the relationship between copyright and culture resulting from different ways of defining culture, it is also worth noting that producers of the music that, according to some, has no or not much cultural values more often point to the influence of copyright on creative processes. The following statements of DJs who are also music producers are good examples of such an observation: "It should be possible to work with this material; this is the flexibility of the law and adaptation to the conditions in which someone wants to use this material" (PM3), and "Copyright law is closely related to economic rights, which is the subject of much speculation in the music industry" (PM5).

Because both intermediaries and organizations representing users of culture are, due to the nature of their activities, biased when it comes to their opinions about the relations between copyright and culture, special importance should be attached to lawyers. Namely, granted that at least some lawyers are able to go beyond the interests of their clients, as well as trusting in the ethos held by academic lawyers, it can be assumed that it is lawyers who will look at the issue of the interaction between copyright and culture in the most objective way. The manifestation of the latter can take the form of "dissentient" opinion, an example of which is an untypical reaction of one of the copyright professors. This professor, when asked how copyright law affects culture, indicated that it is impossible to answer such a question: "We do not know what it would be like when this copyright protection was absent, i.e. to what extent it would have resulted in a lower development of creativity" (L6). What is more, the doubt raised by him concerned the fundamental assumption of the utilitarian justification of copyright discussed in first part of the chapter. In line with this premise, copyright contributes to the overall well-being of society by motivating authors to create. However, according to the mentioned professor: "It is believed that [copyright] also serves the society, because by introducing copyright protections somehow creativity is stimulated. Whether the latter is true is a moot point" (L6). Inferring from the statements of other lawyers, such a premise is quite often unquestioned: "In this respect, copyright plays a culture-forming role, as the exclusivity given to a record producer, a film producer, or an author makes people more willing to undertake creative efforts" (L7). It is even used as a tool to criticize the ideas of free and open culture:

> Copyright law makes it profitable to be an artist—or at least it should be—and that creators receive some kind of remuneration for it, and in fact from this perspective, copyright is an important catalyst for filling open resources or open culture (L3).

It is the ideas of free and open culture—promoted by some Polish organizations—as well as the belief that copyright hampers cultural development on which these views are based that the Polish lawyers are most opposed to:

> It is a big simplification to say that this is freedom, an exchange of thoughts, [that] it will benefit all of us (. . .). I am sure that it will not (. . .). I would warn against such enchantment that if we free everything here, we will have real freedom (L4).

What is interesting is that one of the main reasons why lawyers are cautious about implementing these kinds of ideas is the need to use state resources:

> This is a very short-sighted, surely beautiful slogan "free culture" (. . .). Only if we introduce such a mechanism, without reflection, we have a problem. Of course, if we have 100% of public funds, in my opinion, it is not such a stupid idea (. . .). The question is whether it is a good idea for the state to finance 100% of films or literature (L3).

Namely, the copyright lawyers believe the use of public subsidies can cause getting involved in political issues:

> A very important feature of the cultural market, which is pluralism, is guaranteed when the creator can profit from his work without having to rely on subsidies, i.e., if I read a title [that is] subsidized, (. . .) I obviously know that it is a matter of some political will (L7).

Both publishers and music producers agree with this observation: "We use subsidies from the ministry of culture (. . .) There has always been a problem that these funds are being given away a bit with some political interpretation" (BP1); "I know that all countries do not like those to whom they do not subsidize (. . .), but the issue is that the creator needs to be independent and free" (MP1).

Another reason for the lack of acceptance and sometimes a lack of understanding of the slogans proclaimed by organizations such as the MPF and DC is the lawyers' opinion that the main task of copyright is to regulate the economic exchange of cultural goods: "Copyright law should regulate relations between groups of entities participating in the exchange (. . .) of cultural goods" (L1). The fact that copyright has such a function excludes—according to some lawyers—its "social involvement": "People very often think that copyrights or other similar rights protecting intellectual property have more of a social basis (. . .), but no, they serve the author to make profit off of it" (L8).

However, the opponents of free and open culture are not the dominant group among the interviewed lawyers. They are dominated by those convinced of the need to strive for a balance between the rights and interests of authors, intermediaries, and users. Some of them refer to the so-called "copyright equilibrium" by recalling the initial copyright's assumptions:

> If we go back to the 19th century to the development (. . .) of theories of the protection of intangible goods, they first of all came from the assumption that temporary exclusivity is the incentive to create in the future, and then it [creation] enters the domain and everyone can use it and that it is some system of balance between the interests of creators and the interests of society (L8).

At the same time, others treat it as a necessary premise of the modern system:

> It is necessary to consider all aspects to balance it somewhere – on the one hand access, which is obviously necessary, if only because there is no work without an audience, but on the other hand taking into account the needs and interests and importance of these entities acting as intermediaries in the process of distribution of this creation (L4).

These group of lawyers also make different evaluations of the extent to which such balance is achieved: "[there] is some kind of balance, on the one hand, [of] the author's right to his work (. . .) [and,] on the other hand, providing access to artistic creativity" (L10), "Protection seems excessive in some spheres, that if it were less intense, then (. . .) it would not unduly restrict the rights to, let's call it, access to culture" (L6).

Nevertheless, regardless of the indicated genesis of the equilibrium and the evaluation of its implementation, it is clearly visible that the lawyers lack specific ideas on how to balance interests within the copyright system. The exception was the proposal of a lawyer working for one of the non-governmental organizations, which consisted of a de-commercialization of at least part of the exchange of cultural goods. According to him: "If we introduced such a distinction, distinctly cutting the field of non-monetary, non-commercial economy in the trade of culture and clearly legalized it, it would be a move towards a greater balance in copyright" (L11). Bearing in mind the attitude of both intermediaries and lawyers to reducing market mechanisms by those who produce culture, one can have doubts as to the feasibility of such concept in the Polish creative industry.

4 Conclusions

The analysis of the empirical data presented in the second part of the chapter enables one to draw at least several important conclusions regarding the interrelations between copyright and culture—in particular, the relation between Polish copyright law and Polish cultural practices. Only two of these conclusions are discussed at length below. According to the first one, the way in which culture is defined and valued is the most important factor determining the perception of the copyright–culture relationship. On the basis of this criterion, two main groups of entities can be distinguished that also differ in terms of adopting particular types of copyright justifications, including assumptions about the degree to which copyright should be limited due to the cultural needs of the society. The first group includes lawyers and intermediaries, while the second group consists of organizations promoting free and open culture. Organizations whose main goal is to protect the interests of authors and intermediaries, depending on the context, may be classified either in the first or in the second group. The context is primarily the copyright discourse described in this chapter. Within this discourse, organizations representing entities managing copyright, due to the discursive strategy they have adopted, focused largely on building counter-narratives to the narratives presented by "freedomists" and "openists", or at least this was the case during the examined period.

Lawyers and most intermediaries, including first of all book publishers, when speaking of culture, most often refer to high culture (sometimes also the national culture). In their opinion, high culture is a unique good that deserves special treatment, either by making economically unjustified publishing decisions or by taking into account the social interest related with this type of culture in the law-making process. These opinions are made with the reservation that this special treatment should consist as little as possible in financing culture from public funds, because publicly subsidized culture is exposed to being dependent on the current political mood. All of these assumptions are consistent with the utilitarian approach to copyright adopted by this group, which in the case of lawyers usually takes the form of an economic rationale for copyright.

At the opposite extreme is the group of organizations representing the interests of users and promoting free and open culture. Members of this group define culture in a broad way, taking into account, among others issues, popular, global, and amateur culture. Since these types of culture are consumed by a large number of citizens, the main task of cultural policy—according to these organizations—should be striving to enact copyright laws that would allow the greatest possible access to culture. Such a postulate is compatible with the overriding aim of copyright, which, in the view of this group, is to seek to increase the pool of cultural goods available to the public. Organizations representing users of culture also believe that copyright should refrain from making regulations that could in any way inhibit people's creativity.

Finally, organizations representing authors and intermediaries—that is, the group that has the least consistent approach to the relationship between copyright and culture—is distinguished mainly by the fact that they identify culture (including national culture) with the artists who create it. The adoption of such an assumption allowed the members of these organizations to reconcile the postulate of caring for culture's development with making culture's accessibility dependent on users respecting authors' rights. Focusing on the latter in case of some copyright societies entailed references to deontological justifications of copyright in the context of the right to culture. Such references also appeared among the statements of publishers and producers.

As the above description of the types of attitudes towards copyright and culture shows, it is the non-governmental organizations that have the greatest awareness of the socio-legal aspects of creating and consuming culture. They are also most willing to take such aspects into account in the course of law-making. As a result, Polish social organizations—and this leads to the second key conclusion from the analisis presented in this chapter—are playing an important role in describing and explaining the copyright-culture relationship. This role seems even more important considering that both representatives of the creative industry and copyright lawyers are mostly not aware of the shortcomings of classical copyright theories, including the economic theory of creativity. What is more, some of them are critical of the ideas promoted by non-governmental organizations. Although the academic lawyers are more open to concepts like free culture, most of them do not feel competent to make more in-depth statements on this topic: "I don't know the details of the activities of these organizations. I don't know any results or reports that would show what they have achieved" (L9). At the same time, many copyright lawyers are generally aware of the important role of organizations. The latter can be exemplified with the following quotations: "This is an element of reality (...) that should be analyzed, i.e., that something is bothering them, that there is something up" (L4); "This is an alternative. This is a desired alternative (...). This is one of the ways of solving [problems] (...) that deserves attention" (L9).

The importance of non-governmental organizations is especially visible if one juxtaposes the assumptions underlying three types of theoretical conceptions presented in the first part of the chapter with the statements of representatives of particular groups described and analysed in the second part of the chapter. Such juxtaposition, first, allows one to notice that despite, according to almost all conceptions, culture being an extremely important variable, such belief is not widely shared by the practitioners. Although the utilitarian theory of copyright, to which most interviewees referred, emphasizes the need for providing members of society with a vast pool of cultural goods, according to most lawyers this theory tries to do so mostly by caring for the well-being of the artists who produce these goods. Only the public policy argument cited by representatives of organizations advocating for the liberalization of copyright stresses the necessity of taking into account citizens' right to culture.

An even greater discrepancy between theoretical assumptions and their implementation was observed in the case of theories concerning relations between copyright and processes of cultural creation and participation. Namely, the only group that not only referred directly to these theories, but also postulated their practical realization was the group of organizations representing the interests of users of culture. At the same time, the representatives of other groups either focused on economic and civil aspects of the exchange of cultural goods between individuals or they sought to improve the quality of goods produced by creators, without paying attention to making them widely available.

This short juxtaposition already shows that organizations such as the MPF and DC not only describe and explain the relationship between copyright and culture, but also, as a part of "large-scale community activities" (Młynarska-Sobaczewska 2018, p. 11), form its shape. Moreover, the presence of these organizations in the Polish public sphere provokes the reflection that "the need for 'free culture' is greater than it would result from the previous paradigm of copyright protection" (Młynarska-Sobaczewska 2018, p. 167). It also confirms the assumption of the important role of culture in the creation of the common good. Taking the latter for granted and keeping in mind that the way of perceiving relations between copyright and culture depends on the adopted definition of culture, four essential areas in which these relations are the most intense can be distinguish on the basis of inference from empirical and theoretical material presented in this chapter. These areas are the following: (1) protection of the creators, including protection of their autonomy; (2) protection of artistic freedom; (3) protection of the process of commercial production of cultural goods; and (4) protection of the right to access and participate in culture. The role of copyright in areas 1 and 3 consists in the introduction and enforcement of relevant legal regulations, and in areas 2 and 4, this role consists in the lack of regulation of specific spheres of cultural activity. In case of the former, one can talk about the primacy of copyright over culture, and in the latter, about the primacy of culture over copyright.

The protection of the creators and the protection of the process of commercial production of cultural goods are areas, in which culture is defined narrowly, as it does not include social content production processes, including "internet-inspired creativity" (Simon 2011). Amateur culture is also excluded from area 3, which embraces mainly regulations addressed to intermediaries, that is, entities managing copyright. Both 1 and 3 are areas of particular importance to representatives of the creative industry. Additionally, area 1, which includes not only economic and moral rights but also their proper enforcement, is of great importance to creators, especially to authors working for commercial entities. Apart from intermediaries, lawyers and organizations representing the interests of authors (e.g., the ZAiKS) or intermediaries (e.g., the ZPAV) also pay special attention to both of these areas, although area 3 seems to be less significant.

In the areas that are important from the point of view of the implementation of the right to culture and the concept of free culture—that is, areas 2 and 4—the notion of "deregulated" culture embraces practically every type of culture. The only exception may be ethnic culture, which is often overlooked by the copyright system (Coombe 1998) and is not the subject of this chapter. The protection of artistic freedom and the protection of the right to access and participate in culture are essential preconditions of the democratization of culture that has reached unimaginable dimensions in the digital age. Both areas are also a necessary condition for the cultural development of contemporary societies, which can be stimulated by the unlimited possibilities of artistic expression. These are the most important reasons why areas 2 and 4 are of particular interest to non-governmental organizations representing users of culture.

Although the typology of the key areas of intersections between copyright and culture proposed in this chapter was created on the basis of empirical material about Polish society, it can undoubtedly be applied to other countries and societies, especially those with the *droit d'auteur* tradition. Nevertheless, because the main subject of this chapter is the relationship between copyright and culture on the example of Poland, it is worth adding a few words concerning the distinctiveness of Polish copyright law in the context of its relation to culture.

Polish culture, in the course of history, more than once has been forced to function under the rule of foreign legislation. As a result, many non-legal standards have developed regarding the creation and dissemination of artistic works. For example, in nineteenth century, the lack of copyright regulation entailed that booksellers and publishers were consistently obeying customs regarding book publishing (Święćkowska 2018). Such normative standards to some extent may be corelated to the fact that nowadays in Poland great importance is attached to copyright compliance within the area of high and national culture. These cultural spheres are willingly placed under special protection by the legislature and cultural institutions. Unfortunately, the Polish system of financing culture is not transparent (see, e.g., Głowacki et al. 2009; Wąsowska-Pawlik 2013), and as indicated by the results of the interviews, both lawyers and intermediaries are aware of this fact. As a consequence, in Poland high culture is quite often available primarily to people not only with cultural but also with economic capital (see, e.g., Bachórz et al. 2014).

On the other hand, there is a wide Poles' acceptance of free—including free-of-charge and quite often unlawful—use of popular culture (see, e.g., Danielewicz and Tarkowski 2013). The sources of the causes of such consent can be found in alternative and informal circulation of culture that was functioning in Poland during the communist era when underground communities and movements created communication networks called "the second" and the "third circulation of culture" (Gracz 2013). These circulations provided the space for artistic creations prohibited by "the first", official circulation of cultural goods.; the third circulation was also an alternative to the second circulation, connected mainly with the political opposition. Furthermore, some traces can also be found in the contemporary processes of digitization and cultural globalization observed around the world. Both factors may have contributed to the fact that over the last years activities, including discursive activities, undertaken by Polish organizations aimed either at opening culture or liberalizing copyright have been extremely visible. The spectacular demonstration of the social reaction to these actions was the Polish protests against ACTA, which were one of the largest in Europe and resulted in numerous debates and social initiatives concerning Poles' awareness of copyright and the right to culture.[22]

Another manifestation of Polish specificity concerning the copyright–culture relation is the division into legal and illegal culture that is visible in the public debate on piracy. Legal culture is promoted by organizations supporting the interests of the creative industry, while illegal culture is sometimes glorified by organizations seeking to liberalize copyright in the name of wider access to culture. This division

[22]Exemplary media releases on anti-ACTA protest in Poland from the Guardian and the BBC: https://www.theguardian.com/technology/2012/jan/27/acta-protests-eu-states-sign-treaty [Accessed 14 Aug 2021]; https://www.bbc.com/news/av/technology-16757611 [Accessed 7 Oct 2021].

can be treated as the result of a polarized copyright discourse between representatives of both groups of organizations. At the same time, one can also risk a statement that such a division is an external indication of a deeper problem connected with the answer to an uneasy question—whether Polish citizens were and are rich enough to access culture only through legal sources, or as political economists put it, whether Poland has the need for enhanced copyright (Towse 2001). Notwithstanding the merits of the assumption that the division into legal and illegal culture has an economic dimension, this question seems to be no longer relevant. First, Poland is no longer classified as a developing country.[23] Second, new business models adopted by companies like Spotify or Netflix that distribute content on the internet have caused people to start developing the habit of accessing cultural goods from legal internet sources. At the time when these companies have started to enter the Polish market (for example, the Spotify entered Polish market in 2013 and the Netflix—in 2016), a significant part of internet piracy was eliminated.

Being aware that there are many social, economic, and historical factors that influence the undoubtedly complex relationship between copyright and culture, the more general conclusion that can be drawn from all provided (theoretical and empirical) material is the need to establish the right balance between copyright fixity and cultural variability. Taking this into account, the typology of the most important areas in which (continental) copyright and (non-ethnic) culture intersect and interact, as proposed in this chapter, can be treated as an indication of the spheres where maintaining such a balance has the greatest importance. The analysis of the discourse and the analysis of expert opinions have shown that in Poland the area of protection of the creator and the area of protection of the right to culture are the ones that are mostly grounded in the narratives on copyright and culture. Therefore, these areas are those in which the most action is taken to achieve a copyright equilibrium. Paying less attention to the other areas—namely, to the area of the protection of artistic freedom and the area of the protection of commercial production of cultural goods—can be explained primarily by the little awareness among both Polish artists and Polish users of culture. The former have relatively little knowledge of copyright regulations (Felczner et al. 2013), and the latter are not aware of the strong position of the largest corporations from the creative industry (Danielewicz and Tarkowski 2013). Hence, one can risk a statement that, over time, when the representatives of these groups gain more knowledge about how the copyright system works, more attention will be paid to the need of the protection of artistic freedom and the commercial production of culture.

---

[23] FTSE Russell announced the promotion of Poland to developed market status in 2017 (https://content.ftserussell.com/sites/default/files/research/poland%2D%2D-the-journey-to-developed-market-status_final.pdf) [Accessed 7 Oct 2021].

References

Arewa OB (2007) The freedom to copy: copyright, creation, and context. U C Davis Law Rev 41:477–558

Bachórz A et al (2014) Punkty styczne: między kulturą a praktyką (nie)uczestnictwa. Instytut Kultury Miejskiej, Gdańsk. https://www.nck.pl/en/badania/raporty/raport-punkty-styczne-miedzy-kultura-a-praktyka-nie-uczestnictwa. Accessed 7 Oct 2021

Benkler Y (2006) The wealth of networks: how social production transforms markets and freedom. Yale University Press, New Haven and London

Bollier D (2008) Viral spiral. How the commoners built a digital republic of their own. The New Press, New York and London

Bourdieu P (1984) Distinction. Harvard University Press, Cambridge

Bowrey K (2001) The outer limits of copyright law – where law meets philosophy and culture. Law Critique 12:75–98

Boyle J (2008) The public domain: enclosing the commons of the mind. http://boyle.yupnet.org/. Accessed 7 Oct 2021

Chartrand HH, McCaughey C (1989) The arm's length principle and the arts: an international perspective — past, present and future. In: Cummings MC, Schuster JMD (eds) Who's to pay? For the arts: the international search for models of support. American Council for the Arts, New York

Cohen JE (2007) Creativity and culture in copyright theory. U C Davis Law Rev 40:1151–1205

Coombe RJ (1998) The cultural life of intellectual properties. Duke University Press, Durham, London

Czyżewski et al (1997) Rytualny chaos. Studium dyskursu publicznego. Wydawnictwo AUREUS, Cracow

Danielewicz M, Tarkowski A (2013) Prawo autorskie w czasach zmiany (Copyright law in transition). Digital Centre Foundation. https://www.sbc.org.pl/dlibra/publication/87555/edition/82623/content. Accessed 7 Oct 2021 (English summary is available via https://centrumcyfrowe.pl/czytelnia/copyright-law-in-transition-on-social-norms-related-to-content-usage-new-survey-report/. Accessed 7 Oct 2021)

Donders Y (2007) The legal framework of the right to take part in cultural life. In: Donders Y, Volodin V (eds) Human rights in education, science and culture, legal developments and challenges. UNESCO/Ashgate, Paris-Aldershot, pp 231–272

Dutfield G, Suthersanen U (2008) Global intellectual property law. Edward Elgar, Cheltenham, Northampton

Felczner et al (2013) Świadomi twórcy. Badanie kompetencji prawnych artystów. Fundacja Międzynarodowe Centrum do spraw Badań i Analiz ICRA, Warszawa

Filiciak M et al (2012) The circulations of culture on social distribution of content. Digital Centre Foundation. https://depot.ceon.pl/bitstream/handle/123456789/615/the_circulations_of_culture_report.pdf?sequence=1. Accessed 7 Oct 2021

Frey B (1999) State support and creativity in the arts: some new considerations. J Cult Econ 23 (1/2):71–85

FTSE Russell (2018) Poland: the journey to developed market status. https://content.ftserussell.com/sites/default/files/research/poland%2D%2D-the-journey-to-developed-market-status_final.pdf. Accessed 7 Oct 2021

Głowacki J et al (2009) Finansowanie kultury i zarządzanie instytucjami kultury, National Centre for Culture (Narodowe Centrum Kultury). https://nck.pl/en/badania/raporty/finansowanie-kultury-i-zarzadzanie-instytucjami. Accessed 7 Oct 2021

Gracz K (2013) Bridging the gaps between the social and legal norms concerning protection of intellectual and artistic creations: on the crisis of copyright law in the digital era. J World Intell Prop 16(1–2):39–57

Hettinger EC (1989) Justifying intellectual property. Philos Public Aff 18(1):31–52

Hughes J (1988) The philosophy of intellectual property. Geo Law J 77(2):287–366

Kwall R (1985) Copyright and the moral right: is an American marriage possible? Vand Law Rev 38(1):1–100
Landes WM, Posner RA (1989) An economic analysis of copyright law. J Leg Stud 18:325–363
Lessig L (2004) Free culture. How big media uses technology and the law to lock down culture and control creativity. The Penguin Press, New York
Lessig L (2008) Remix: making art and commerce thrive in the hybrid economy. Bloomsbury, London
McLeod K (2005) Freedom of Expression®: overzealous copyright bozos and other enemies of creativity. Doubleday
Merryman JH (1986) Two ways of thinking about cultural property. Am J Int Law 80(4):831–853
Mezey N (2001) Law as culture. Yale J Law Hum 13:35–67
Młynarska-Sobaczewska (2018) Right to culture. Scholar Publishing House, Warsaw
Mulcahy KV (2006) Cultural policy: definitions and theoretical approaches. J Arts Manag Law Soc 35(4):319–330
O'Keefe R (1998) The "right to take part in cultural life" under Article 15 of the ICESCR. Int Comp Law Q 47(4):904–923
Pałecki K (2007) Od recenzenta. In: Głuszczyńska I, Lankosz K (eds) Międzynarodowe stosunki kulturalne. Wybór dokumentów. Wyższa Szkoła Administracji, Bielsko-Biała
Shaver L, Sganga C (2010) The right to take part in cultural life: on copyright and human rights. Wisconsin Int Law Rev 27:637–662
Simon DA (2011) Culture, creativity & copyright. Cardozo Arts Entertain Law J 29(2):279–374
Spence M (2002) Justifying copyright. In: McClean D, Schubert K (eds) Dear images: art, copyright and culture. Ram Distribution, pp 389–403
Stokes S (2001) Art and copyright. Hart Publishing, Oxford-Portland
Strycharz J et al (2015) Polskie organizacje zarządzania zbiorowego i ich dane finansowe, Digital Centre Foundation. https://centrumcyfrowe.pl/wp-content/uploads/2015/04/Polskie-OZZ-i-ich-dane-finansowe.pdf. Accessed 7 Oct 2021
Święćkowska T (2018) Kochani krwiopijce. Własność literacka i prawo autorskie w XIX-wiecznej Polsce. Universitas, Cracow
Towse R (2001) Creativity, incentives and reward. An economic analysis of copyright and culture in the information age. Edward Elgar, Cheltenham, Northampton
UN Committee on Economic, Social and Cultural Rights (CESCR) (2009) General comment no. 21, Right of everyone to take part in cultural life (art. 15, para. 1a of the Covenant on Economic, Social and Cultural Rights). Available via https://www.refworld.org/docid/4ed35bae2.html. Accessed 7 Oct 2021
van den Haag E (1957) Of happiness and of despair we have no measure. In: Rosenberg B, White DM (eds) Mass culture: the popular arts in America. Free Press, Glencoe, pp 504–536
Wąsowska-Pawlik A (2013) Polityka kulturalna Polski 1989–2012. In: Hausner J et al (eds) Kultura a rozwój. National Centre for Culture (Narodowe Centrum Kultury), Warszawa, pp 107–126
Williams R (1965) Long revolution. Penguin Books, London
Zeidler K (2016) Restitution of cultural property. Wolter Kluwer, Gdańsk-Warsaw

Organization Sites and Statues

Creative Commons. https://creativecommons.org/. Accessed 7 Oct 2021
Creative Poland (Stowarzyszenie Kreatywna Polska). http://www.kreatywnapolska.pl/. Accessed 7 Oct 2021
Creative Poland (2014) Statue of the Creative Poland. http://www.kreatywnapolska.pl/statut-stowarzyszenia/. Accessed 7 Oct 2021

Digital Centre Foundation (Fundacja Centrum Cyfrowe). https://centrumcyfrowe.pl/. Accessed 7 Oct 2021

Legal Culture Foundation (Fundacja Legalna Kultura). http://fundacja.legalnakultura.pl/. Accessed 7 Oct 2021

Legal Culture Foundation (2011) Statue of the Legal Culture Foundation. http://fundacja.legalnakultura.pl/o-fundacji/statut. Accessed 7 Oct 2021

Modern Poland Foundation (Fundacja Nowoczesna Polska). https://nowoczesnapolska.org.pl/. Accessed 7 Oct 2021

Modern Poland Foundation (2019) Statute of the Modern Poland Foundation. https://nowoczesnapolska.org.pl/wpcontent/uploads/2019/02/Statut-FNP-07.01.2019.pdf. Accessed 7 Oct 2021

Panopticon Foundation (Fundacja Panoptykon). https://panoptykon.org/. Accessed 7 Oct 2021

Polish Society of Authors (Stowarzyszenie Autorów ZAiKS). https://www.zaiks.org.pl/. Accessed 7 Oct 2021

Polish Society of Authors (ZAiKS) (2019) Statue of the ZAiKS. https://app.zaiks.org.pl/media/vooppujq/statut-w-brzmieniuuchwalonym-na-nadzwyczajnym-zjez-dzie-delegato-w-w-dn-21-10-2019-r-wpisany-do-krs-w-dniu-23-12-2019-r_pdf. Accessed 7 Oct 2021

Polish Society of the Phonographic Industry (Związek Producentów Audio Video (ZPAV)). http://www.zpav.pl/. Accessed 7 Oct 2021

Polish Society of the Phonographic Industry (ZPAV) (1991) Statue of the ZPAV. http://www.zpav.pl/pliki/dopobrania/statut.pdf. Accessed 7 Oct 2021

Legal Acts and Drafts of Proposed Legal Acts

ACTA Anti-Counterfeiting Trade Agreement. (2011). Tokyo, 1 October 2011

Act of 4 February 1994 on Copyright and Related Rights (Dz.U. No. 24, item 83) (Dz.U.2017.880-tłum.)

Amendment Act of 11 September 2015 amending Act on Copyright and Related Rights and Gambling Act (Dz.U. 2015 item 1639)

Directive (EU) 2019/790 of the European Parliament and of the Council of 17 April 2019 on copyright and related rights in the Digital Single Market and amending Directives 96/9/EC and 2001/29/EC (Dz. U. L 130 z 17.5.2019)

The Constitution of the Republic of Poland of 2nd April, 1997 (Dz. U. No. 78, item 483). https://www.sejm.gov.pl/prawo/konst/angielski/kon1.htm. Accessed 7 Oct 2021

The Ministry of Administration and Digitisation (2012) Bill on open resources. https://legislacja.rcl.gov.pl/lista/1/projekt/86492. Accessed 7 Oct 2021

The Minister of Culture and National Heritage (2003) Ordinance on defining the blank media and devices that enable making copies of copyrighted works, and the fee that should be paid for the sale of these media and devices by their producers and importers (Dz.U. 2003 No. 105 item 991). http://isap.sejm.gov.pl/isap.nsf/download.xsp/WDU20031050991/O/D20030991.pdf. Accessed 7 Oct 2021

The United Nations. (1948). Universal Declaration of Human Rights

The United Nations General Assembly. (1966). International Covenant on Economic, Social, and Cultural Rights. Treaty Series, 999, 171

Court Decisions

Eldred v. Ashcroft, 537 U.S. 186 (2003)
Shaver L (2010) The right to science and culture. Wis L Rev 1:121–184

Ewa Radomska PhD candidate at the Faculty of Law and Administration (the Department of Sociology of Law) of the Jagiellonian University; holder of an MA in law and an MA in sociology. Her research interests focus on communication of law, legal consciousness, discourse on law, social aspects of intellectual property law (e.g., copyright discourse, relations between intellectual property and culture), criminology and security science (e.g., crime mapping and Police studies). She is currently principal investigator in the research project "Social conflict over intellectual property rights on the example of Polish discourses on copyright" and holder of scholarship in the research project "Legal Consciousness of Polish Society. Diagnosis, Types, Paths of Formation"—both funded by the Polish National Science Centre.

The Procedural Justice in South Korean Popular Culture. An Analysis of Court Hearings Using the Example of the K-drama *Your Honor*

Katarzyna Rużyczka

Abstract Korean dramas, commonly known as K-dramas, are becoming popular around the world while simultaneously promoting South Korean culture. One of the aspects of society that is often depicted in K-drama is the work of lawyers and the judiciary. In this era of globalization, the Korean wave, the term used to describe the increase in worldwide popularity of South Korean culture, is an effective tool of soft power, creating an image of South Korea among fans from different countries. Depicting the judiciary through cultural productions appears to be an extremely important aspect of this wave. The goal of this chapter is to examine the fulfillment of the justice indicators proposed by Tom R. Tyler in selected court hearings presented in the television series *Your Honor*. Events taking place in the series, which are closely related to the selected hearings and their cultural aspects are examined as well.

1 Introduction

The connection between law and culture is an important topic in legal research. As Naomi Mezey notes, "Law is simply one of the signifying practices that constitute culture and, despite its best efforts, it cannot be divorced from culture. Nor, for that matter, can culture be divorced from law" (2001, p. 46). Additionally, the relationship between law and culture can be described as always dynamic, interactive, and dialectical—law is both a producer of culture and an object of culture. One of the ways in which the law is depicted is through popular culture, especially television series or movies.

This chapter is a result of the research project "Empathy as a challenge. Example of Polish judges" (Grant number 2019/33/B/HS5/01664) financed by the National Science Centre, Poland and carried out at the Faculty of Law and Administration of the Jagiellonian University.

K. Rużyczka (✉)
Jagiellonian University, Department of Sociology of Law, Cracow, Poland

M. Stępień, J. B. Klakla (eds.), *Law and Culture*, Law and Visual Jurisprudence 5,
https://doi.org/10.1007/978-3-030-81193-8_8

As Ewa Radomska claim in Chapter 'Copyright and Culture: The Case of Poland' of this book (p. 130) "nowadays, in the era of cultural commodification and globalization, the main role of culture, not only in the Polish society, is – apart from providing content that can be monetized – to enable people to take part in extended social relations that cross national borders". One of the interesting example of popculture crossing borders is Korean wave know as Hallyu (한류). The term was created in the 1900s by the Chinese press to describe the growing popularity of South Korean pop culture in China (Parc and Moon 2013, p. 127). This phenomenon, which is increasing all over the world, includes music (K-pop), series (K-drama), fashion (K-fashion), and movies (Diniejko 2013, p. 123). Due to the growing popularity of Hallyu, the Korean government has changed its cultural policy to use it as a soft medium to strengthen the national image (Jin and Yoon 2017, p. 2242). To help promote the culture, Korea's Presidential Council on Nation Branding was created in 2007; its purpose was to prepare a plan to create an image of the country as democratic, with advanced technology, an innovative economy, and an interesting culture (Diniejko 2013, p. 131). Therefore, the phenomenon of the Korean wave is not an example of pop culture created only for South Korean recipients, but it is also directed outside the country, constituting a soft-power tool.

In particular, K-drama productions, in which the image of South Korea is carefully created, are a tool to promote the culture of the country. Images of food, luxury products, architecture, or social behavior are an important element in promoting the country and creating demand among the fans of the Korean wave for products and services depicted in South Korean television series (Shim 2006, p. 30). Youna Kim points out that through exposure to Korean pop culture such as a television series, Asian audiences can develop a better awareness of the sociocultural and economic conditions in which they live, critically reflect on the legitimacy of their own social systems, and envision new opportunities (Lee 2018, p. 76).

One of the societal elements often depicted in these series is the law. Viewers can see the work of police officers, prosecutors, lawyers, and judges as well as the relationship between the justice system and the individual. In line with the Confucian tradition, in South Korea, judges have used a combination of mediation and adjudication in their judicial activities in the past (Jung 2018, p. 280). As a result of changes that took place in this country in 1894, the judicial system was modernized based on new solutions inspired by European standards (Jung 2018, p. 280).

This interpretation of law and culture mentioned above is an interesting example, considering the growing popularity of K-drama around the world and how it presents the law and the judicial system to viewers from other countries who are not necessarily familiar with South Korean legal culture. Therefore, in this chapter I attempt to answer the following question: Can procedural justice be found in the scenes of court hearings in the productions of Korean pop culture, such as K-drama?

Procedural justice has been developed both in a legal and psychological context. In legal language, it refers to the fairness of the process during which a decision is made, while in psychology it focuses on the subjective judgments of people regarding the fairness of decisions made during the process (Hollander-Blumoff and Tyler 2011, p.3). According to Tom R. Tyler, research in the field of social psychology indicates that procedural fairness has a significant influence on how people think and behave in relation to the outcomes of legal disputes. It is also noted that procedural fairness causes people to be satisfied with judicial decisions and determines future compliance with their results and agreements (Hollander-Blumoff and Tyler 2011, p. 3).

Tyler's theory of procedural justice was used to analyze the Korean series Your Honor (친애 하는 판사 님께), which is an interesting example of pop culture interpretations of the judiciary and the work of a judge due to role reversal. Your Honor aired on SBS TV from July 25, 2018, through September 20, 2018. Today, it can be watched with English subtitles on YouTube, where it was shared by the official SBS YouTube channel.[1] The series has 16 episodes of about 50 min each, and is set in Seoul Central District Court, that is, in the first—instance courts in South Korea. Your Honor presents the story of identical twin brothers—one is a judge and the other lives on the edge of the law. The characters switch places, with the corrupt judge being replaced by his brother, who interprets the law and issues judgments as he pretends to be a judge. He is helped by a young lawyer who is undergoing training in the court.

2 Procedural Justice

Tyler's theory of procedural justice assumes that a trial must include four basic components: participation, also known as voice; neutrality; respect; and trust (Tyler 2000, p. 121). The first component, voice, is a form of active participation in the process through the possibility of interested persons expressing their opinions. Tyler states that research reveals that people feel more fairly treated if they have the opportunity to participate in resolving their problems or conflicts by being able to share their suggestions about what should be done. This helps build a sense of fairness of proper treatment during the trial, with the proviso that this belief remains intact as long as the person who is subject to authority believes the decision-maker took into account his reasons (Tyler 2007, p. 31). The second is neutrality, which assumes that citizens bring cases to the courts because they perceive court decisions

[1] Your Honor television series first season online link: https://www.youtube.com/watch?v=AjZcuQ2motI [Accessed 17 May 2021].

to be independent of private views and opinions. To emphasize this belief in the fairness of jurisprudence, judges can ensure transparency and openness by providing information about legal classification of individual factual state, and ultimately how the regulations influenced the final decisions. The third component is respect, which applies to authority figures (judges, court employees) who, in connection with their positions, send important messages through their behavior. Respecting the rights of people who are subject to jurisprudence at every stage of the process conveys the feeling that they are important and valuable and that their rights are protected. What can help a citizen feel that they are being treated with respect is informing them about the various stages of the process; this can take the form of brochures, websites, or the availability of information desks in court buildings. The fourth component is trust, which results from how an entity evaluates the judiciary in terms of the decision-making procedures. There is a better assessment of the course of the proceedings when the decision-makers exhibit care and sincerity in their decisions, which also prompts the citizens to be open and honest in their actions (Tyler 2007, pp. 30–31).

3 Methodology

The purpose of the analysis of the cases presented in the series is to verify whether the method of conducting the court hearing can contain elements of the theory of procedural justice as understood by Tyler. The series Your Honor was chosen because the work of a judge and the judicial process are portrayed from the point of view of a person without a legal background. The analysis of the television series with such a plot is connected with the following research problems:

- Can elements of Tyler's theory of procedural justice be seen in how the Korean pop culture series presents court hearings?
- Does a person without legal education taking the role of a judge behave in a way that, according to the theory of procedural justice, can be considered fair?
- If the incorporation of procedural justice in K-drama can be recognized, will it also be associated with the occurrence of cultural elements characteristic for South Korea?

The research method adopted combines traditional sociological observation with Tyler's concept of procedural justice, and thus structures it. Four components of procedural justice have been distinguished, along with the indicators I have developed based on Tyler's theory concerning the concept of procedural justice, in Table 1. Sociological observation is based on watching the entire K-drama to understand the overall plot, after which I selected two cases from among those depicted in the series. Sociological observation is realized by watching the series, examining how the trials and the judiciary were portrayed by Korean television producers. This approach provides insight into the image-shaping of the judiciary and the work of a judge in Korean popular culture. Then, I watched the K-drama again, taking detailed notes on the trials I chose and the behavior of the characters associated with them, both inside and outside the courtroom. Based on these notes, I analyzed the scenes of the trials in Your Honor by using the components and indicators of procedural fairness listed in Table 1 from the point of view of the defendants and other people related to the case (for example, witnesses or the victim's family members).

It should be noted that, regarding the situations presented at the hearings, two types of events were analyzed; the first are behaviors resulting from the legal definitions of the trial procedure, which can be called a "ritual", and the second are situations in the courtroom caused by the behavior of the judge and court employees going beyond the trial procedure, and which may be analyzed in terms of procedural fairness. The components of procedural justice that I noticed during my observation of the court hearings were assigned to individual elements in Tables 2 and 3 and discussed below them.

The sample cases for analysis included the comprehensive presentation of a criminal trial, the action of which takes place in a few episodes of the series; a case from early in the impostor judge's career; and the final case adjudicated by the impostor judge. These choices were made to analyze whether the judge's experiences influenced his use of procedural justice.

Table 1 Indicators of the four components of procedural fairness in the analyzed court hearings

Voice	Neutrality	Respect	Trust
*Whether the defendant, witnesses, victim, and family members were allowed to speak during trial; *Whether the defendant, witnesses, victim, and family members were allowed or asked by the judge to express their opinion	*Whether the judge was transparent in his actions during the trial; *Whether the judge justified the application of certain legal provisions	*Whether the defendant, witnesses, victim, and family members were treated with respect and their rights were respected; *Whether the defendant, witnesses, victim, and family members had access to information about the court, legal procedures, and individual stages of the trial to understand what was happening during trial	*Whether the judge justified his final legal decisions; *Whether the judge demonstrated care and interest in making the decision

4 Analysis of Cases Presented During Hearings

4.1 Trial 1

The first hearing concerns a fatal vehicle crash in which a pregnant woman was killed by the accused, who was driving under the influence of alcohol. The trial began with the prosecutor's presentation of the facts, then the judge gave the floor to the defense lawyer, who asked the defendant why she did not act to help the victim after the crash. A flashback depicted the defendant fainting from shock after she approached the victim. After the accused confirmed this, the lawyer emphasized that the defendant had attempted to contact the victim's family many times to settle the matter out of court, but they had rebuffed the efforts. Then the judge asked the prosecution to state the legal qualification of the accusation, and the prosecutor said that, according to Article 5, Clause 11 of legal act relating to fatal driving penalties the recommendation is that the accused be sentenced to three years' imprisonment. The judge then allowed the defense counsel to make a final statement. The attorney pointed out that the accused could not reconcile with the deceased's family, but she had sent a letter of apology every day from the date of the accident to the date of the hearing. However, the accused had not received any feedback from the deceased's family, so to demonstrate the depth of her remorse, she had deposited a much larger than customary amount of money as penance for her role in the woman's death. The attorney emphasized that the defendant regretted what had happened and was extremely sorry. This was her first offense, so she asked for mercy, addressing the audience in the courtroom and stressing that she was "a healthy part of society". The defense lawyer also addressed the judge, admitting that the defendant should pay for her crime, even though he sought a lenient penalty. The judge asked the accused for a final statement. She replied that she would feel guilty about killing another person for the rest of her life, and she apologized again, crying and covering her face with her hands.

In episode 5, the judge sentenced the defendant to 18 months in prison, suspended for three years, and ordered her to take 80 h of safe-driving lessons. After delivering the sentence, the judge reread the facts of the case.

Table 2 Assignment of individual elements of the Trial 1 to the four components of procedural justice on the basis of indicators according to Table 1

Voice	1. The prosecutor, while describing the facts, asked the accused whether she could confirm that such a situation took place. (He emphasized that the accused had not contacted the medical services or the police after the crash and that she had failed to settle the case with the victim's family.) 2. The defense lawyer, while asking the accused about the facts, also asked her to confirm said facts. 3. The judge gave the defense counsel the opportunity to present a final statement on behalf of his client. 4. The judge gave the accused the opportunity to present her final statement and allowed her to deliver it while standing next to her attorney. 5. The judge twice allowed the husband of the victim to speak. The first time was at the hearing after the defendant had delivered her final statement, and the second was after the judgment had been announced. In both cases, the court allowed the husband to express his opinion. 6. At the beginning of the court hearing the accused repeatedly apologized for her behavior and attempted to exhibit regret for the act she had committed.
Neutrality	1. The prosecutor explained the legal basis for the proposed sentence for the accused. 2. The judge announced the verdict, maintaining eye contact with the victim's husband, but did not broadly justify why he chose such a verdict. However, after its announcement, he re-quoted the facts of the case. 3. When answering questions posed by the prosecutor and the defense lawyer, the accused stood in the center of the room in the place for the testifying persons, not the defendant. After this stage of the trial was over, she returned to her place next to the defense attorney.
Respect	1. During the questioning of the accused, the judge was yawning, and by means of non-verbal communication he exhibited fatigue and lack of interest, for example, by not looking at the pages or resting his head on his hand. Additionally, after the prosecutor's questioning was complete, one could see that the judge was drawing checkered signs or funny illustrations of a figure showing discontent. The position of the judge changed during the last speech of the accused; he began to listen carefully, looking directly at the woman. 2. The judge asked the defense attorney to lead his crying client out of the courtroom. 3. During the first hearing, the judge instructed the husband of the deceased that he should not say in the courtroom that he wanted to kill someone. 4. Court workers tussled with the victim's husband when he refused to sit down at the judge's request. 5. The judge reacted sharply when he saw that the security personnel had gotten physical with the victim's husband and ordered them to stop, then allowed the man to speak. 6. The judge advised the victim's husband about the possibility of appealing the verdict. 7. When leaving the courtroom, the judge bowed to those present. 8. The judge informed those present that the sentence would be announced the following week, providing the date of April 27.
Trust	1. The judge did not exhibit any interest in the case during the trial: He did not listen actively, did not focus on the question asked by the victim's husband, and did not answer immediately. The victim's husband concluded that the judge did not know the name of the victim over whose case he was presiding. 2. The judge did not broadly justify the judgment he issued but provided only the legal basis and the sentence. 3. The judge did not fully answer the victim's husband's questions about the case.

Based on Table 2, the following conclusions can be drawn. This trial was presented at the beginning of the series, in episode 4. The main character, who was just beginning to play the role of a judge, did not indicate due diligence or interest in the case, and his activities were related more to procedural rules, such as interrogating the accused and listening to the defense attorney's speech, rather than a real desire to properly fulfill is judicial obligation. Perhaps the protagonist's behavior resulted from the fact that he was just beginning to understand the role of a judge. He did not yet identify himself with the role he was supposed to fulfill, which made his behavior inappropriate, and the elements required for the accused's feeling of a fair trial were not fully implemented.

Voice: The accused had the opportunity to comment at every stage of the hearing, from confirming the facts cited by the prosecutor or defense lawyer to answering questions to delivering her final statement. Moreover, during the hearing, the accused had the opportunity to ask the judge if she could leave the courtroom. For the victim's husband, the situation was different, as he was seated in the audience and was more of an observer than an active participant in the hearing. Nevertheless, the judge, at the request of the victim's husband, allowed the man to speak twice, listening to his arguments and answering his questions. Allowing the victim's husband to speak at this stage of the proceedings was of great importance, as the man referred to facts not presented in the courtroom and presented evidence that had not been included in the case. Believing that the court would not impose a penalty appropriate for the accused, the man directly declared to the court that he was ready to deliver his own punishment by killing her. Additionally, after the final sentence was announced, the husband stood up and asked why the court forgave the accused. The man shared his life story, pointing out that he had always been guided by logic, but he added that he could not find any arguments justifying such a lenient penalty. Since someone who gets behind the wheel of a car under the influence of alcohol must take into consideration that they may kill someone, the man alleged that the judge had looked for many excuses to return this criminal to society. Consequently, he asked the judge if a man who killed for the first time should be forgiven just because it was an act committed for the first time? The judge, by giving the voice to the husband of the victim, gave him an opportunity not only to demonstrate how he himself viewed the sentence by presenting his arguments and his thoughts about law but also to showcase his assessment of the judge's work. This issue seems to be extremely important, especially since the husband asked the judge not only about the essence of the case but also about his profession, while arguing his point of view.

Neutrality: In procedural terms, it can be stated that the defendant was informed about the legal grounds for the imposed sentence. Additionally, when answering questions, she did not stand in the traditional place for the accused but in the spot intended for witnesses in the middle of the courtroom. Conversely, the victim's husband did not understand the sentence passed in the case and also directly questioned the judge's administration of justice. During the trial, the husband even presented his point of view, which he argued with reference to his "logic."

Respect: Even as the accused acknowledged that the fatal accident was her fault, the judge propped his head on his hand and reacted only by nodding, a sign that he agreed with her statements. He exhibited a passive attitude rather than active. Throughout the questioning of the defendant, the judge revealed a lack of interest in the case by doodling without looking at the court documents. After hearing about the defendant's deposit of money for the victim's family, the judge reacted by nodding his head in appreciation, raising his eyebrows, and making a note. Moreover, during the defendant's final statement, when she admitted that she had killed a man, the judge was just beginning to listen "actively", but still supported his head with his hand. Concerning the victim's husband, the judge talked with him, maintained eye contact—including during the pronouncement of the sentence—and also informed and instructed him about his rights. This is important because after hearing the accused's final statement, the victim's husband called her the devil and said he had imagined murdering her, adding that if no 'fair' sentence was ordered, he would kill the defendant himself. Hearing this, the judge warned the husband that he should not say such things in the courtroom. Additionally, earlier in the trial, when the judge asked the husband of the victim to sit down and he refused, the court guards approached him to force him to sit. When the husband further refused and called the sentence unfair, the security guard attempted to force him out of the courtroom. Seeing this, the judge shouted, "Guard!", asked him to leave the husband alone, then granted the husband permission to speak. This entire exchange is important in terms of respect. On the one hand, the guard uses force, which is contrary to the element of respect. Additionally, the use of force was not justified, as the judge merely asked the husband to sit down. On the other hand, the judge immediately reacted strongly, ordered the court staff to stop using force and allowing the victim's husband to speak. This reaction from the judge to effectively manage the courtroom and react to unacceptable behavior fulfills the requirement of the element of respect. Moreover, after delivering the sentence and listening to the victim's husband, who is clearly upset about the situation, the judge told the husband he could file an appeal within a week. Communicating the possibility of an appeal is also a significant sign of respect. In a situation where the husband of the victim believes the penalty imposed by the judge does not correspond to the act committed by the accused, he was informed about what legal steps he could take to achieve justice by legal means.

Trust: During the trial, the judge did not pay close attention to the defendant, nodding in response to her statements without listening carefully Instead, he focused more on other activities, such as doodling, than on the trial itself. Moreover, after the victim's husband objected to what he considered a too—lenient sentence, the judge surrendered to his emotions, ordered a break, and fled the courtroom. The judge's exhibition of such an emotional response in relation to the defendant's situation detracts from the confidence that the judge actually analyzed the case sufficiently, especially since the accused sought the lowest possible sentence.

During his second speech, the husband emphasized that the defendant did not regret what she had done and asked the judge if he knew the name of his deceased spouse. From the judge's reaction, the man concluded that the judge did not even know the name of the person on whom the case centered. Then, he proceeded to share the story of his relationship with the victim, stressing that the court did not even know who she was and asking the judge if he knew what life was like without a family.

It should be noted, however, that the judge's behavior, exhibiting boredom throughout the trial, concerned not only the accused herself but also the husband of the victim, who counted on the proper conduct of the trial—including the judge's ability to remember the victim's name—to ensure that the judge adequately and fairly arrived at the verdict and the sentence. Taking these facts into account, as well as those listed in the table above, it can be said that the trial does not seem to evoke a sense of procedural fairness, because it contains many flaws and does not meet the requirements of the four components listed above.

Attention should also be paid to the issues presented outside the courtroom, revealing how the judge's behavior closely related to the analyzed cases.

First, it should be pointed out that the court refused to take into account the evidence presented by the victim's husband, which revealed that the accused was not remorseful. The judge reviewed the documentation in his office and checked the legality of this evidence with his apprentice, who determined that it was not obtained in accordance with applicable law, therefore, it could not be considered in the case. Second, it should be pointed out that the judge, being in a state of emotional agitation after ordering a break in the trial, consulted with the apprentice concerning the penalty corresponding to the crime. Third, the series depicted the defense attorney's conversations with the accused in which they discussed the use of a special ointment to cause tears in court and that she did not regret the accident herself. The defense attorney directly suggested to the defendant that she should refrain from the party lifestyle so that her behavior would indicate active grief that could result in a lower sentence.

The last event that is relevant to the context of this hearing is the behavior of the judge when he saw the husband of the victim protesting the outcome of the case. The judge approached the husband, bowed, apologized, and handed him a bottle of water to drink. Furthermore, the judge unofficially provided information about new facts in the case, which could be taken into account when appealing. The judge's behavior indicates that he himself did not perceive the case's outcome as fair. The cited scenes influence the way the main character is perceived, because they reveal that even though he did not fulfill his duty during the trial, he attempted to correct his mistakes outside the courtroom.

4.2 Trial 2

The second trial involved an on-duty paramedic who had been called to help a drunk man but who was now accused of violence and destruction of property. The trial began with the prosecutor presenting the facts, then asking the paramedic about the patient's appearance at the scene and his refusal to measure the patient's blood pressure in the ambulance. The prosecutor alleged that the defendant had attempted to forcefully bind the patient to the bed, and as a result, he had caused bodily harm lasting more than seven weeks and had damaged the victim's watch, worth 5 million won. The last question was whether the accused had settled the case with the victim, to which the paramedic replied in the negative.

The defense counsel then asked the defendant if the victim had complained about pain; the attorney also asked about what happens when a patient refuses a blood pressure check and what the paramedic's responsibilities are in such a situation. The accused replied that he should do his best job, including carrying out an appropriate health examination. The defense lawyer also asked about the use of violence against the patient when tying him to the bed and providing help. The paramedic replied that he held the patient down with all his strength, but only after the fact heard that, in the context of his duties, this is called violence. Answering the question about why he did not settle the case with the victim, the accused stated that the victim did not answer his calls. The defense lawyer emphasized that the defendant received only this message: "You are a jerk; you should be fired. I will not settle the case, you jerk", which the defendant confirmed. The judge then asked the prosecutor to define the demand for the sentence, to which he asked for one year imprisonment.

The pronouncement of the sentence took place at the next hearing, during which the judge read the case number, the name and surname of the accused, and then the facts, before announcing the sentence. The judge emphasized that what the accused had committed was a result of performing his duties as a paramedic, whose task is to ensure the safety and life of other people. In the judge's opinion, there was no reason to doubt that the actions committed by the defendant resulted from his attempt to perform his best work and he had been in similar situations before and was aware that his actions were subject to criminal liability, yet he had tried to prevent further accidents, which demonstrated his courage. The judge emphasized that the law cannot punish courage, which is judged by the universal agreement that we should thank those to whom we should be grateful, and therefore he acquitted the accused.

Table 3 Assignment of individual elements of the Trial 2 to the four components of procedural justice on the basis of indicators according to Table 1

Voice	1. While presenting the facts, the prosecutor asked for the accused's confirmation. 2. Questions were directed by the defense lawyer to the accused regarding the facts and his work. 3. The judge gave the defense counsel the opportunity to present a final statement for his client, which stated that the paramedic had inadvertently injured the patient while fulfilling his duties, that he regretted his actions very much, and that the accused's contribution to society should be considered with mercy in mind. 4. The accused had the possibility to deliver a final statement. 5. The judge attempted to encourage the defendant to open up, asking detailed questions about what the defendant honestly thought about the case.
Neutrality	1. The prosecutor provided the legal basis for the proposed sentence for the accused. 2. The judge called a witness to hear the testimony of another subject, who knew the situation. 3. When announcing the verdict, the judge cited the exact number of the case and the facts. 4. The judge accurately justified his sentence.
Respect	1. The judge's behavior in the courtroom demonstrated interest and active listening, and he looked directly at people in the courtroom. 2. When the judge called the witness and he did not appear, he exhibited surprise and dissatisfaction. When the judge heard about the arrival of the witness, he impatiently began to look out for him, and even rose from his seat. 3. The court employee did not inform the judge directly about the arrival of the witness, but did inform the defense counsel of the accused, who had just in turn announced the witness' arrival. 4. The court employee opened the door for the acquitted defendant so that the man could freely leave the part of the courtroom where the trial was held and move to the part intended for the public. 5. The judge smiled when pronouncing the sentence, made eye contact with other court employees, and at the end bowed to everyone leaving the courtroom. 6. The judge informed the witness that he could sit down and pointed to the right place. 7. When the witness began to testify, they addressed the judge "honorable judge." Hearing these words, the judge interrupted and said he was not someone to be respected. He then asked the witness to continue his testimony, thus shortening the distance between them. 8. When leaving the courtroom, the judge bowed to the people present at the trial.
Trust	1. The judge asked the defendant a number of questions regarding his work and experience, referring to the facts of the case, in an attempt to understand the realities of the paramedic's work. 2. The judge emphasized that his duty was to perform his work properly, therefore he wanted to ensure that it was also true in the case of the accused—that he performed all necessary actions without exceeding his obligations. 3. After the verdict was announced, the judge supported the defendant, explaining that he had been acquitted and could safely leave, then showed him the way out. 4. The judge reacted sharply to the defense attorney's final speech, instructing him to do his job better, for example, by confirming that the value of the damaged watch was indeed as high as the victim claimed. 5. The judge asked for the defendant's final statement, and when the paramedic stated that he had nothing more to say, the judge asked how often the accused had to deal with similar situations at work, noting that his task as a judge was to perform his work in the best possible way.

Based on Table 3, the following conclusions can be drawn. This case was the last in which the main character playing the role of a judge issued a sentence (he later decided to resign as a result of other plot events taking place in this television series). The judge already had some experience with how he should fulfill his role and how other participants in the hearing should behave. The judge asked detailed questions and was involved in the course of the hearing, demonstrating initiative, which indicates that he had managed to take on the role of judge and he was guided not only by the procedure itself but also by his judgment.

Voice: During the trial, the accused was asked to confirm the facts mentioned by the prosecutor; additionally, his defense counsel asked questions about his work and the allegation of using violence toward the victim. The defense attorney asked the accused those questions in the context of the charges against his client presented by the prosecutor. Moreover, the defendant had the opportunity to express his opinion throughout his final statement. This was important, especially because, in the judge's opinion, the paramedic had not yet done so but had only emphasized his guilt. The judge asked him what he really thought about the case, while attempting to provide him with a sense of comfort and security. This attitude of the judge, who took the initiative to understand the accused's point of view and listen to his thoughts about the healthcare system, is important in the context of the procedural fairness indicator of voice. Furthermore, the court called a witness, another paramedic who worked with the defendant and could testify about him, their work, and the case from his point of view. One should also pay attention to the lack of the victim's voice; he was depicted only in flashbacks and was not present at the trial nor did he testify. Should he not also be allowed to speak or call experts or witnesses in such a case? Is the victim's absence from the courtroom related to the partial presentation of the case by the creators of the television series, to allow it to focus only on the accused? It appears that the answer to these questions may be an interpretation in which it is assumed that the series producers consciously "hid" the victim to focus on the accused, which differs from the situation presented in Trial 1.

Neutrality: In relation to the defendant, both the legal qualification proposed by the prosecutor and the legal basis of the judgment were provided. Additionally, the judge called a witness who had also been present during the events to learn his point of view as a witness and as a paramedic who knew the realities of work and procedures in this profession. In relation to the victim, the issue of an acquittal may be raised in particular—were the arguments given in the justification sufficient for the person who had brought the case to court? Was the statement of the judge, that the law cannot punish courage when the defendant had been attempting to fulfill his duty, a sufficient justification for the sentence? It should especially be considered that the judge linked this argument with the universal social contract, according to which the assessment of this type of behavior of life—saving persons should be made, and by which the citizens should be grateful and thank those working in the emergency services or law enforcement. The lack of legal arguments in the justification of the judgment that could refer to the facts may be indicative of the judge's private views of justice and the role played by law in society.

Respect: During the trial, the judge was involved, listening carefully, offering information, encouraging the accused to speak freely, and broadly justifying his verdict of acquittal. The court employee opened the gate in front of the acquitted paramedic, while at the same time the judge demonstrated non-verbally that he could leave by motioning with his hand, but also verbally by explaining that the verdict meant that the paramedic is free and may go. The judge interrogated the witness, who had not appeared on time, without negative consequences; one can see that the witness ran to the court in his uniform stained with blood. Additionally, the judge shortened the distance between him and the witness by allowing the abandonment of formality as the witness began his speech. This situation can be interpreted in two ways. First, one should consider whether the shortening of the distance in the situation presented in the courtroom can be read as positive or negative. Second, such shortening of the distance may also be of great importance in the context of the assessment of procedural justice by both sides—the accused and the victim. One can ask whether the fact that the judge shortens the distance with the witness testifying in favor of the accused means that the judge may be considered biased against and disrespectful to one of the parties.

Trust: The judge was involved in the case, instructing and disciplining the defense lawyer by defending the rights of the accused. When, during his final statement, the defense attorney noted that the defendant confessed and expressed deep regret for his act, the judge was indignant, asking the attorney whether he was sure the watch was worth 5 million won and whether he had a bill confirming its value. The defense attorney replied that the watch had a certificate of authenticity, but the judge replied by saying he knew a thousand people who made hundreds of fake certificates a year, so he ordered the defense attorney to check the watch bill and implored him to do his job better. The judge noted that the attorney saying his client regretted his actions and asking for mercy was inappropriate in this case. Additionally, the judge asked the attorney if this was all he had to say in defense of his client, admonishing him for considering this a simple case, since a defense attorney should do everything in his power to represent the client, which, in the judge's opinion, he had not done. Even if defendant had admitted guilt himself, in the judge's opinion, the defense lawyer could become more involved in the case, for example by better checking the evidence and saying more in defense of the client during the final statement. Additionally, it is worth paying attention to the justification of the acquittal decision, in which the judge emphasized the essence of the healthcare profession and the challenges faced by these professionals in their daily work. The judge also outlined a picture of the law's role in punishment, which was also part of the justification. In relation to the victim, it can be noted that the judge was involved in the case and familiarized himself with the documentation, the evidence attached to the case, and broadly justified the acquittal. After the defendant's final statement, the judge asked him to state what he really thought about the case without any embarrassment; as a result, the defendant began to cry and said he hated his country and was afraid of the people who lived in it, because, as a paramedic, he had no rights over the display of the emergency number on his uniform, which caused problems with the performance of duties. The judge took action to understand not only the accused but the reality of his job. An attempt by the judge to actively encourage the defendant to speak enabled him to speak freely. This is important in the context of the element of trust in procedural justice, because both the statements of the accused himself and the witness can reveal important elements concerning the mental state of the accused.

Another aspect of the trial should be noted in the context of procedural justice. According to the witness, the accused blamed himself for the death of another patient who had died the same day because the ambulance had not arrived on time as a result of an unjustified call made by the drunken man who was now suing him. Because of that, the accused had begun to suffer from depression, which he had not had time to treat. The witness indicated that various types of attacks take place while working in the ambulance, which means that paramedics must deal with difficult situations themselves; moreover, it was their decision, based on the assessment of the situation, whether they tied someone to the bed. In the event of poor assessment of the situation, they may be fined for exceeding their powers; if such a ruling is reached, they may also be brought before a disciplinary tribunal under the Fire Officers Act. Therefore, the verdict in this case would have an impact on the disciplinary proceedings of the accused. The witness also asked the court to not allow a situation where a great man like the defendant would be forced to appear before a disciplinary commission or to leave the team. The testimony of this witness seems to be extremely important to the verdict announced by the judge and to procedural justice, as it could have impacted both on assessment of the situation in which the accused found himself and the judgment itself. The issue raised by the witness relating to possible disciplinary action that is dependent on the court's judgment could also have influenced how the judge ruled.

Taking into account the components and elements assigned to the indicators in Table 3, and the conclusions drawn on its basis, it can be summarized that this trial met the four required components of procedural fairness toward the defendant. However, this is not necessarily true when assessing this hearing from the victim's point of view.

In the context of the trial and the delivered judgment, it is also relevant to refer to the issues depicted outside the courtroom that were related to this case. Before depicting the first scene from the trial, the series creators showed the judge's apprentice reading a letter from the second paramedic, in which he stated that the defendant was falsely accused of using violence, and that as a result of the events that took place, the accused had undergone treatment for depression. The author of the letter said he would like to appear as a witness, to which the judge agreed. Despite problems with the witness' arrival to court, he did have an opportunity to testify, which turned out to be groundbreaking for the case. This issue may have also affected the judge's behavior in terms of neutrality and trust from the victim's point of view, especially considering that the witness did not faced any consequences for being late to court.

5 Cultural Aspects of the Cases

In the television series Your Honor, one can find elements of procedural justice as understood by Tyler, but also the cultural elements of this country, which I observed while watching the court hearings.

One aspect of the South Korean judicial system is the special petitions (탄원서) in the form of letters that can be addressed to the judge handling the case (one can find the right to petitions in Article 26 of South Korean Constitution which encompasses "claimant's basic rights" clauses such as the right to petition. (Choi 2014, p. 91)). The title of this series refers directly to such letters written to the judge, which begin with the words "To your honor". The main character, who plays the role of a judge in this series, had helped his fellow prisoners in the past to write petitions of this type, and while playing the role of a judge, he himself received such petitions. In the case of the two analyzed hearings, both the question of the evidence attached by the husband of the victim in Trial 1 and the request to be called as a witness by the paramedic in Trial 2 were precisely the application of this right to submit a petition. The form is intended to enable the judge to better understand the petitioner's situation and his perception of the case.

In the context of the analyzed procedural justice, it can be stated that this form of petition—and even direct contact with a judge outside the courtroom—implements the voice component, because it allows not only an honest and free expression from the person concerned, but gives them a real opportunity to present their point of view on a case outside the courtroom, which may affect the final judgment.

Second, in the context of South Korean courts, the subject literature refers to the characteristics of using courts based on "a rule, [that] Korean people have traditionally avoided court trials as a form of dispute settlement due to a legal culture and tradition of avoiding a lawsuit in accordance with the maxim 'litigant makes himself ruin by the lawsuit'" (Jung 2018, p. 299). This cultural determinant of how South Korean citizens approach the courts also seems significant in the context of finding elements of procedural justice in the scenes of court hearings in the product of a pop-culture K-drama. Depicting court hearings in pop culture may, in this context, lead to broadening the knowledge about the course of court hearings. Moreover, the elements of procedural fairness that I have analyzed above may also reflect in this context the stereotypes about the judiciary in society, both positive and negative.

Third, by depicting corruption and internal problems of the judiciary, the series exposes various types of threats to the justice system, within which the main character and his assistant attempt to fight for justice. In the context of the Korean justice system, this may be of great importance both in connection with the political changes that the country has experienced over the past decades, but also with various concerns that the South Korean judiciary favors the rich and the powerful. Moreover, the literature on the subject of cultural tradition and law indicates that, "In fact, it has been pointed out that Korean traditional culture consists of relationism, in-group favoritism, nepotism, familism, authoritarianism, blood relation emotion, ritualism, in-group collectivism, sectionalism, compartmentalism, and altruism, and these cultural features still remain in the contemporary society of Korea" (Yi and Hong 2013, p. 113). In the series, one can see the above-mentioned phenomena, but also the actions taken to eliminate them and the attitudes of people working in the justice system.

Fourth, the moment when the judge offered water and an umbrella to the husband of the victim after the hearing's conclusion in Trial 1 can be read as behavior characterized by empathy or understanding, resulting from the fact that the judge himself realized that the sentence he had issued had not fulfilled the promise of justice. Additionally, this behavior could be interpreted as a good deed for the husband of the victim, but in the context of procedural justice, even if this did not take place at the courtroom, it could be a sign of a lack of neutrality toward the parties.

Fifth is the matter of an apology and the settlement of the case, which are both deeply related to the influence of Confucianism on South Korean society (Lee 2005, pp. 21–28). During the hearing, it can be noticed that the accused is asked questions about whether an agreement was reached with the aggrieved party, what steps had been taken to that end, and, if no settlement was reached, the reasons why.

Another interesting cultural aspect is the argumentation of the defense attorney in Trial 1, who, in his final statement, emphasized that the defendant regretted what had happened and had expressed extreme sorrow. The attorney added that this was her first offense so she asked for mercy, stressing that she was "a healthy part of society". This argument is followed by the attorney's acknowledgment that defendant should pay for her crimes, but he asked that a lenient penalty be imposed. Furthermore, in Trial 2, the arguments of defense attorney were interesting in a cultural context, because he stated that the paramedic had inadvertently injured the patient while fulfilling his duties, that he regretted his actions very much, and that the accused's contribution to society should be considered with mercy in mind. These arguments seem to have a group-collective dimension, which is intended to benefit society as a whole and not only be considered in the context of an individual.

Additionally, attention should be paid to the justification of the acquittal issued by the judge in Trial 2. It does not refer to the legal arguments but to the social contract that is in force in this country, which clearly refers to South Korean culture not only in a legal but social sense.

6 Conclusions

This work is an introduction to broader research on how South Korean culture portrays court trials through pop-culture productions such as K-drama. On the basis of the analysis carried out using the method I developed and adopted, it can be concluded that in the series Your Honor, in the scenes of the trials and beyond them, one can see elements of the theory of procedural justice as well as visible influences of South Korean culture, which can be also interpreted in a procedural justice context.

The possibility of noticing the theory of procedural justice by Tyler in the trials depicted in Your Honor indicates the universality of this theory. At the same time, Tyler's theory of procedural justice and the influences of Korean culture are not exclusive of each other. Despite the different cultural circles from which Tom R Tyler and the series Your Honor come from, analyzing this product of the Korean pop culture through the American understanding of procedural justice, one can find elements in the series that, in Tylor's understanding, will or will not be elements of a fair trial. One can venture to conclude that it results from a certain creation of South Korean TV-series not only on the domestic but also on the external market, including the American one.

Moreover, in the cultural context of how South Korean citizens use the courts, it can be considered that this series allows viewers to see the work of a judge both inside and outside the courtroom, bringing them closer to the South Korean judiciary. Additionally, the series offers the opportunity to reveal the "human" side of a judge and the challenges they must face in their daily work.

On the basis of the observations made while watching the series and the analysis of selected scenes from court hearings, it can be concluded that the main character attempted to perform his role as a judge fairly, despite the lack of legal background. Motivated by this desire, he consulted a lawyer associate on the matter of legal qualifications, evaluation of evidence, the writing of judgments and their justifications, and the behavior that was required of him in the courtroom.

With the development of the plot, one can observe how the main character began to assume the role of judge, fueled by the experience he had gained and relying on his understanding of justice. The adamant attitude he adopted seems to be extremely important in the context of the various pressures depicted in the series or the attempts of bribery that the main character faced as a substitute for his brother.

Additionally, it can even be concluded that the main character, who had prior experience with the judicial system as a defendant and a jail inmate before playing the role of a judge, not only took active steps to protect the rights of the accused, as in the case of Trial 2 in which where he asked the defense counsel to do his job better, but also became an empathetic judge who attempted to understand the situations of the accused, the witnesses, and the victims' families. The relationship between procedural justice and empathy can be also connected to the protagonist's individual ability and his development of empathy, since he could picture himself in the position of the defendant. According to Megan Pearson "empathy is a significant tool in achieving many of these, particularly those relating to treating litigants with respect, being perceived as trustworthy and giving litigants a voice" (Pearson 2020, p. 335).

When analyzing the assignment of the elements observed in the trials to the components in Table 1, I noticed that what meets the components of procedural justice for some defendants—in particular, behavior beyond the court "ritual" resulting from the procedure—may not meet the components of procedural justice for another defendant involved in the case. It can be concluded that, in these cases, the proceedings met the procedural justice requirements of only some of the participants or they were carried out partially. Additionally, it should be emphasized that the series presents more court hearings in which the main character is directly or indirectly involved, and which concern various aspects of life, politics, business, or sexual violence, than just the two that were analyzed for the purposes of this chapter.

It is worth noticing that flashbacks played a special role in this television series, as they were presented before the courtroom scenes or during the testimony of witnesses or defendants through which the events were depicted. Moreover, it can be seen that the flashbacks depicted the events from different points of view, both from the objective creators of the series as well as from the subjective characters. It can be concluded that the creators of the series, through flashbacks, attempted to objectify the reality of the series by revealing different versions of the events of individual characters as part of the trial.

The analysis presented in this chapter has its limitations, such as how scriptwriters build the plot or main characters. Such limitations are of particular importance in the case of, for example, a television series where the protagonist is unfairly sentenced to imprisonment, which by definition could disturb the analysis of the incorporation of procedural justice. Furthermore, an analysis conducted by a researcher coming from a European culture includes certain limitations that may result from the misinterpretation of certain behaviors or the failure to read all cultural codes.

In context of image of law in culture it should be taken into account what Magdalena Wojdala concluded at Chapter 'Does Visual Culture Pose a Threat to Law?' of this book (p. 202): "The fears concerning the proliferation of images in law relate to problems the law has struggled with before: proving the truth of statements, and argumentation based on the effectiveness or the efficiency of communication." It should be noted that the image of the law in television series is often criticized, because it is believed that the law shown through visual media distorts its actual image. But one should also note that the image of judge work and moral choices showed in pop culture can also have impact on how people can understand and perceive trials and judge behavior in real life. This can be understood as a kind of education which can make people closer to justice system.

Therefore, wider research on K-dramas could help to isolate the characteristic treatments that are used by the creators of Hallyu in incorporating procedural justice into the scenes of court hearings in television series. However, on the basis of the analysis conducted, in which four indicators of procedural justice were used, I have concluded that despite depicting problems within the justice system, Your Honor also reveals the human face of judges who have their own individual weaknesses but who exercise the elements of the theory of procedural justice in trial scenes and beyond.

References

Choi D-K (2014) The state of fundamental rights protection in Korea. In: Current issues in Korean law, studies in comparative legal history. Robbins Collection, Publications, pp 87–124

Diniejko A (2013) Polityka kulturalna Korei Południowej w dobie globalizacji. Gdańskie Studia Azji Wschodniej 3:123–139

Hollander-Blumoff R, Tyler TR (2011) Procedural justice and the rule of law: fostering legitimacy in alternative dispute resolution. J Dispute Resolut 1:1–18

Jin DY, Yoon JT (2017) The Korean wave: retrospect and prospect. Int J Commun 11:2241–2249

Jung YH (2018) The responsive judge: comparative perspectives of Korea and Japan. In: Sourdin T, Zariski A (eds) The responsive judge international perspective, vol 67. Springer, Singapore, pp 277–309

Lee I (2005) The law and culture of the apology in Korean dispute settlement (with Japan and the United States in mind). Mich J Int Law 27(1):6–52

Lee HK (2018) The Korean wave, encountering Asia and cultural policy. In: Kawashima N, Lee HK (eds) Asian cultural flows cultural policies, creative industries, and media consumers, 2018. Springer, Singapore, pp 75–89

Mezey N (2001) Law as culture. Yale J Law Humanit 13:35–67

Parc J, Moon HC (2013) Korean dramas and films: key factors for their international competitiveness. Asian J Soc Sci 41(2):126–149

Pearson M (2020) Empathy and procedural justice in clash of rights cases. Oxf J Law Relig 9 (2):350–371. https://doi.org/10.1093/ojlr/rwaa012

Shim D (2006) Hybridity and the rise of Korean popular culture in Asia. Media Cult Soc 28 (1):25–44

Tyler TR (2000) Social justice: outcome and procedure. Int J Psychol 35(2):117–125

Tyler TR (2007) Procedural justice and the courts. Court Rev: J Am Judges Assoc 44(1/2):26–31

Yi S, Hong SS (2013) The legal development in Korea: juridification and proceduralization. In: Yang H (ed) Law and society in Korea. Edward Elgar, Cheltenham, pp 108–128

Online Websites

Financial Times, South Korea judiciary accused of favoring rich and powerful critics say efforts to tackle graft are hamstrung by lenient prison sentences for wealthy, https://www.ft.com/content/d7fb173a-184c-11e8-9376-4a6390addb44 (17.06.2020)

Your Honor television series first season online link: https://www.youtube.com/watch?v=AjZcuQ2motI (28.05.2020)

Katarzyna Rużyczka A PhD student at the Department of Sociology of Law of the Jagiellonian University. She graduated from Culture Studies with specialization in Film Studies (bachelor's degree) and Law (master's degree) at Jagiellonian University. Currently holding a scholarship in the research project "Empathy as a challenge. A case of Polish judges" funded by the Polish National Science Centre. Her main research interests focus on South Korean and Japan legal systems, ageing society, public policies, woman rights, alternative dispute resolutions and connection between law and psychology.

Does Visual Culture Pose a Threat to Law?

Magdalena Wojdala

Abstract The proliferation of images in law is widely recognized in the discourse on law and image. Some considerations on this issue do not concern specific problems that arise with the increase in the presence of an image in law, but describe the issue in a general manner. Their example is the narrative that law is endangered by visual culture. The narrative in which visual culture is a threat to the law can be simplified and analytically described in three points. Firstly, it is recognized that the law is affected by socio—cultural changes external to it, resulting in the entry of visual culture into law. Secondly, it is assumed that these changes are unfavorable for law, principally because they introduce into law—an area traditionally based on rationality—an element of irrationality and emotionality. The third point in the narrative is to express the concern that the law is therefore in a state of crisis and its future is unclear. The aim of this chapter is to refute the above arguments.

1 Introduction

The proliferation of images in law is widely recognized in the discourse on law and image (see Brunschwig 2014, p. 901; Dudek 2015, pp. 37–71; Feigenson and Spiesel 2009, pp. 105–124; Marder 2013, p. 331; Silbey 2012, p. 171; Porter 2014, pp. 1687–1782). It can be noted that the discussion about this phenomenon is led by some authors at a comparatively general level (see Boehme-Neßler 2011; Feigenson and Spiesel 2009; Porter 2014; Sherwin 2006). This means some considerations on this issue do not concern specific problems that arise with the increase in the presence of an image in law, but describe the issue in a general manner. It does allow for widely applicable conclusions; however, the consequence of this is the

The work was supported by the National Science Centre, Poland, under research project Preludium 13, 2017/25/N/HS5/01474.

M. Wojdala (✉)
Jagiellonian University, Department of Sociology of Law, Cracow, Poland

M. Stępień, J. B. Klakla (eds.), *Law and Culture*, Law and Visual Jurisprudence 5,
https://doi.org/10.1007/978-3-030-81193-8_9

appearance of certain statements in the discourse that are not accompanied by in—depth research. Their example is the narrative that law is endangered by visual culture as exemplified by the following sentences:

> The final risk of welcoming images into the legal lexicon – the risk that multimedia advocacy will vitiate the quality of legal discourse – is more subtle, but perhaps more pernicious and less susceptible to regulation. (...) Modern visual communication raises the level of detachment to the point of cynicism, and it replaces deep reading with fragmented and often frenetic surfing. To the extent that law adopts these communication tools, there is a real danger that legal writing – and perhaps more importantly, legal reading – will enter what Nicholas Carr calls "the shallows", "chipping away at [our] capacity for concentration and contemplation" (Porter 2014, pp. 1768–1700).

> The proliferation of mass culture, particularly through the visual media of film and television, can be viewed as a powerful tool of cultural postmodernisation. The force of that tool is now coming to bear upon law (Sherwin 2000, p. 39).

The narrative in which visual culture is a threat to the law can be simplified and analytically described in three points. Firstly, it is recognized that the law is affected by socio—cultural changes external to it that result in the entry of visual culture into law. Secondly, it is assumed that these changes are unfavorable for law, largely because they introduce into law—an area traditionally based on rationality—an element of irrationality and emotionality. The third point in the narrative is to express the concern that the law is therefore in a state of crisis and its future is unclear. The aim of this chapter is to refute the above arguments, which is presented in three points.

2 The Assumption of the Entry of Visual Culture Into Law

The first part of the narrative concerning the threat to law from visual culture was formulated as the recognition that external socio—cultural changes affect law and involve the intrusion into law of visual culture. This claim is based on certain assumptions about culture and society that are not directly expressed. These assumptions are reinforced by terminological chaos, particularly in relation to the concepts of socio—cultural change, culture, image, and visuality. A simple definition of these terms is impossible, because their semantic scope is wide. However, ordering the terminological framework makes it possible to illustrate that part of the narrative of the threat to law from visual culture is based on terminological inconsistency.

2.1 The Concept of Socio—Cultural Change

The first point to be addressed is explaining what socio—cultural change is. This concept is one of the central issues for sociology. Considerations regarding change have not only been present in this field from its beginnings, but the concept itself of systematic reflection on society began with the observation of changes that accompanied such nineteenth-century phenomena as urbanization, industrialization and the development of capitalism. The systemic model is a research perspective that has become highly influential in thinking about change. It is based on the assumption that society can be treated as a system, that is, a complex and closed whole, which consists of many elements connected by various relationships. In this perspective, social change is the difference between the successive states of a given system (Sztompka 2005, pp. 20–22).

The issue of socio—cultural change is closely related to the concept of time. The individual states of the systems that constitute a given society can only be compared with each other from a time perspective. The legacy of early sociology is distinguishing two research orientations. The first is a synchronous approach, which consists of conducting research from a static perspective, that does not account for the passage of time, in order to learn the structure or function of a given phenomenon. The second orientation is the diachronic approach, in which the time factor is emphasized in research. The issue of socio—cultural change should be placed in a diachronic orientation. As Piotr Sztompka (2005, pp. 200–201) noted, there is a contemporary tendency in sociology to blur the boundaries of this division and not to separate the static and dynamic aspect of social phenomena in research. This approach is a consequence of changes in assumptions about society, according to which it is recognized that dynamics are an inherent feature of society. In this vision, they are understood, not as an object, but as a process, which means that society does not "exist" but "becomes".

The above remarks allow the conclusion that we can currently observe a number of socio—cultural changes. However, this is not an exceptional situation, but a certain dimension of society. These changes can have a different intensity, which is why they are now referred to as rapid.

2.2 Different Meanings of the Concept of Culture

In the narrative discussed in the chapter, it is assumed that socio—cultural changes are external to law. However, this assumption is problematic because it means treating law and culture as separate systems, each influencing the other (Stępień 2019, p. 325). In this case, law may either adapt to socio—cultural changes or resist them depending on the assessment of these changes adopted. In this chapter, a hypothesis is raised that the assumption in question may result from the inconsistent use of the concept of culture.

The concept of culture is the central tool of description in the humanities and the social sciences. However, individual disciplines and research orientations significantly differentiate its meaning. Difficulties of definition are compounded by various uses of the term in everyday language. The four most popular ways of understanding the term "culture", highlighted by Martyn Hammersley (2019), are presented below.

The first was developed primarily in philosophy, and the other three in social sciences, principally anthropology.

The first meaning of the concept of culture comes from the nineteenth century and is based on the idea of "aesthetic cultivation" (Hammersley 2019, pp. 11–19). Quoting Matthew Arnolad's definition, culture here includes "the best that has been known and said in the world" (Hammersley 2019, pp. 11–12). The term is used here in the singular and primarily refers to the world of ideas, science, and art. It is also related to the aretic approach—the assumption of understanding culture as aesthetic improvement is to support the development of virtues by individuals. The concept of culture understood in this way initiates the later division into high and low culture, sometimes referred to as mass culture or popular culture, adopted by some research orientations. While the distinction between high and low culture has entered the colloquial language, this division is currently highly controversial.

The second means of understanding the term "culture", described by Hammersley as "developmental", also has nineteenth-century roots (2019, pp. 7–8). It was elaborated upon in evolutionary anthropology, largely as a response to Europeans' exploration of non—European communities. It also attracted scientific interest to rural European communities. The concept of culture was already understood broadly here and included those aspects of human life that do not have a biological basis. According to the famous definition of Edward B. Tylor, culture is "that complex whole which includes knowledge, belief, art, morals, law, custom, and any other capabilities and habits acquired by man as a member of society" (1871, p. 1). In the evolutionist orientation adopted in the nineteenth century, various universal stages of the development of culture were distinguished, which is why this trend is defined as developmental. These assumptions were rejected at the turn of the twentieth century.

In the third sense, culture is used in the plural – as cultures. This understanding became central to twentieth-century anthropology and also entered everyday language and means "cultures as distinct ways of life" (Hammersley 2019, pp. 8–9). This meaning also settled in the colloquial language. In this tradition, concepts such as multiculturalism and cultural relativism have developed.

Fourth, culture can be understood as "meaning—making" (Hammersley 2019, p. 9). Culture is understood here not as an object, but a process consisting in the production by people of the meaning of their actions and experiences. This concept of culture has evolved in anthropology, sociology and cultural studies. Culture as a network of meanings is the assumption of such research orientations as interactionism.

The inconsistent use of the concept of culture occurs when a given author claims in their argument that one adopts an anthropological understanding of culture, and therefore recognizes that law is a part of it. However, during later analysis, one begins to use the understanding of culture as "aesthetic cultivation", according to which culture is only a fragment of that which is recognized as culture in social sciences. Moreover, culture in the "aesthetic cultivation" understanding can be assessed, which results in the recognition that the socio—cultural changes can be assessed abstractly. Meanwhile, accepting the assumptions formulated in the social sciences, according to which law is part of culture, implies accepting that changes in culture cannot be external to law. This means that if there is an increase in the number of images in culture, this fact can be reflected in law. Therefore, law is not influenced by some external and easy—to—evaluate cultural trend that must be adapted to or rejected.

2.3 Visual Culture as the Content of the Indicated Socio—Cultural Changes

The dissemination of photography and film made sociologists and philosophers begin diagnosing a change in social reality, which consists of its enormous saturation by images, from the 1970s (see Barthes 2008; Baudrillard 2012; Sontag 2005). In addition, there has been a change in social practices in the creation, dissemination and perception of images (Sztompka 2012, p. 12). The term for this is visual culture.

Visual culture is another vague term. Most often it is treated as an object of interest in science, but sometimes it is defined as a research orientation (Mitchell 2002, p. 166). This chapter rejects the latter because it is rare and also introduces additional terminological confusion. In the discourse on law and image, the authors do not always use this term. Terms such as "age of image" (Boehme-Neßler 2011, p. 190), "digital baroque culture" (Sherwin 2011, p. 4), or simply "images" in general, are also used. The meaning of the above terms is similar in use. The considerations are based on what is "visual" and refer to the issue of contemporary media—primarily television and the internet—and the content they broadcast, such as film productions, broadcasts of political rallies, advertising spots or computer games. The issue of the emergence of visual culture is presented as closely related to technological development; an almost deterministic position can be encountered (see Boehme-Neßler 2011).

The concept of visual culture can be clarified by presenting several categories of the phenomena it covers, according to Sztompka (2012, pp. 13–14). The first category can be referred to as the "iconosphere". It is a collection of different types of images that are present in social reality. Examples include advertising billboards, paintings, photographs and road signs. The second group of phenomena that can be distinguished within visual culture is the "sociosphere", which covers the visually observable layer of social life (i.e. the image of people and the appearance of objects). The third category are the "imaging regimes"; that is, the rules by which images are created. "Regimes of looking" are the fourth and last group and refers to the rules for observing and recording the images of specific people or objects.

As can be noted above, the key concept for describing the changes in question is "image". However, "picture" is a term also used in the discourse. According to the dictionary definitions, it is generally assumed that image is a concept with a broader meaning or refers to non—material images (see Cambridge Dictionary. Image; Oxford Learner's Dictionary. Image), while the word picture refers to images having a physical form, the paradigmatic example of which is a painting (see Cambridge

Dictionary. Picture; Oxford Learner's Dictionary. Picture). This differentiation of meanings, however, has little use, because both in everyday and scientific language, these concepts are sometimes used synonymously which can be seen in the indicated definitions. In this chapter, the concept of image has been adopted because it seems to better correspond to the subject of discussion and is much more often used by English—speaking authors.

The concept of an image is sometimes understood differently depending on the adopted scientific discipline or research orientation. It can be approximated by distinguishing several categories of phenomena, which are described using the concept of an image developed by William J. T. Mitchell in the work "What is an image?" (1984, pp. 503–537). The first category is graphic images, which are traditionally of interest to aesthetics and art history. These are images with a physical substrate or are digital and include photos, films, projects or works of art. The second group of phenomena is optical images, an example of which is mirror reflection or projections—they lay within a scope of physics. The third category mentioned by Mitchell is verbal images, which are metaphors and pictorial descriptions. The discipline dealing with this issue is literary criticism or literary studies. Verbal images may not seem an obvious category; their distinction is based on the concept of imagination. Mental images are the fourth category, and cover non—material images such as dreams, memories and ideas. These kinds of images are of interest to psychology and philosophy. The last group are perceptual images, which are the most difficult to define because they denote images of persons and the appearances of objects or representations (for example, actors' representations), which the author describes as sense data.

3 Factors of Perceiving Changes in the Law as Unfavorable

The second point of the narrative regarding the threat to the law by visual culture is the recognition that these changes are unfavorable for the law. This opinion is associated with numerous beliefs about images and visual culture, several of which are controversial.

3.1 Treating Images as Carrying Emotionality, Subjectivity and Irrationality

The assumption that the increase in the number of images in law is undesirable concerns the features attributed to an image, which are a cornerstone of visual culture. In this regard, there are many superficial opinions in the legal literature, according to which the image has a strong emotional impact, and its use carries a large dose of subjectivism and irrationality in communication. An example of this opinion are the statements that images and emotions are inseparable (Boehme-Neßler 2011, p. 64), as well as images are irrational (Porter 2014, p. 175; Tushnet 2012, p. 69). This is contrasted with the message expressed linguistically, which would be the mainstay of rationality and objectivity: the ideas valued in the world of law. However, the above assumptions represent a notable simplification.

The perception of images, about which many popular claims are circulated in the legal literature, is of interest to sciences such as psychology and neurobiology (Barry 2020, pp. 3–27). As a rule, it is assumed that an image is perceived differently from a text. Language is considered to be perceived linearly while image is perceived holistically. Image is considered to be a means of facilitating the memorization of content. It should be noted that, according to research, the intelligibility and memorability of a message increases when it has a visual and auditory character (Grabe 2020, p. 55). The researchers of image perception pay considerable attention to the relationship between an image and emotionality. It is assumed that an image has a greater emotional impact on the recipient than a text because the mind interprets the images as if they were real objects. This thesis is widespread; however, it should be noted that while many studies support it, there are also some that contradict it. Research in this area is still ongoing (Fahmy et al. 2014, pp. 107–118). For this reason, the division which unequivocally assigns to the text a reference to cognitive abilities, and to the image a reference to emotionality, is most often rejected (Grabe 2020, pp. 55–56).

A reproducible belief is that understanding an image does not require any prior knowledge because it is intuitive and therefore subjective and irrational (on this issue see Tushnet 2012, p. 687). However, effective communication of an image requires not only knowledge, allowing one to place its content in the appropriate context, but also training in perception. A major problem, caused by insufficient education, is lawyers' lack of skepticism towards images. Instead, they often rely on their own intuitions and consider the content of images to be obvious. This approach is sometimes referred to as naive realism and primarily concerns images such as photos and film recordings (Feigenson 2014, p. 18). Naive realism is the belief that photos and recordings are simple records of events that provide insight into reality, which is highly controversial. The conclusion that can be drawn from these considerations is that images are used differently in the communication process than texts—which is in line with popular beliefs—but this does not mean that the image, as Peter Goodrich (2017, p. 14) wrote accurately, "lures and leads the unsophisticated viewer into a realm of fantasy and emotion, and in doing this exercises a power of illusion and a derailment of reason that can lead (...) to chaos and the devaluation of legal reason and judgement".

3.2 *Fear of the Excessive Spread of Visuality in Law*

Law is traditionally considered to be a verbal—centric discipline. It is often emphasized in the literature that the law is based on the word, both spoken and written (see

Katsh 1995, p. 146; Feigenson and Spiesel 2009, pp. 105–124; Boehme-Neßler 2011, p. 90; Brunschwig 2014, p. 901; Dudek 2015, p. 38; Porter 2014, pp. 1687–1782). The concept of law is understood here broadly, not only as a collection of normative acts, but also as various practices accompanying their creation, dissemination and application. Legal provisions and legal documents are formulated in language. Language is a communication tool in legally relevant situations, such as a court hearing or a lawyer's contact with a client. Thus, the theory of law made language one of the fundamental subjects of research. The increase in the number of images in law is considered unfavorable because there is a fear that visual tools will start to replace text, as it has in general culture according to some beliefs described below. It is assumed to be dangerous due to concerns that it will cause the "memization" of law or for legal documents to be treated as internet blogs (Porter 2014, p. 1694, 1744, 1780).

There is a set of controversial assumptions about visuality and visual culture that are the basis for the described concerns. William J. T. Mitchell even calls some of them myths about visual culture (2002, pp. 169–170). A popular assumption in the discourse on visual culture is the contention that there has been an unprecedented contemporary pictorial inflection point that has divided history into the age of writing and the age of visuality (Mitchell 2002, p. 172). From this assumption is derived the view of the decline of the era of writing and the disappearance of competences other than visual ones (Elkins 2002, p. 97). The consequence of the above assumption is the belief that we currently live in an all—encompassing visual age (Mitchell 2002, p. 172). The domination of visuality is understood here as an exceptional situation resulting from technological development. The basic idea of visual culture is that the contemporary iconosphere is much richer than it used to be; that is, it includes a greater number of images and a greater variety of them. Artistic representations constitute only a small fragment of them, and it does not seem appropriate to associate the image largely with the area of art (Moxley 2008, pp. 131–146). Both assumptions are closely related to the belief that contemporary media is visual in nature. Related to this is a far—reaching hypothesis about the diminishing usefulness of senses other than sight (Mitchell 2002, p. 172).

The richer iconosphere is not seen as the only pillar of visual culture. Małgorzata Bogunia-Borowska (2012, pp. 44–53) argues that today we can talk about a society of a "new paradigm", which she describes as photo—society. The foundation of this society is constituting itself around the meanings of images. The author writes that it happens on many levels: individual, collective, private, public, institutional, ethical, political, artistic, cultural and ideational. According to Bogunia-Borowska, visuality in photo—society involves all social practices, including communication, social ties, power, knowledge and customs. A significant number of authors have accepted the assumption that we live in an all—encompassing visual age. According to James Elkins (2002, p. 97), the last 100 years have been the most visual era in history and at the same time the period of the greatest spread of visual competences. Martin Jay (2002, p. 88) wrote that we live in a culture whose technological development has resulted in the creation and dissemination of images to an unimaginable degree. Piotr Sztompka (2012, p. 12) pointed out that contact with pictures is now more frequent than contact with text. Nicholas Mirzoeff (1999, pp. 3–4) proposed that the human experience is more visualized than ever before. Moreover, the aforementioned author (1999: 4—9) recognized that the socio—cultural changes that resulted from an increase in imaging and visualization translated into a cultural crisis that led to the emergence of postmodernity.

As previously noted, some of these assumptions are controversial. Firstly, the arguments that the pictorial turn that ostensibly divided history into distinct ages of writing and images, is flawed. Today we are dealing not only with an increase in the number of images, but also text. Technology has made it easier to disseminate more text than ever before. Therefore, while contemporary socio—cultural changes have resulted in an increase in the number of images, this does not mean that text is no longer important. Determining what number of messages is conveyed in a given form would require in—depth and extensive empirical research. Moreover, it should be noted how people communicated prior to the alleged pictorial turn. The common—sense conclusion is that it was primarily speech and not text, as writing for a long time was a tool of only a narrow and privileged group of people. This means that even if we are dealing with a turn that has caused a rapid increase in images in social circulation, a substantial contrast between it and an era of widespread writing is unconvincing.

In addition, arguments can be found in the literature that the contemporary pictorial turn is not something unique. On the contrary, the idea of the pictorial revolution is a metaphor and a narrative figure often repeated in history. It appears when the creation or dissemination of an image is facilitated by an invention or when some new cultural practice develops in this respect. Peter Burke (2012, pp. 34–38) describes two visual turns in the history of the "western world". The first of these was initiated by the spread of the printed image in the 15th and 16th centuries. The use of forms such as woodcut, copperplate and engraving allowed the reduction of costs and facilitated the sharing of specific visual content. The invention of printing had as great an impact on the dissemination of images as it had on the dissemination of texts. The second turn, which Burke writes about, was the appearance of the photographic image in the nineteenth century, followed by film. In addition to these ground—breaking inventions, others, such as oil paintings or the convergent perspective, met with responses ranging from euphoria to hysteria. The contemporary visual turn is therefore a continuation of previous ones.

Secondly, as Mitchell (2002, p. 174) noted, the present day is not a unique visual era. Visuality and images in a broad sense are a constitutive element of culture, which means that a person living in culture inevitably lives in the world of images. The sense of sight and the visible have not only become relevant today; quite the contrary. The importance of the visual aspect in social reality can be observed even at the linguistic level. In English, the terms "I see" and "I understand" can often be used synonymously (see Cambridge Dictionary. See, Oxford Learner's Dictionary. See). Moreover, a hypothesis can be raised that nowadays, just like the increase in the number of images, it is possible to detect an increase in the number of sounds in the social space, an obvious example of which is the unprecedented availability of various musical works. However, the assumption that we live in a unique audial age is not derived from this fact.

Thirdly, the assumption that contemporary media is visual in nature can be criticized as disregarding the importance of other senses that still play an important role in cultural practices. Most of the media is sense—mixed (Mitchell 2002, pp. 174–176), and it almost seems like a truism that the audial element in the media cannot be ignored. Contemporary emphasis on the unisensory nature of the media is not new in culture. An example of this approach is the deeply entrenched assumption that links particular types of art with one sense. The aesthetician Arnold Berleant (1964, p. 187) criticized this belief, and he emphasized that more than one sense is involved in aesthetic experience. The example of sculpture is significant here, which is traditionally considered a visual form, while directly referring to the sense of touch. The tactility of the sculpture may be proved by the countless surreptitious attempts to touch objects at exhibitions. The antithesis of the view that argues for the hegemony of visual media is the recognition of multisensory nature of media. What is more, the lack of consistency in the position advocating the hegemony of visual media is visible in disregarding the visual aspect when using text. Reading is an activity that is most often undertaken through the sense of sight. For this reason, contrasting the text with visuality seems to be a logical error, as it is a juxtaposition of two sets distinguished on the basis of other categories, one of which is the medium and the other, the sense. It can be assumed that this opposition is a simplification when analyzing the linguistic and pictorial message, which is possible, inter alia, from a semiological perspective.

The above considerations reveal that the increase in the number of images does not necessarily mean a decrease in the importance of the text. Despite the fact that the increase in the use of images in law is noticeable, it is still a rare phenomenon. It should also be noted that there are no postulates in the literature to replace text with image in law. Rather, it is a vision of how text and image complement each other and use the image in a situation where language is not an effective communication tool. Fears that images might turn legal text into a blog treat visual culture as an invisible force that works without human intermediation. This chapter emphasizes the humanistic and subjective aspect of socio—cultural changes, meaning that they are the result of people's actions (Sztompka 2005, p. 201). The consequence of this assumption is that lawyers, and particularly judges, are still bound not only by legal regulations, but also by the rules of legal and judicial ethics. The increase in the presence of images in the law does not release lawyers from acting in accordance with such regulations. The same legal and ethical standards apply when using images as when using text.

4 Vision of Law in Crisis

The third point in the narrative about the threat to law from visual culture was the recognition that, due to socio—cultural changes, law is in a state of crisis. The concept of crisis can be understood as a turning point in a process of socio—cultural change, or a transitional state followed by an improvement or deterioration of the situation (Sztompka 2005, p. 47, see also Holton 1987). What is important is that social researchers indicate that this term became one of the basic tools for describing social reality in the twentieth century. The pejorative character of the concept of crisis is contrasted with the optimistic idea of progress that was widespread in the nineteenth century. The term "crisis" is used so often in characterizing various situations that researchers write about the paradoxical continuity of crisis, which, instead of being a moment, lasts and becomes the norm. One can risk a hypothesis that the popularity of the concept of crisis results from the static perception of a social reality that is in a state of constant change. Therefore, the use of the concept of crisis is not distinctive in relation to the contemporary relationship between law and image.

The vision of a crisis caused by negatively assessed elements of visual culture entering the law may be the result of such a static view of social reality fostered by the traditionally recognized verbal—centricity, or even text—centricity, of the law. If one adopts this popular opinion, the sense of a crisis in law may be caused by the vision of the law moving from the era of reason into one of irrationality and emotionality. Such a concept is an idyllic look at yesterday's law. Using text in the past does not mean that the law worked perfectly then. It is also worth noting that the image was also present in law in the past. It was a marginal element not because lawyers did not notice its potential, but because image processing techniques were insufficient or too expensive. Jennifer L. Mnookin (2013) revealed how quickly photography was applied in law once it had been invented. In the United States, at the turn of the twentieth century, it was already routinely being used as a proof.

The narrative of the crisis in law caused by the proliferation of images may also be related to fear of using technical innovations in law. The increase in the number of images in law is directly related to technological development. In literature, you can encounter terms such as "digital world" (Katsh 1995) or "digital culture" (Feigenson and Spiesel 2009). Facilitating image processing through technical innovations is a truism. However, it should be emphasized that this does not mean simple determinism. Technical innovations have also significantly influenced the lengthening of relevant legal texts, if only due to the high availability of data in electronic databases that can be easily cited. As Elizabeth G. Porter writes: "lawyers, judges, and legal scholars have largely harnessed new digital technology to create more and longer textual documents, rather than to communicate the law in a new, denser, and potentially more powerful manner" (2014: 1700). The new tools in the work of a lawyer provided by technological development are not received with enthusiasm by everyone. Technical innovations often arouse distrust because they constitute a new, untamed quality. The above argument is related to the issue of the psychological dimension of recognizing changes affecting the law as being unfavorable. This is a reaction of fear to the changes occurring in general. In this context, images may be perceived by some as disrupting the "old order".

5 Conclusions

The authors who express themselves in the discourse on law and image reference the achievements of visual studies. In this way, the concept of visual culture found its way into legal considerations. The suggestion of this chapter is to manage such a process with caution. The term "visual culture" is entangled in a number of theoretical issues considered in the social sciences and humanities. It inherits the definitional difficulties associated with various notions of image, culture and visuality, as well as their related concepts. In addition, issues related to visual culture, for example the level of the use of various senses in the perception of reality, are the subject of research in the sciences of human biology. This aspect cannot be overlooked when building concepts related to visual culture.

Recognizing that there are an increasing number of images in social reality and assessing this phenomenon are two different issues, and presenting valuable cognitive conclusions in this area requires extensive empirical research. Without it, vague claims about visual culture are merely speculation. An example of this type of speculative assumption is the recognition that visual culture is a threat to the law. While it is possible to evaluate certain situations in which image is used in law, without specifying the problem, the conclusions are merely a collection of the author's beliefs concerning law and culture.

Taking into account all the considerations contained in the chapter, it should be considered whether the conceptualization of visual culture is adequate enough for lawyers to hold definitive views on. adequate for lawyers. Because such conceptualizations can be seen as too general and controversial, it is difficult to determine their possible effects on the legal field, and they can cause entanglements in discussions that go far beyond legal considerations. The issue of visual culture is still being explored in other disciplines, but the current controversy requires either abandoning the issue or clearly defining what is meant by the concept.

The fears concerning the proliferation of images in law relate to problems the law has struggled with before: proving the truth of statements, and argumentation based on the effectiveness or the efficiency of communication. In the case of using images in law, it is not that the essence of the problems themselves changes, but rather the context of these problems: the specificity of images. Education in this area does not exist, which favors the belief that understanding images is intuitive. Changing this manner of thinking requires the creation of standards regarding the use of images in various legal contexts and specifying what is meant by the term "image". Speculative claims about a threat to the law, based on a controversial notion, contribute little to the legal reality. On the other hand, a useful research path in this area would be an analysis of the specific legal problems that arise from the wider usage of images in law.

References

Barry AM (2020) Perception theory: a neurological perspective on visual communication. In Josephson S, Kelly JD, Smith K (ed) Handbook of visual communication. Theory, methods, and media. Routledge, New York, London, p 3–27
Barthes R (2008) Światło obrazu: uwagi o fotografii. Aletheia, Warszawa
Baudrillard J (2012) Fotografia, czyli świetlny zapis. In Bogunia-Borowska M, Sztompka P (ed) Fotospołeczeństwo. Antologia tekstów z socjologii wizualnej Znak, Cracow, p 380—386
Berleant A (1964) The sensuous and the sensual in aesthetics. J Aesthet Art Critic 23(2):185–192
Boehme-Neßler V (2011) Pictorial law, modern law and the power of pictures. Springer, London
Bogunia-Borowska M (2012) Fotospołeczeństwo. Społeczno—kulturowe konteksty dyskursu o społeczeństwie. In: Bogunia-Borowska M, Sztompka P (eds) Fotospołeczeństwo. Antologia tekstów z socjologii wizualnej. Znak, Cracow, pp 43–89
Brunschwig CR (2014) On visual law: visual legal communication practices and their scholary exploration. In: Schweighofer E (ed) Zeichen und zauber des rechts: festschrift für friedrich lachmayer. Weblaw, Bern, pp 899–933
Burke P (2012) Naoczność. Materiały wizualne jako świadectwa historyczne. Wydawnictwo Uniwersytetu Jagiellońskiego, Cracow
Cambridge Dictionary. Image. https://dictionary.cambridge.org/pl/dictionary/english/image. Access 18 Mar 2020
Cambridge Dictionary. Picture. https://dictionary.cambridge.org/pl/dictionary/english/picture. Access 18 Mar 2020
Cambridge Dictionary. See.https://dictionary.cambridge.org/dictionary/english—polish/see. Access 30 Sept 2020
Dudek M (2015) "Nie samymi §łowami prawo żyje" – o prawie i wizualności. In: Środnicka E (ed) Wzajemne relacje prawa i kultury. Kasper, Cracow, pp 37–71
Elkins J (2002) Preface to "a Skeptical introduction to visual culture". J Vis Cult 1:93–99
Fahmy S, Bock MA, Wanta W (2014) Visual communication. Theory and research. A mass communication perspective. Palgrave Macmillan, New York
Feigenson N (2014) Visual common sense. In: Sherwin RK, Wagner A (eds) Law, culture and visual studies. Springer, Dordrecht, pp 105—124
Feigenson N, Spiesel C (2009) Law on display: the digital transformation of legal persuasion and judgment. New York University Press, New York
Goodrich P (2017) Imago Decidendi: on the common law of images. Brill, Leiden
Grabe ME (2020) Visual cognition. In: Josephson S, Kelly JD, Smith K (eds) Handbook of visual communication. Theory, methods, and media. Routledge, New York, pp 51–70
Hammersley M (2019) The concept of culture. A history and reappraisal. Palgrave Macmillan, Cham
Holton RJ (1987) The idea of crisis in modern society. Br J Sociol 38(4):502–520
Jay M (2002) That visual turn. J Vis Cult 1:87–92
Katsh ME (1995) Law in a digital world. Oxford University Press
Marder NS (2013) The court and the visual: images and artifacts in U.S. Supreme Court opinion. Chicago-Kent Law Rev 88(2):331–364
Mirzoeff N (1999) What is visual culture? In an introduction to visual culture. Routledge, London, pp 1–33
Mitchell WJT (1984) What is an image? New Liter Hist 15(3):503–537
Mitchell WJT (2002) Showing seeing: a critique of visual culture. J Vis Cult 1(165):165–181

Mnookin JL (2013) The image of truth. Photographic evidence and the power of analogy. Yale J Law Humanit 10(1):1–74
Moxley K (2008) Visual studies and the iconic turn. J Vis Cult 2:131–146
Oxford Learner's Dictionary. Image. https://www.oxfordlearnersdictionaries.com/definition/american_english/image. Access 18 Mar 2020
Oxford Learner's Dictionary. Picture. https://www.oxfordlearnersdictionaries.com/definition/english/picture_1?q=picture. Access 18 Mar 2020
Oxford Learner's Dictionary. See. https://www.oxfordlearnersdictionaries.com/definition/english/see_1?q=see. Access 30 Sept 2020
Porter EG (2014) Taking images seriously. Columbia Law Rev 114(7):1687–1782
Sherwin RK (2000) When law goes pop. The vanishing line between law and popular. University Press Culture, Chicago
Sherwin RK (2011) Visualizing law in the age of the digital baroque. Arabesques and entanglements. Routledge, London
Sherwin RK, Feigenson N, Spiesel C (2006) Law in the digital age: how visual communication technologies are transforming the practice, theory, and teaching of law. J Sci Technol Law 12:227–270
Silbey J (2012) Images in/of law. N Y Law School Law Rev 57(1):171–183
Sontag S (2005) On photography. Rosetta Books, New York
Stępień M (2019) Say it with images: drawing on Jerome Frank's ideas on judicial decision making. Int J Semiot Law 32(2):321–334
Sztompka P (2005) Socjologia zmian społecznych. Cracow, Znak
Sztompka P (2012) Wyobraźnia wizualna i socjologia. In: Bogunia-Borowska M, Sztompka P (eds) Fotospołeczeństwo. Antologia tekstów z socjologii wizualnej. Znak, Cracow, pp 11–41
Tushnet R (2012) Worth a thousand words: the images of copyright law. Harv Law Rev 125 (3):683–759
Tylor EB (1871) Primitive culture: researches into the development of mythology, philosophy, religion, art and custom. J. Murray, London

Magdalena Wojdala A PhD candidate at the Faculty of Law and Administration of the Jagiellonian University. She graduated from Law (master's degree) and Ethnology (master's degree) at Jagiellonian University. She is a head of the research project "Law during the transition. The practice of using non—textual elements in judicial opinions".

The manufacturer's authorised representative in the EU is Springer Nature Customer Service Centre GmbH, Europaplatz 3, 69115 Heidelberg, Germany. If you have any concerns regarding our products, please contact ProductSafety@springernature.com

Printed and bound by CPI Group (UK) Ltd, Croydon, CR0 4YY
05/10/2026
02227747-0002